W9-CTM-967

THE NEW COVENANT

THE NEW COVENANT

JIMMY SWAGGART

JIMMY SWAGGART MINISTRIES
P.O. Box 262550 | Baton Rouge, Louisiana 70826-2550
www.jsm.org

ISBN 978-1-941403-62-4

09-167 | COPYRIGHT © 2019 Jimmy Swaggart Ministries®

19 20 21 22 23 24 25 26 27 28/ Sheridan / 10 9 8 7 6 5 4 3 2 1

All rights reserved. Printed and bound in U.S.A.

No part of this publication may be reproduced in any form or
by any means without the publisher's prior written permission.

TABLE OF CONTENTS

THE NEW COVENANT

INTRODUCTION

INTRODUCTION

JESUS CHRIST IS THE new covenant. I do not mean that He has the new covenant, understands the new covenant, or is in charge of the new covenant, but rather in His person—He *is* the new covenant.

The meaning of the new covenant is the cross of Christ—what Jesus there did, and what makes everything possible. Every single thing that comes to the child of God of any repute, irrespective as to what it is, is all made possible by the cross of Christ. The cross is the oldest doctrine in the Word of God, and in essence is the oldest doctrine among men. Every single doctrine of the Bible must be built upon the doctrine of the new covenant given to us by the cross of Christ.

Inasmuch as the meaning of the new covenant is the cross, that meaning was given to us by the apostle Paul. The Lord entrusted Him with the single most important doctrine, one might say, on the face of the earth, and that a million times over. The problem with believers is, we do not quite understand the worth—the value—of the new covenant. I would pray that through this book we might shed some light on this, and that you, the reader, would understand more about this most important subject.

The new covenant is perfect. That means it will never have to be amended and never have to be replaced because it is all in Christ.

If we follow the new covenant and all of its aspects and teachings, we will reap the result, which is everlasting victory. The trouble is that the church most of the time abandons the new covenant for that which it engineers of its own accord. God help us that we may adhere strictly to that which is given to us by the Lord Jesus Christ and at such a price.

There is one name all names above,
Unto believers precious,
Which causes hearts to glow with love,
It is the name of Jesus.

We have no goodness of our own,
His merits we come pleading;
He who the wine-press trod alone
Is for us interceding.

To guard us He is ever near
In waking hours or sleeping
This one to trusting hearts so dear,
Is constant vigil keeping.

He breaks the power of canceled sin,
From Satan's bondage frees us;
O where, my soul shall I begin
To praise the name of Jesus?

THE NEW COVENANT

CHAPTER 1

FOURTEEN YEARS

FOURTEEN YEARS

"THEN FOURTEEN YEARS AFTER I went up again to Jerusalem with Barnabas, and took Titus with me also" (Gal. 2:1).

We begin with the apostle Paul, because as we have stated in the foreword, it was to Paul that the meaning of the new covenant was given. Paul is now speaking of his apostolic authority. But now he wants to demonstrate the essential unity that is existing between himself and the Twelve, and we speak of the twelve apostles. Previously Paul had illustrated and emphasized his independence from them, at least as it speaks to the origin of his message. Understanding that the Lord gave to Paul the meaning of the new covenant, this puts a different perspective on everything as it regards this man's ministry and message.

Now we have four particulars that we might look at:

1. We now enter into a new subject—not the source of Paul's gospel, but the nature of the gospel itself centered in the issue of circumcision for Gentiles.
2. There is a new aspect of Paul's relationship to the Twelve— not independence from them as during the early years of his ministry, but rather harmony and cooperation.

3. This proclaims the new period in Paul's ministry and of early church history.
4. There is a new conclusion—namely, that in the essential content of the gospel and of the plan for missionary activity, Paul and the Twelve were one.

In other words, I think one can say that it was established that Paul was given the meaning of the new covenant, therefore the foundation is sure.

COMPROMISE

This is also the first point historically at which Paul came into sharp conflict with the heresy now troubling the Galatian churches. Of course, we are speaking of the law-grace heresy, which, if Paul had not met it head on, it would have destroyed the new covenant. In fact, that was Satan's aim all the time.

What was to be done about this distinct point of view? Was it a minor matter to be passed over quickly? Was it an issue on which to seek compromise? Should a battle be fought?

At the time, it would seem that few besides Paul (and perhaps Barnabas) recognized the full importance of this issue. So it is to Paul's steadfastness in conflict that Christians owe, humanly speaking, the continuation of the full gospel of grace in subsequent church history. The issue is important today because many would claim that doctrine is not of great importance, that compromise should always be sought, and that the value of human works alongside the reality of grace should be recognized. Of course, Paul refused to compromise one iota;

to have done so would have destroyed the great gospel of Christ—the new covenant.

FOURTEEN YEARS AFTER

The phrase, *"Then fourteen years after I went up again to Jerusalem with Barnabas,"* has spurred arguments for centuries about whether this particular visit to Jerusalem was the financial-relief visit (Acts 11:27–30) or the Jerusalem Council visit (Acts 15:1–35).

I suppose this argument will not be settled until we arrive in glory. Even though there is evidence for both, I personally feel that Acts Chapter 15 presents the probability.

BARNABAS

The question of whether this trip recorded in Galatians 2 pertained to Acts 11 or 15 might be helpful in attempting to establish a chronology of Paul's life. It really has little impact however on the critical issue in these ten verses.

The important matter can be detected from the fact that Paul took the gentile Titus with him, probably as a test case. In addition, Barnabas was with him.

Barnabas was a tremendous help to Paul. He truly was a *"son of consolation"* (Acts 4:36), a term from which we derive the word *paraclete,* one of the titles for the Holy Spirit who filled his life. He befriended the former Pharisee when most of the apostles still feared Paul (Acts 9:27). Barnabas invited him to share in a broader ministry in Antioch (Acts 11:25–26). Then, apparently after an extended ministry in Antioch, the Holy Spirit sent the two of them on the first major missionary journey of the early church (Acts 13:1–3).

BEFORE CHRIST, AFTER CHRIST

Previously, Paul had made it clear that he did not receive his credentials to preach the gospel from human beings. That kind of affirmation might cause some people to accuse him of being a rebel, a charge which simply would not be true.

Paul's position relative to this controversy was absolutely essential for the simple reason that the great gospel of grace—the new covenant—was at stake. The Lord gave Paul the meaning of this great covenant and not to the original twelve, or anyone else for that matter. This was denied by many, and Paul had to defend his position, not so much on his account, but because of the Word of the Lord. That great message for which Jesus died, must not be weakened, compromised, or hindered.

In attempting to explain the fourteen years, as stated by Paul, I think this can be concluded as another brief indication of the chronology of the apostle's life. It seems he basically dated events from his conversion to Christ (BC/AC: Before Conversion/ After Conversion; Before Christ/After Christ). In regard to that, it is safe to assume, I think, that the reference to *"fourteen years after"* means fourteen years after his conversion. If that is correct, this would probably place the time frame of the historical event in Galatians 2 at Acts 15.

THE DIVINE COMMISSION

The *"three years"* of Galatians 1:18 and the *"fourteen years"* of Galatians 2:1 contrast with the *"fifteen days"* of Galatians 1:18, and so emphasize the independence of Paul in relation to the Twelve and his non-indebtedness to them in the matter of doctrine.

Also, had he gone up to Jerusalem earlier, at least as it regards doctrine, the proofs of his independent ministry would not have existed. All these years he had labored fruitfully without having any ordination from the hands of the Twelve; now they recognize his apostleship as being divinely commissioned for the proofs were there, and God had set His seal upon them. Consequently, the Twelve were compelled to acknowledge his position and authority, and also the intelligence of his ministry—an intelligence which surpassed even theirs.

However, in no way do the following statements mean to insinuate that the Twelve were originally opposed to Paul, for that was not the case at all. We are speaking here of unity of purpose, which could only be brought about by the Holy Spirit, and in fact was.

TITUS

The phrase, *"and took Titus with me also,"* was evidently done to make him a test case on the whole question of gentile circumcision. This shows a determined spirit with which Paul came to this meeting in Jerusalem.

We have no detailed information on how Titus became associated with the apostle. It is quite clear that this Grecian Christian was one of Paul's early converts (Tit. 1:4). At the close of the second missionary journey, Titus was already a leader in the young church. Here then, is a case in point.

If it was demanded that Titus be circumcised, the whole matter of the gospel of grace would then be suspect. Consequently, this was about as important a test case as there could ever be. As we shall see, this situation came out in favor of Paul, i.e., "*The Holy Spirit,*" for Titus was not compelled to be circumcised.

I'm sure the reader understands that some were demanding in those days that the law of Moses be heeded as well as accepting Christ in order for one to be saved. Circumcision, which we will discuss more later, was the symbol of that law.

THE GOSPEL OF GRACE

In the great gospel of grace, as given to Paul, the Holy Spirit through him proclaimed the fact that Jesus was the end of the law—He had fulfilled all the law—and it was no longer binding on believers. In other words, it had served its purpose, and inasmuch as the reality (Christ) had now come, the symbolism, which was the law, was no more appropriate. If, in fact, the propagators of the law had been successful in their efforts, the gospel of grace for which Jesus died would have been voided. To attempt to attach anything to His finished work in essence says that what He did was not enough and needs other things added. That is blasphemy, pure and simple.

Titus helped Paul greatly in his travels, and was employed by him in important services.

It is known that Titus ultimately went into Dalmatia (II Tim. 4:10) and is supposed to have returned again to Crete, where it is said he propagated the gospel in the neighboring islands, and died at the age of ninety-four.

BY REVELATION

"And I went up by revelation, and communicated unto them that gospel which I preach among the Gentiles, but privately to them which were of reputation, lest by any means I should run, or had run, in vain" (Gal. 2:2).

This meeting was, without a doubt, one of the most important in history. Actually, I think it would not be possible to overstate the case. It is a matter of doctrine, not about peripheral matters but rather the great foundation of the faith.

Unfortunately, many have been led to believe that if they are sincere in what they believe, that is all that is necessary; however, nothing could be further from the truth.

As sincere as one might be, to be on a wrong road in no way guarantees the correct destination. In fact, someone who is sincerely wrong is just as wrong as someone who is insincerely wrong. So, what one believes concerning Christ matters more than anything else in the world.

The tragedy is, most Christians (and I don't think I'm exaggerating), let someone else do their thinking and interpretation for them as it regards the Bible.

AN EXAMPLE

Let me give an example of this, of which there are many.

A few days ago, a dear lady related to Frances how the teaching of a certain preacher had blessed her. She was speaking about a particular book that had recently come out claiming that there are codes found in the Bible and, if correctly interpreted, can divulge a wealth of meaning other than what is obviously imparted in Scripture.

She was attempting to relate what the preacher had said and how much she thrilled to this new "truth."

First of all, there are no hidden messages in the Bible which can be divulged by some secret code, etc. Such does not exist. While it is certainly true that the unconverted cannot understand the Word of God, at the same time, *"God hath revealed them unto us* (believers) *by his Spirit: for the Spirit searcheth all things, yea, the deep things of God"* (I Cor. 2:10).

As well, Paul said concerning the gospel, *"Which in other ages was not made known unto the sons of men, as it is now revealed unto his holy apostles and prophets by the Spirit"* (Eph. 3:5). He is not speaking of some code, but rather the plainly written Word of God.

If this dear lady had known the Word of God as she should have, then she would not have been listening to this particular preacher in the first place. Or, upon hearing what he had to say concerning this "code," she would have known instantly that such was false.

Jesus said, *"Man shall not live by bread alone, but by every word that proceedeth out of the mouth of God"* (Mat. 4:4).

To be sure, the Bible we hold in our hands is the Word of God, and not some mysterious code.

OUR BOOKS

At least one of the reasons, I believe, that the Lord has instructed us to write the books which we have written and are writing, is because of the necessity—even the absolute necessity—for sound doctrine. By that I in no way mean to infer that we are the only ones who have sound doctrine, for there certainly are others, but in the final analysis not very many. In fact, it has always been that way.

Yet I am one of the few who has the wherewithal to put all of this in print. Inasmuch as the Lord has instructed me to do this, and I definitely believe that He has, it is incumbent upon the body of Christ to avail itself of this which the Lord has given.

Christians get into trouble because they do not know the Word of God. To be sure, the solution to every single problem as it pertains to *"life and godliness"* is found in the pages of the Word of God (II Pet. 1:3–4).

A PERSONAL EXAMPLE

Even though I have previously related the following, due to the subject matter I think it would be appropriate to recount this happening again in brief.

If I remember correctly, it was some time in 1992. As was my custom, immediately upon arising early in the morning

(I've always been an early riser), I would go to the Lord for a short period of prayer, and then a short time of study of the Word of God.

This particular morning, as I attempted to enter into the spirit of prayer while slowly walking on the circular drive in front of our house, I seemed to have no victory at all. The problems at the ministry were gargantuan. In fact, the Lord was having to supply a financial miracle each and every day for us to survive, even as He continues to do. As well, it seemed like the opposition from the church world was so intense that it was literally impossible to continue.

With a heavy heart, all of these things were on my mind. As stated, even though I attempted to pray, I seemingly could not get through; consequently, there was little or no victory.

A short time later, I walked back in the house. Still very heavy hearted, I picked up my Bible and proceeded to read, as I usually did every morning. For the last forty years or longer I suppose, I have always read the Bible completely through, from Genesis to the book of Revelation; I never skip around in the text.

THE SONG OF SOLOMON

I had finished reading the book of Ecclesiastes the day before, so I began with the Song of Solomon.

I remember sitting down with the Bible on my lap, and even though I greatly love the Song of Solomon, in my heart and spirit I would have been much happier had I been reading elsewhere in the Word of God.

With these thoughts in mind, and desperately needing a touch from the Lord, I slowly began to read, beginning with the first verse. When I arrived at the third verse, it happened: the Holy Spirit illuminated the words, *"thy name is as ointment poured forth."* I mean it seemed to stand out greatly so in the text and besides that, the Spirit of God came all over me.

I began to weep as I sat there savoring that beautiful phrase, *"thy name is as ointment poured forth."* In fact, the Holy Spirit poured that ointment all over me in that early morning hour, which gave me a rejuvenation such as words cannot begin to express.

Of course this has happened enumerable times, but what makes this stand out so beautifully in my mind is because I thought in my heart, at least on that particular morning, that the Lord didn't really have anything for me in this ancient book, Song of Solomon, but He did and greatly so. In fact, it was a "rhema" word to my heart for that particular time.

We get into trouble because we don't know the Word of God, we don't think doctrine is important, or we don't abide by the Word of God that we do know.

REVELATION

The phrase in Galatians 2:2, *"and I went up by revelation,"* refers to revelation from the Lord. In other words, the Lord told Paul to do so and not in obedience to an authoritative order from the Twelve. In fact, he did not recognize their authority over him, and they never for a moment attempted to portray such. It is to be remembered that the design for which Paul states this is to show that he had not received the gospel from men. Again, he was not attempting to play the part of a lone ranger, not at all. He is careful therefore to state that he went up by the express command of God, and we are speaking of going to Jerusalem as it regards the council that would be conducted there.

He did not go up to receive instructions from the apostles there in regard to his own work, or to be confirmed by them in his apostolic office; he went to submit an important question pertaining to the church at large.

The reason why, he says, that he went up by direct revelation seems to be to show that he did not seek instruction from the apostles; he did not go of his own accord to consult with them, as if he were dependent on them. But even in a case when he went to advise with them, he was under the influence of express and direct revelation, which proved that he was as much commissioned by God as they were.

In the Greek, the word *revelation* is *apokalupsis*, and it means "to unveil, reveal, uncover." Even though we have dealt with the word *revelation* previously, due to the extreme seriousness of this matter, perhaps more thought would be helpful. In fact, it would be impossible to exhaust information concerning revelation as given by the Lord, even as Paul here proclaims.

THE NATURE OF REVELATION

Salvation, as proclaimed in the Word of God (for that is the purpose of the Word) is supernatural, i.e., *"all from God, and by revelation."*

But this does not mean that, according to it, all men as creatures live, move, and have their being in God. It is meant that, according to it, God has intervened extraordinarily in the course of the sinful world's development, for the salvation of men otherwise lost.

In Eden the Lord God had been present with sinless man in such a sense as to form a distinct element in his social environment (Gen. 3:8). This intimate association, which was the source of man's leading and guidance, was broken up by the fall. God did not, therefore, withdraw Himself from concernment with men. Rather, He began at once a series of interventions in human history by means of which man might be rescued from his sin, and despite it, brought to the end destined for him, at least for those who will believe. These interventions involved the segregation of a people for Himself, by whom God should be known, and whose distinction should be that God should be *"near unto them"* as He was not to other nations (Deut. 4:7; Ps. 145:18).

ISRAEL

This people (Israel and even the church) was not permitted to imagine that it owed its segregation to anything in itself fitted to attract or determine the Divine preference; no consciousness was more poignant in Israel than that Jehovah had chosen it, not it Him, and that Jehovah's choice of Israel rested solely on His gracious will.

Nor was this people permitted to imagine that it was for its own sake alone that it had been singled out to be the sole recipient of the knowledge of Jehovah; it was made clear from the beginning that God's mysteriously gracious dealing with Israel had as its ultimate end the blessing of the entirety of the world (Gen. 12:2–3; 17:4–16; 18:18; 22:18; Rom. 4:13), the bringing together again of the divided families of the earth under the glorious reign of Jehovah, and the reversal of the curse under which the whole world lay for its sin (Gen. 12:3).

JEHOVAH WAS KNOWN ONLY IN ISRAEL

To Israel God showed His Word, made known His statutes and judgments, and after this fashion He dealt with no other nation; and therefore none other knew His judgments (Ps. 147:19). This meant that Israel was light years ahead of all other nations, and as well, all modern believers who know the Lord fall into the same category.

Accordingly, when the hope of Israel (who was also the desire of all nations, whether they realized such or not) came, His own lips unhesitatingly declared that the salvation He brought, though of universal application, was *"of the Jews"* (Jn. 4:22). The nations to which this salvation had not been made known are declared by the chief agent in its proclamation to them to be, meanwhile, far off, *"having no hope"* and *"without God in the world"* (Eph. 2:12), because they were aliens from the commonwealth of Israel and strangers from the covenant of the promise.

Salvation as afforded in the Bible, thus announces itself, not as the product of men's search after God, if haply they may feel after Him and find Him, but as the creation in men of the gracious God forming a people for Himself, that they may show forth His praise.

In other words, the salvation of the Bible presents itself as distinctively as that of revelation. Or rather, to speak more exactly, it announces itself as the revealed salvation, as the only revealed salvation; and sets itself as such over against all religions, which are represented as all products, as the art and device of man. In other words, salvation is of the Lord, while all religions of the world are of man.

PERSONAL REVELATION

As a result of what we have just said, and due to the fact that no more word from the Lord is to be given, at least as it regards something being added to the Scriptures, any personal revelation given by God, or rather claimed to be given by God, must always agree in every respect with the written Word of God. Otherwise, it has to be discarded.

Sometime back I read a statement made by a particular lady preacher as it regards the "Jesus died spiritually" doctrine. This teaches that Jesus died like a sinner, actually as a sinner on the cross, and took upon Himself the nature of Satan. After the lady went through this litany, she said, "You won't find this in the Bible. The Lord will have to reveal it to you."

Now think about that for a moment. The redemption of man, which is the greatest thing that God ever did, and it's not in the Bible. She was right, it was not in the Bible because it's not scriptural; it was wrong. In fact, this teaching is ungodly.

The Bible is full of the account as to what Jesus did at the cross, and it's not fiction, and neither is it that which must be given to somebody by revelation, because it's not in the Bible. That's about the most preposterous thing I have ever heard.

It is the intention of the Holy Spirit, however, to constantly give revelation to believers regarding every aspect and walk of life, hence Paul speaking of going up to Jerusalem by revelation.

The Scriptures are very clear on this as they regard at least a part of the office work of the Holy Spirit. Jesus said of the Spirit of God:

> *Howbeit when he, the Spirit of truth, is come, he will guide you into all truth: for he shall not speak of himself; but whatsoever he shall hear, that shall he speak: and he will shew you things to come. He shall glorify me* (glorify Jesus): *for He shall receive of mine, and shall shew it unto you. All things that the Father hath are mine: therefore said I, that he shall take of mine, and shall shew it unto you* (Jn. 16:13-15).

Let us say it again because it is so very important: While the Lord will constantly reveal things to His chosen people, still, whatever He gives will always be according to the Word of God. And again, if it isn't, it needs to be discarded.

For instance, the Lord gave me a revelation of the cross, and to do it He took me to Romans 6. As well, He gave me a revelation as to how the Holy Spirit works. To do that, He took me to Romans 8. It must line up with the Word of God or else it is specious.

HOW CAN ONE BE LED BY THE SPIRIT?

Satan does all within his power to keep believers from being led by the Lord, especially preachers. He wants them to be led by other men, which, in fact, most are. Consequently, very little is truly done for the Lord, simply because the Holy Spirit can little function in the realm of man-devised plans. This is one of the reasons why religious denominations oftentimes hinder the work of God. More and more of them demand total allegiance from their preachers, with denominational heads serving as the leadership in every capacity. While this is certainly not an appeal for a lone ranger mentality or attitude—that's not the idea—but rather Christ given His proper place as head of the church, with Him functioning through the Holy Spirit to lead and guide His people. This is God's way, even as Paul here presents the example.

The Holy Spirit is to lead and guide every single believer. That's one of the reasons He has taken up abode within our hearts and lives. So, how can this be done?

Before we answer that question, let me say this: It is the office of the apostle that is meant by the Lord to serve as the de facto leader of the church. The Holy Spirit knows what the church needs. Consequently, He moves upon the heart of one called to be an apostle and gives him that word, that message—that which He wants the church to know, to heed, and to have. Unfortunately, true apostles—and there aren't very many—are seldom given opportunity to give the church what the Lord has given them. But somehow and someway the Holy Spirit has a tendency, for the most part, to get it through.

Incidentally, the way that one recognizes if one is truly a God-called apostle, is the message that God gives him. For instance, it was the great message of grace that God gave to the apostle Paul. Satan did everything that hell could do to stop it, but he did not succeed. Paul delivered the message, and thank God he did!

Now let's try to answer the question as to how the Holy Spirit can do this.

PRAYER AND THE WORD

I think it is virtually impossible for believers, be they preachers or otherwise, to be led by the Spirit, at least to any degree, unless they have a proper prayer life and fully know and understand the Word of God. Regrettably, both of these great attributes are missing in most hearts and lives of believers.

It is through prayer that we have communication with the Lord, with Him dealing with us and drawing us ever closer to Himself. Developing such a relationship cannot be done any other way.

I think I can also say that if one has a proper prayer life, he will at the same time have a proper "Word life," and the study of the Word of God will be preeminent.

As well, I think I can say without any fear of contradiction that all of the leading that the Lord gives to us, which He constantly desires to do, and which He will do if we only yield to Him, will always and without fail come through His Word. In other words, He will give us a "rhema" word, tailor-made for our immediate need.

The idea is to be led by the Spirit; however, there are no shortcuts to this process—a proper prayer life and a proper study of the Word is always demanded.

To be led by the Spirit is the most rewarding, fulfilling, thrilling, and happy life in which one could ever begin to engage; it is that which the Lord intended. Sadly, so few Christians take full advantage of it.

Many if not most Christians make their plans, and then ask God to bless those plans. That's not the right way. The right way is to let God make the plans; then the blessing on them is guaranteed.

THE CROSS OF CHRIST

I do not personally believe that much leading can be done by the Holy Spirit unless the individual has his or her faith exclusively in Christ and the cross. There are several things, I think, that are demanded:

- First, Jesus Christ is the source of all things that are received from God, and I mean all things (Jn. 1:1-5; 14:6).
- Second, the cross of Christ is the means and the only means by which all of these things are given to us (I Cor. 1:17-18; 2:2; Col. 2:10-15).
- Third, the cross of Christ must ever be the object of our faith (Rom. 6:1-5; Gal. 6:14).
- Fourth, with Jesus Christ as the source, and the cross as the means, and the cross of Christ ever the object of our faith, then the Holy Spirit who works exclusively

within the parameters of the finished work of Christ will wondrously help us (Rom. 8:1-11).

That which I have given is very simple. A child can understand it. It is the secret, the strength, and the direction of the Holy Spirit—it's always the direction of the cross. That's where Jesus paid the price, satisfied the demands of a thrice holy God, and did for us what we could not do for ourselves. That's the reason that Jesus Christ and Him crucified must ever be the object of our faith.

THAT GOSPEL WHICH I PREACH

In Galatians 2:2, the phrase, *"and communicated unto them that gospel which I preach among the Gentiles,"* refers to the gospel of grace.

"That gospel" could be summed up in this: Jesus Christ has been crucified, resurrected, and is coming again; and there is righteousness for all men through faith in Him without the works of the law. That is what Paul had always preached and what he continued to preach because it was given to him by the Lord. It would undergo no change in its essential features, especially in the one doctrine that he was most anxious to impress upon the Galatians—and all concerned for that matter—the doctrine of justification by faith.

THE GENTILES

If one is to notice, Paul singles out the Gentiles. Among the Jews, it seems that he had suffered the law and circumcision for a time, as the other apostles did, yet ever holding the true doctrine of the gospel, which was the gospel of grace.

I think the facts will show that the apostle was patient with the Jews; however, it was a patience which was born of frustration I think, that is if such terminology would be permissible to use.

Paul knew that the gospel was one gospel, not two. There was no such thing as one gospel for the Gentiles and another for the Jews. As it regards the Council held at Jerusalem and recorded in Acts 15, by the grace of God he had succeeded in freeing the Gentiles from that yoke, and I speak of the yoke of the law. However, every evidence is that the Jewish segment of the church was continuing to preach the law. In other words, they were attempting to tag Jesus onto the law of Moses, which within itself was a travesty. In fact, it ultimately destroyed the Jewish segment of the church. However, in real terms, there should not have even been a Jewish segment as such, with the church actually intended by the Holy Spirit to be one, which would include all—Jews and Gentiles.

WHO WAS RESPONSIBLE?

Concerning the Jewish segment of the church and the original twelve apostles, every evidence is that the Twelve sided with Paul, but it seems at times with some questions (II Pet. 3:15–16). So, at least as it regards leadership, that would leave James, the Lord's brother.

Even though James was a godly man, and of that there is no doubt; nevertheless, it seems he had some problems as it related to the law and grace issue. In other words, he seemed to come down in favor of the law continuing to be kept, at least as it regarded the Jews (Acts 21:20–22). If this is right, and it definitely does seem to be the case (if one will carefully peruse the account in Acts 21 and elsewhere), then I personally think that James missed the Lord in that respect. We do know, even as Galatians 2:12 reveals, that James seemed to have favored the law side. As a result, some (not the original Twelve) who came from Jerusalem felt free to propagate their gospel of works, which of course contradicted that which Paul taught and preached.

This issue possibly would have festered in any case. However, if James had taken a firm stand regarding the Jews, even as he did with the Gentiles, I think the situation would not have been nearly as divisive as it proved to be.

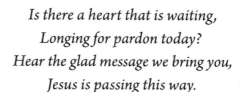

Is there a heart that is waiting,
Longing for pardon today?
Hear the glad message we bring you,
Jesus is passing this way.

Coming in love and in mercy,
Quickly now unto Him go;
Open your heart to receive Him,
Pardon and peace He'll bestow.

Listen, the Spirit is calling,
Jesus will freely forgive,
Why not this moment accept Him?
Trust in God's mercy and live.

He is so tender and loving,
He is so near you today;
Open your heart to receive Him,
While He is passing this way.

THE NEW COVENANT

CHAPTER 2

REPUTATION

REPUTATION

"... *BUT PRIVATELY TO THEM which were of reputation*" (Gal. 2:2).

The pronoun *them* refers to the original Twelve; however, James the brother of John, had by now been martyred (Acts 12:2). Whether this refers as stated, to the visit of Acts 11:30 or Acts 15:4 is not clear; however, it was probably the latter.

The idea is, that Paul met privately with the other apostles (Peter and John), and no doubt James, the Lord's brother, and gave them a private explanation of the new covenant as had been given to him by the Lord. The point on which Paul seems to have made this private explanation was not whether the gospel was to be preached to the Gentiles, for on that they had no doubt after the revelation to Peter (Acts 10), but whether the rites and ceremonies of the Jews were to be imposed upon the Gentile converts, such as circumcision, etc.

Paul explained his views and his practice on that point, which were that he did not impose those rites on the Gentiles;

he taught that men might be justified without their observance; and that they were not necessary in order to have salvation.

THE REASONS

The reasons why Paul sought this private interview with the leading men in Jerusalem seems to be obvious; and we may suppose it was something like the following:

- The Jews in general had a very strong attachment to their own customs, and this attachment was found in a high degree among those who were converted from among them to the Christian faith. They would be strongly agitated, therefore, by the doctrine that those customs were not necessary to be observed.

- If the matter were submitted to a promiscuous assembly of converts from Judaism, it could not fail to produce great excitement. They could not be made readily to understand the reasons why Paul acted in this manner; there would be no possibility in an excited assemblage of that sort, to offer the explanations which might be desirable; and after every explanation which could be given in this manner, they might have been unable to understand all the circumstances of the case—hence, the private meeting.

- If a few of the principal men were made to understand it, Paul felt assured that their influence would be such as to prevent any great difficulty. He therefore, sought an early opportunity to lay the case, the law/grace issue, before them in private, and to secure their favor; and this course contributed to the happy issue of the whole affair (Acts 15).

MUCH DISPUTATION

There was indeed much disputation when the question came to be submitted to *"the apostles and elders"* (Acts 15:6), many of the sect of the Pharisees in that assembly maintained that it was needful to teach the Gentiles that the law of Moses was to be kept (Acts 15:5). No one can tell what would have been the issue of that discussion among the excitable minds of the converts from Judaism, had not Paul taken the precaution, as he says here, to have submitted the case in private to those who were of *"reputation,"* and if Peter and James had not in this manner been satisfied, and had not submitted to the views which they did as recorded in Acts 15:7–21, and which terminated the whole controversy.

Paul's concern can be detected in the next few verses, which actually show the heart of the issue. Paul was concerned that the Judaizers might make some progress in their efforts to contaminate the liberating gospel of God's grace with their petrifying message of legalism.

These people seem to be constantly dogging his steps and causing problems for him. Unfortunately, their successors still exist; and they still work against those individuals who preach the true gospel of Christ that frees people from their sins and from empty religion.

Some of the above material was submitted by Dr. Bernard Rossier.

PAUL'S MEANING

Some have attempted to take Acts 15:2, couple it with Acts 15:6, 9 and insinuate sarcasm on the part of Paul relative to the other apostles.

While the wording in the English of the authorized version seems to be somewhat ironical, yet the Greek text gives no hint of that. This would be inconsistent with Paul's assertion of fellowship with these apostles, and with his own humility, and it would have defeated his own purpose by that much, which was to show the Galatians that he was on terms of fellowship with them and was recognized by them in his apostolic authority. Consequently, at least in the Greek text, these words or phrases used by Paul, are actually terms of honor and convey no tinge of depreciation.

RUN IN VAIN

In Galatians 2:2, the phrase, *"lest by any means I should run, or had run, in vain,"* I think is clear in its meaning.

First of all, Paul does not mean that his past fruitful labors which resulted in the conversion of many sinners and the establishment of churches would be rendered null and void simply because they would not have the approbation of the Jerusalem church—that is if they were to decide against him. However, Paul did know, that if the original Twelve and even James, the Lord's brother, repudiated his gospel of grace, at least as far as the Gentiles were concerned, this would create an almost insurmountable barrier, as should be obvious.

I think it is very clear as to how much significance Paul attached to proper recognition by the Jerusalem church and the Twelve; when we think of the strong prejudices of that church situated in the stronghold of apostate Judaism, this feeling of anxiety lest his work be disowned, is certainly a natural thing. His fear was that those in authority in the Jerusalem church, by insisting on the Mosaic ritual, might thwart his past and present efforts at establishing a church that would be free from all connections with the Mosaic economy which had been set aside at the cross.

Paul saw that in the existing situation, there was danger that his work would be rendered ineffectual by the opposition of the Jerusalem church; that the disapproval of the Twelve would have such repercussions in the church that his work would be seriously handicapped. He was always careful lest the Jewish law be forced upon the Gentiles, and lest the unity of the Christian church be broken by a division of the latter into a Jewish and a Gentile branch, which definitely was not the will of God, and thankfully did not occur. It should be obvious that if the original Twelve, or any part of that number, failed to agree with Paul, that the results could be disastrous.

LEST BY ANY MEANS

The apostle did not really lack confidence in his own teaching. And yet he was aware that it rested solely upon his own individual conviction, and upon the interpretation that he had put upon the intimation to him of the divine will. In fact, one might even detect a certain small element of uncertainty which gave room for confirmation, which the apostle desired to receive, and thankfully did receive.

Paul recognized here that the decision reached could have terrible consequences for the church's missionary outreach—if the doctrine of grace was not boldly and clearly upheld. Thank God it was upheld. Consequently, every evidence is that Paul and the Twelve preached and proclaimed the same gospel, as should be obvious. Yet it was Paul who spearheaded the gospel of grace, and for the simple reason that it was to him that the meaning of this great covenant was given.

THE NEW COVENANT

Inasmuch as we have used the phrase "new covenant" quite often, and especially that it was given to Paul, perhaps a little more explanation may be helpful.

The term *new covenant* necessarily implies an old covenant, and we are reminded that God's dealings with His people in the various dispensations of the world's history have been in terms of covenant. The Holy Scriptures by their most familiar title keep the thought before us. Actually the terms *Old Testament* and *New Testament* could be said "old covenant" and "new covenant" with the writings produced within the Jewish church being the writings or Scriptures of the old covenant, and those within the Christian church being the Scriptures of the new covenant.

THE LORD'S SUPPER

Looking at the matter more particularly, we have to note the words of Christ at the institution of the Lord's Supper. In three of the gospels, as also in Paul's account (Mat. 26:28; Mk. 14:24; Lk. 22:20; I Cor. 11:25), the word *testament*—covenant—occurs. Matthew and Mark record *"My blood of the* (new) *covenant,"* Luke and Paul say, *"The new covenant in my blood."*

The revisers following the critical text, have omitted "new" in Matthew and Mark, but even if it does not belong to the original manuscript, it is implied, and there need be little doubt that Jesus used the word.

The old covenant was so well known to these Jewish disciples, that to speak of the covenant in this emphatic way, referring manifestly to something other than the old Mosaic covenant, was in effect, to call it a "new covenant." The expression, in any case, looks back to the old and points to the contrast; but in the contrast there are points of resemblance—for instance, the similarity between the Passover and the Lord's Supper.

HIS BLOOD

It is most significant that Christ here connects the "new covenant" with His "blood." We at once think, as doubtless the disciples would think of the transaction described in Exodus 24:7, when Moses *"took the book of the covenant, and read in the audience of the people"* these words, indicating God's undertaking on behalf of His people and what He required of them; *"and they said, all that the* LORD *hath said will we do, and be obedient,"* thus taking up their part of the contract.

Then comes the ratification, *"And Moses took the blood* (half of which had already been sprinkled on the altar), *and sprinkled it on the people, and said, Behold the blood of the covenant, which the* LORD *hath made with you concerning all these words"* (Ex. 24:8).

The blood was sacrificial blood—the blood of the animals sacrificed as burnt offerings and peace offerings (Ex. 24:5-6). The one-half of the blood sprinkled on the altar tells of the sacrifice offered to God, the other half sprinkled on the people, of the virtue of the same sacrifice applied to the people, and so the covenant relation is fully brought about.

Christ speaking of His blood in this connection plainly indicates that His death was a sacrifice and that through that sacrifice His people would be brought into a new covenant relationship with God. His sacrifice is acceptable to God and the virtue is to be applied to believers—so all the blessings of the new covenant are secured to them; the blood *"is shed for you"* (Lk. 22:20).

He specifically mentions one great blessing of the new covenant, the forgiveness of sins, *"which is shed for many for the remission of sins"* (Mat. 26:28).

DIFFERENCE BETWEEN THE NEW COVENANT AND THE OLD COVENANT

This great thought is taken up in Hebrews and fully expounded. The writer (who I believe was Paul) draws out fully the contrast between the new covenant and the old by laying stress upon the perfection of Christ's atonement in contrast to the material and typical sacrifices (Heb. 9:11–23).

He was a *"high priest of the good things to come,"* connected with *"the greater and more perfect tabernacle."* He (Jesus) entered the heavenly holy place *"by his own blood,"* not that of *"goats and calves,"* and by that perfect offering He has secured *"eternal redemption"* in contrast to the temporal deliverance of the old dispensation.

The blood of those typical offerings procured ceremonial cleansing; much more, therefore shall the blood of Christ avail to cleanse the conscience *"from dead works to serve the living God"*—that blood which is so superior in value to the blood of the temporal sacrifices, yet resembles it in being sacrificial blood.

THE BLOOD OF JESUS

It is the blood of Him *"who, through the eternal Spirit offered himself without spot unto God"* (Heb. 9:14).

It is the fashion in certain quarters nowadays to say that it is not the blood of Christ but the spirit of self-sacrifice for others that invests the cross with its saving power, and this verse is sometimes cited to show that the virtue lies in the surrender of the perfect will, the shedding of the blood being a mere accident, or rather incidental. But this is definitely not the view of the New Testament writers.

The blood-shedding is to them a necessity. Of course, it is not the natural, material blood or the mere act of shedding it that saves. The blood is the life. The blood is the symbol of life; the blood shed is the symbol of life outpoured—of the penalty borne; and while great emphasis must be laid, as in this verse it is laid, upon Christ's perfect surrender of His holy will to God, yet the essence of the matter is found in the fact that He willingly endured the dread consequences of sin, and as a veritable expiatory sacrifice, shed His precious blood for the remission of sins, which within itself was an absolute necessity. In other words, people are able to be saved because Jesus shed His life's blood on the cross of Calvary. Inasmuch as the life is in the blood, in essence Jesus poured out His life for us.

THE MEDIATOR OF A NEW COVENANT

On the ground of that shed blood, as the writer goes on to assert, *"He is the mediator of the new testament* (covenant), *that by means of death, for the redemption of the transgressions that were under the first testament* (covenant), *they which are called might receive the promise of eternal inheritance"* (Heb. 9:15).

Thus, Christ fulfills the type in a twofold way: He is the sacrifice upon which the covenant is based, whose blood ratifies it, and He is also like Moses—the mediator of the covenant. The death of Christ not only secures the forgiveness of those who are brought under the new covenant, but it was also for the redemption of the transgressions under the first covenant, implying that all the sacrifices gained their value by being types of Christ, and the forgiveness enjoyed by the people of God in former days was bestowed in virtue of the great sacrifice to be offered in the fullness of time—namely the sacrifice of Christ at Calvary.

THE ETERNAL INHERITANCE

Not only does the blessing of perfect forgiveness come through the new covenant, but also the promise of the *"eternal inheritance"* in contrast to the earthly inheritance, which, under the old covenant, Israel obtained. The mention of the inheritance is held to justify the taking of the word in Hebrews 9:16 as *"testament,"* the writer passing on the thought of a testamentary disposition, which is only a force after the death of the testator.

Undoubtedly there is good ground for the analogy, and all the blessings of salvation which come to the believer may be considered as bequeathed by the Saviour in His death, and accruing to us because He has died. In that sense, it has to be tacitly assumed that the testator lives again to be His own executor and to guarantee possession of the blessings.

In other words, Jesus is the only one who has ever left a will (last will and testament), which benefit is to be received upon His death and then come back from the dead (resurrection) to guarantee that the terms of the will be carried out in totality. One can only shout, hallelujah!

COVENANT

Still, we think there is much to be said in favor of keeping to the sense of covenant even here, and taking the phrase, which, rendered, is: *"a testament* (covenant) *is of force after men are dead"* (Heb. 9:17), as meaning that the covenant is established on the ground of sacrifice, that sacrifice representing the death of the maker of the covenant, in this case Christ.

The allusion may be further explained by a reference to Genesis 15:9–10, 17, which has generally been considered as illustrating the ancient Semitic method of making a covenant: the sacrificial animals being divided, and the parties passing between the pieces, implying that they deserved death if they broke the engagement.

The technical Hebrew phrase for making a covenant is "to cut a covenant."

Whatever the particular application of the word in Hebrews 9:17, the central idea in the passage is that death— blood-shedding—is necessary to the establishment of the covenant, and so he affirms that the first covenant was not dedicated without blood, and in proof quotes the passage already cited from Exodus 24, and concludes that *"without shedding of blood is no remission"* (remission of sins) (Heb. 9:22).

THE PROPHET JEREMIAH

This new covenant established by Christ was foretold by the prophet Jeremiah, who uses the phrase "new covenant" in describing it, and very likely Christ had that description in mind when He used the term, and meant for His disciples to understand that the prophetic interpretation would be realized in Him (Mat. 26:28). There is no doubt that the author of Hebrews had the passage in mind, for he has led up to the previous statement by definitely quoting the whole statement of Jeremiah 31:31–34 (Heb. 8:10–13).

He had in Hebrews 7 spoken of the contrast between Christ's priesthood *"after the order of Melchisedec"* (Heb. 7:11) and the imperfect Aaronic priesthood, and he designates Jesus as *"a surety of a better testament* (covenant)*"* (Heb. 7:22).

Then in Hebrews 8, he emphasizes the thought of the superiority of Christ's heavenly high priesthood, declaring that God is the *"mediator of a better covenant, which was established upon better promises"* (Heb. 8:6).

THE NEED FOR THE SECOND COVENANT

The first covenant, he says, was not faultless, otherwise there would have been no need for a second; but the fault was not in the covenant but in the people who failed to keep it, though perhaps there is also the suggestion that the external imposition of laws could not suffice to secure true obedience. *"For finding fault with them, he saith, Behold the days come, saith the Lord, when I will make a new covenant with the house of Israel and with the house of Judah"* (Heb. 8:8).

The whole passage (Heb. 8:8–12) would repay careful study, but we need only note that not only is there prominence given to the great blessings of the covenant, perfect forgiveness and fullness of knowledge, but, as the very essence of the covenant—that which serves to distinguish it from the old covenant and at once to show its superiority and guarantee its permanence—there is this wonderful provision: *"I will put my laws into their mind, and write them in their hearts: and I will be to them a God, and they shall be to me a people"* (Heb. 8:10).

This at once shows the spirituality of the new covenant. Its requirements are not simply given in the form of external rules, but the living Spirit possesses the heart; the law becomes an internal dominating principle, and so true obedience is then secured.

To sum it all up, if one wants to know the need for the second covenant, the first covenant could not cleanse from sin, simply because the blood of bulls and goats was incapable of carrying out that which is indicative of the new covenant. Thank God the blood of Jesus Christ cleanses from all sin.

EZEKIEL

The prophet Ezekiel had spoken to the same effect, though the phrase *new covenant* is not used in his passage. He said, *"I will put my spirit within you, and cause you to walk in my statutes, and you shall keep my judgments, and do them"* (Ezek. 36:27).

Ezekiel also speaks of the great blessings to be enjoyed by the people of God, including cleansing, walking in God's statutes, recognition as God's people, etc., and he distinctly says of this era of blessing, *"I will make a covenant of peace with them; it shall be an everlasting covenant with them"* (Ezek. 37:26).

Other important foreshadowings of the new covenant are found in Isaiah 54:10; 55:3; 59:21; 61:8; Hos. 2:18–23; Mal. 3:1–4. We may well marvel at the spiritual insight of these prophets, and it is impossible to attribute their forecasts to natural genius; they can only be accounted for by divine inspiration.

REFERRING BACK TO THE PROMISE

The writer to the Hebrews recurs again and again to this theme of the "new covenant"; in Hebrews 10:16–17 he cites the words of Jeremiah already quoted about writing the law on their minds and remembering their sins no more. In Hebrews 12:24, he speaks of *"Jesus the mediator of the new covenant,"* and *"the blood of sprinkling,"* again connecting the blood with the covenant, and finally, in Hebrews 13:20 he prays for the perfection of the saints through the *"blood of the everlasting covenant."*

In II Corinthians 3 Paul has an interesting and instructive contrast between the old covenant and the new. He begins it by saying that *"Our sufficiency is of God; who also hath made us able ministers of the new testament* (covenant); *not of the letter, but of the Spirit: for the letter killeth, but the spirit giveth life"* (II Cor. 3:5–6).

The *"letter"* is the letter of the law, of the old covenant which could only bring condemnation, but the Spirit which characterizes the new covenant gives life, writing the law upon the heart.

He goes on to speak of the old as that *"ministration of death"* which nevertheless came with glory, and he refers especially to the law, but the new covenant is *"the ministration of the spirit,"* the *"ministration of righteousness"* (II Cor. 3:8–9), and has a far greater glory than the old.

THE GOSPEL OF CHRIST

The message of this new covenant is "the gospel of Christ." The glory of the new covenant is focused in Christ; rays shooting forth from Him.

The glory of the old dispensation was reflected upon the face of Moses, but that glory was transitory and so was the physical manifestation. In other words, that glory soon faded, signifying that the law of Moses at least as it was then given, was temporary as well.

The sight of the shining face of Moses awed the people of Israel and they revered him as a leader specially favored of God. When he had delivered his message, he veiled his face and thus the people could not see that the glow and glory did not last; every time that he went into the divine presence, he took off the veil and afresh his face was lit up with the glory, and coming out with the traces of that glory lingering on his countenance he delivered his message to the people and again veiled his face (Ex. 34:29–35), and thus the transitoriness and obscurity of the old dispensation were symbolized.

In glorious contrast to that symbolical obscurity, the ministers of the gospel, of the new covenant, use great boldness of speech; simply because the veil is done away in Christ (II Cor. 3:14).

The glory which comes through Him is perpetual, and fears no vanishing away.

A BRIEF VIEW OF THE NEW COVENANT
AS PREACHED BY PAUL

Paul interprets God and man by his doctrine of Christ. To him Jesus is Christ and Christ is Jesus. The real mystery of God is Christ, not the so-called mystery-religions. Christ has set us free from the bondage of ceremonial legalism. We are free from the curse of the law (Gal. 3:1). Grace is the distinctive word for the gospel (Rom. 3–5), but it must lead to sanctification (Rom. 6–8), not license (Col. 3).

Paul's teaching concerning redemption is the love of God seeking a world lost in sin and finding love's way, the only way consonant with justice, in the atoning sacrifice of Jesus Christ God's Son (Rom. 3:21–31). The sinner comes into union with God in Christ by faith in Christ as Redeemer and Lord. Henceforth he lives to (for) God in Christ by the help of the Holy Spirit (Rom. 8; Gal. 5). Paul presents God as Father of all in one sense (Eph. 4:6), but in a special sense of the believers in Christ (Rom. 8:15).

Jesus Christ is the incarnated Son of God (II Cor. 8:9; Phil. 2:5–10), who is both God and man (Rom. 1:3). With Paul the agent of creation is Jesus (Col. 1:15), who is also the head of the church universal (Eph. 1:22; Col. 1:18).

THE CROSS

In the work of Christ, Paul gives the central place to the cross (I Cor. 1:17; 2:2; Eph. 2:13–18; Col. 2:20). Sin is universal in humanity (Rom. 1:18–3:20), but the vicarious death of Christ makes redemption possible to all who believe (Rom. 3:21; Gal. 3:6–11).

The redeemed constitute the kingdom of God or church universal, with Christ as head. Local bodies (churches) are the chief means for pushing the work of the kingdom.

Paul knows two ordinances, both of which present in symbolic form the death of Christ for sin and the pledge of the believer to newness of life in Christ. These ordinances are water baptism and the Lord's Supper (I Cor. 11:17–34).

Actually, the Lord's Supper give us a clearer view of the atoning work of Christ on Calvary's cross, more so than anything else. That is the main reason we are encouraged to periodically take this supper, simply because of what it represents.

THE SECOND COMING OF CHRIST

Paul is animated by the Rapture of the Church (I Thess. 4:13–18), and the second coming of Christ, which will be sudden (I Thess. 5:1–11). However, even though he taught that such would not happen in his day (II Thess. 2), he did teach that it was always to be considered as imminent (I Thess. 5:2).

Meanwhile, the death of the saint brings us to Christ, which is a glorious hope (II Cor. 5:1–10; Phil. 1:21; II Tim. 4:18).

RIGHTEOUSNESS

Paul preached righteousness, but a righteousness which could only come about in Christ. His notion of the righteousness demanded by God and given by God included both sanctification and justification.

In the end, the sinner who for Christ's sake is treated as righteous must be righteous. Thus, the image of God is restored in man by the regenerating work of the Spirit of God (II Cor. 3:18).

Paul sees God in the face of Christ (II Cor. 4:6), and the vision of Christ brings God to all who see.

JUSTIFICATION BY FAITH

To properly understand the new covenant, a proper understanding of justification by faith is necessary. While Jesus is the central theme of the new covenant, and in effect is the new covenant, meaning that He in His person is the new covenant, in other words the leading actor, justification by faith is what He brought to humanity by His death and resurrection.

Out of the thirty-nine occurrences of the verb *justify* in the New Testament, twenty-nine come in the Epistles or recorded works of the apostle Paul; so do the two occurrences of the corresponding noun, *dikaiosis* (Rom. 4:25; 5:18). This reflects the fact that Paul alone of New Testament writers makes the concept of justification basic to his doctrine. This is explained in the fact that Paul was given the meaning of the new covenant, and therefore had a greater understanding than any of the other writers concerning its concepts.

In no way does this mean that the other writers of the New Testament taught any other gospel, or contradicted Paul in any manner, which they did not. The same Holy Spirit inspired all; therefore, it would not be possible for there to be any contradiction. However, it was Paul who fully proclaimed that covenant, while the other writers complemented that which the Holy Spirit through him gave to the church.

THE MEANING OF JUSTIFICATION

Justification means to Paul God's act of remitting the sins of guilty men, and accounting us righteous, freely, by His grace, through faith in Christ, on the ground, not of our own works, but of the representative law keeping and redemptive blood-shedding of the Lord Jesus Christ on our behalf (Rom. 3:23–26; 4:5–8; 5:18).

Paul's doctrine of justification is his characteristic way of formulating the central gospel truth that God forgives believing sinners. Theologically, it is the most highly developed expression of this truth in the New Testament.

THE RIGHTEOUSNESS OF GOD

In Romans, Paul introduces the gospel as disclosing *"the righteousness of God"* (Rom. 1:17). This phrase proves to have a double reference:

- To the righteous man's status, which God through Christ freely confers upon believing sinners, i.e., *"the gift of righteousness"* (Rom. 5:17; 3:21; 9:30; 10:3–10; II Cor. 5:21; Phil. 3:9).

- To the way in which the gospel reveals God as doing what is right—not only judging transgressors as they deserve (Rom. 2:5; 3:5) but also keeping His promise to send salvation to Israel (Rom. 3:4), and justifying sinners in such a way that His own judicial claims upon them are met (Rom. 3:25). It was at the cross with Jesus giving Himself as a sacrifice, that makes justification possible, and only by the cross. In other words, when the believing sinner expresses faith in Christ who has paid the price, who has satisfied the ransom, who has met every demand of a thrice-holy God, that is the reason that justification is then made possible.

"The righteousness of God" is thus predominantly a forensic concept (argument), denoting God's gracious work of bestowing upon guilty sinners a justified justification, acquitting them in the court of heaven without prejudice to His justice as their judge.

It has been questioned whether Paul's doctrine of justification by faith without works is any more than a controversial device, developed simply as a weapon against the Judaizers. But the following facts indicate that it was more than this— far more.

ROMANS

The epistle to the Romans is evidently to be read as a full-dressed statement of Paul's gospel, and the doctrine of justification is its backbone.

In fact, if the believer doesn't understand the book of Romans, he little understands his salvation. That book (epistle) as given to Paul by the Holy Spirit defines all that we believe, and all that we are in Christ Jesus. It points not only to our salvation, but as well, to victory over sin in any and every capacity. It is truly the emancipation proclamation of mankind.

PERSONAL

In three places Paul writes in personal terms of the convictions that had made him the man and the missionary that he was, and all three are couched in terms of justification (II Cor. 5:16–21; Gal. 2:15–21; Phil. 3:4–14).

In Romans 7:7, Paul describes his personal need of Christ in terms of the law's condemnation—a need which only God's justifying sentence in Christ could relieve (Rom. 8:1; Gal. 3:19–4:7). Paul's personal salvation was evidently rooted in the knowledge of his justification, and so is ours.

GOD'S FUNDAMENTAL ACT OF BLESSINGS

Justification is to Paul God's fundamental act of blessing, for it both saves from the past and secures for the future.

On the one hand, it means pardon, and the end of hostility between God and ourselves (Acts 13:39; Rom. 4:6; 5:9). On the other hand, it means acceptance and a title to all blessings promised to the just, a thought which Paul develops by linking justification with adoption and heirship (Rom. 8:14; Gal. 4:4).

Both aspects appear in Romans 5:1–2, where Paul says that justification brings both peace with God (because sins are remitted) and hope of God's glory (because the sinner is accepted as righteous). This hope is a certainty; for justification has an eschatological significance (pertains to the end-time).

It is the judgment of the last day brought into the present, a final, irreversible verdict. In other words, what we will have then, we have now—salvation, but not fully developed.

The justified man can be sure accordingly that nothing will ever separate him from the love of his God (Rom. 8:33–39). His glorification is certain (Rom. 8:30), that is, if he continues to trust Christ and what Christ did for us at the Cross.

The coming inquisition before Christ's judgment-seat, where every believer will one day stand (Rom. 14:10; II Cor. 5:10) may deprive him of particular rewards (I Cor. 3:15), but not his justified status.

THE BASIC REFERENCE POINT

Paul's doctrine of salvation has justification as its basic reference point. His belief about justification is the source from which flows his view of Christianity as a salvation of grace and faith, in which Gentiles and Jews stand on an equal footing (Rom. 1:16; 3:29; Gal. 3:8–14, 28). It is in terms of justification that he explains grace (Rom. 3:24; 4:4, 16), the saving significance of Christ's obedience and death (Rom. 3:24; 5:16), the revelation of God's love at the cross (Rom. 5:5–9), the meaning of redemption (Rom. 3:24; Gal. 3:13; Eph. 1:7) and reconciliation

(II Cor. 5:18), the covenant relationship (Gal. 3:15), faith (Rom. 4:23; 10:8), union with Christ (Rom. 8:1; Gal. 2:17), adoption and the gift of the Spirit (Gal. 4:6–8; Rom. 8:10, 15), and Christian assurance (Rom. 5:1–11; 8:33), all made possible by the new covenant, which is made possible by the cross. In other words, the cross is the foundation of all things that we receive from God, and especially the new covenant.

It is in terms of justification that Paul explains all hints, prophecies, and instances of salvation in the Old Testament (Rom. 1:17; Gal. 3:11, quoting Hab. 2:4; Rom. 3:21; 4:3–8, quoting Gen. 15:6; Ps. 32:1; Rom. 9:22–10:21, quoting Hos. 2:23; 1:10; Isa. 8:14; Joel 2:32; Isa. 65:1, etc., Rom. 11:26, quoting Isa. 59:20; Gal. 3:8, quoting Gen. 12:3; Gal. 4:21, quoting Gen. 21:10; etc.).

THE KEY TO HISTORY

Justification is the key to Paul's philosophy of history. He holds that God's central overarching purpose in His ordering of world-history since the fall has been to lead sinners to justifying faith.

God deals with mankind, Paul tells us, through two representative men: *"the first man Adam,"* and *"the second man,"* who is *"the Last Adam,"* Jesus Christ (I Cor. 15:45; Rom. 5:12).

The first man, by disobeying, brought condemnation and death upon the whole race; the second man, by His obedience, has become the author of justification and life for all who have faith (Rom. 5:16).

From the time of Adam's fall, death reigned universally, though sin was not yet clearly known (Rom. 5:12). God took Abraham and his family into covenant, justifying Abraham through his faith, and promising that in Abraham's seed (through one of his descendants) all nations should be blessed (justified) (Gal. 3:6–9, 16; Rom. 4:3, 9–22).

Even through Moses God revealed His law to Abraham's family. The law was meant to give, not salvation but knowledge of sin, in other words to define sin as to what it was and how bad it was. By detecting and provoking transgressions, it was to teach Israelites their need of justification, thus acting as a teacher (the household slave who took children to school) to lead them to Christ (Rom. 3:20; 5:20; 7:5, 7–13; Gal. 3:19–24).

This epoch of divine preparatory education lasted until the coming of Christ (Gal. 3:23–25; 4:1–5).

THE WORK OF CHRIST

The effect of Christ's work was to abolish the barrier of exclusivism which Israel's possession of the law and promise had erected between Jew and Gentile (Eph. 2:14), through Christ, justification by faith could now be preached to Jew and Gentile without distinction, for in Christ all believers were made Abraham's seed, and became sons of God and heirs of the covenant (Gal. 3:26–29).

Unhappily, in this situation most Jews proved to be legalists; they sought to establish a righteousness of their own by works of law, and would not believe that faith in Christ was the God-given way to righteousness, and the only way to righteousness (Rom. 9:30–10:21). So many *"natural branches"* had been cut off from the olive tree of the historical covenant community (Rom. 11:16), and the church was for the present predominantly Gentile; but there was hope that an elect remnant from fallen Israel, provoked by the mercy shown to undeserving Gentiles, would themselves come to faith and find remission of sins in the end (Rom. 11:23–32). Thus, both Jew and Gentiles would be saved, not through their own works and effort, but through the free grace of God justifying the disobedient and ungodly; and all the glory of salvation will be God's alone (Rom. 11:30–36).

Regrettably, precious few of Israel have sought justification by faith in Christ. Yet Israel will ultimately come back to the Lord, accepting Christ as Saviour, which will take place at the second coming and will come as all have come, justified by faith in Christ.

These considerations point to the centrality of justification in Paul's theological outlook.

THE GROUND OF JUSTIFICATION

As stated by Paul in Romans, the doctrine of justification seems to raise a problem of theodicy (the defense of God's goodness and omnipotence in view of the existence of evil). Its background, set out in Romans 1:18–3:20, is the solidarity of mankind in sin and the inevitability of judgment.

In Romans 2:5–16, Paul states his doctrine of the judgment day. The principle of judgment, he says, will be *"to every man according to his deeds* (works)*"* (Rom. 2:6).

The standard of judgment will be God's law, in the highest form in which men know it (if not the Mosaic law, then the law of conscience). The evidence will be *"the secrets of men."* Only law keepers can hope to be justified.

And there are no law keepers. None are righteous; all have sinned (Rom. 3:9). So the prospect is of universal condemnation, for Jew as well as Gentile, for a law-breaking Jew is no more acceptable to God than anyone else (Rom. 2:17–27). All, it seems, are doomed.

No human being will be justified in His (God's) sight by works of the law, for the simple reason, that none have ever kept the law (Rom. 3:20, echoing Ps. 143:2).

THE JUSTIFICATION OF THE UNGODLY

But now Paul proclaims the present justification of believing sinners (Rom. 3:21). God reckons righteousness to the unrighteous and justifies the ungodly (Rom. 3:23; 4:5).

Deliberately? Quality of the last phrase is heightened by the fact that these very Greek words are used in the Greek translation of Exodus 23:7, *"I will not justify the wicked"* and Isaiah 5:22–23, *"Woe unto them … Which justify the wicked.…"* The question arises, on what grounds can God justify the ungodly without compromising His own justice as the judge? Or breaking His own Word?

THE SATISFACTION OF GOD'S LAW

Paul maintains that God justifies sinners on a just ground: Namely, that Jesus Christ, acting on our behalf, has satisfied the claims of God's law upon us. He was *"made* (born) *under the law"* (Gal. 4:4) in order to fulfill the precept and bear the penalty of the law in our stead.

By His blood (His death) He put away our sins (Rom. 3:25; 5:9). By His obedience to God He won for all His people the status of law keepers (Rom. 5:19). He became *"obedient unto death"* (Phil. 2:8); His life of righteousness culminated in His dying the death of the unrighteous, bearing the law's penal curse (Isa. 53:4–12; Gal. 3:13).

In His person on the cross, the sins of His people were judged and expiated. Through this one act of righteousness— His sinless life and death— *"the free gift came upon all men unto justification of life"* (Rom. 5:18).

Thus, believers become *"the righteousness of God"* in and through Him who *"knew no sin"* personally, but was representatively made to be sin (a sin offering) in our place (II Cor. 5:21). Thus, Paul speaks of *"Christ Jesus, who of God is made …* (our) *righteousness"* (I Cor. 1:30).

The Old Testament statements given concerning the wicked not being justified, pertains to the claims of heavenly justice being unsatisfied. In other words, they could not be justified, would not be justified, God would see to it that they were not justified, unless heaven's claims of the payment of the sin penalty were carried out, in which it was done in Christ. Consequently, heaven's claims being satisfied, then the wicked could be justified, which they are in Christ.

THE IMPUTATION OF CHRIST'S RIGHTEOUSNESS

This was the thought expressed in older Protestant theology by the phrase, "the imputation of Christ's righteousness." The phrase is not in Paul, but its meaning is.

The point it makes is that believers are made righteous before God (Rom. 5:19) through His admitting them to share Christ's status of acceptance. In other words, God treats them according to Christ's desert. There is nothing arbitrary or artificial in this, for God recognizes the existence of a real union of covenantal solidarity between them (believing sinners) and Christ. For Paul, union with Christ is not fiction, but fact—the basic fact, indeed, of Christianity; and his doctrine of justification is simply his first step in analyzing its meaning. So it is *"in Christ"* (Gal. 2:17; II Cor. 5:21) that sinners are justified, in fact the only way in which they can be justified.

God accounts them righteous, not because He accounts them to have kept His law personally (which would be a false judgment), but because He accounts them to be "in" the one who kept God's law in perfection, and did so representatively, who is Jesus.

SUBSTITUTION AND IDENTIFICATION

The great doctrine of substitution (Christ becoming our substitute) and identification (the believing sinner identifying with all that Christ is and did), presents the mechanics of "justification by faith." Actually, it is the sum total of salvation, the product of the new covenant.

The key words are for emphasis, for the point is crucial, the gospel which proclaims God's apparent violation of His justice really reveals His justice. By His method of justifying sinners, God (in another sense) justified Himself; for by sending forth Christ as a propitiation for sins, in whom human sin was actually judged and punished as it deserved, He revealed the just ground on which He was able to pardon and accept believing sinners in Old Testament times (as in fact He did: Ps. 130:3), no less than in the Christian era.

THE MEANS OF JUSTIFICATION

Faith in Christ, says Paul, is the means whereby righteousness is received and justification bestowed. Sinners are justified *by* or *through* faith.

Paul does not regard faith as the ground of justification. If it were, it would be a work of merit, and Paul would not be able to term the believer, as such, one who does not work for his salvation (Rom. 4:5); nor could he go on to say that salvation by faith rests on grace (Rom. 4:16), for grace absolutely excludes works (Rom. 11:6).

Paul quotes the case of Abraham, who *"believed God, and it was counted unto him for righteousness,"* to prove that a man is justified through faith without works (Rom. 4:3; Gal. 3:6; quoting Gen. 15:6).

ABRAHAM'S FAITH

In Romans 4:5, 9, 22, and 24, Paul refers to the Genesis text as teaching that Abraham's faith was *"reckoned … for righteousness."*

All he means, however, as the context shows, is that Abraham's faith—wholehearted reliance on God's promise—was the occasion and means of his being justified. The phrase *"reckoned to him for* (as) *righteousness"* could either mean *"as"* (by real equivalence, or some arbitrary method of calculation), or else *"with a view to, leading to, issuing in."* The latter alternative is clearly right.

Paul is not suggesting that faith, viewed either as righteousness, actual or as a substitute for righteousness, is the ground of justification; Romans 4 does not deal with the ground of justification at all, only with the means of securing it. The ground of justification is Christ's obedience and death.

PAUL AND JAMES

On the assumption that James 2:14-26 teaches that God accepts men on the double ground of faith and works, some have thought that James deliberately contradicts Paul's teaching of justification by faith without works. This seems to misconceive James' point.

It must be remembered that Paul is the only New Testament writer to use the word *justify* as a technical term for God's act of accepting of men when they believe. When James speaks of being justified, he appears to be using the word in its more general sense of being vindicated, or proved genuine and right before God and men, in face of possible doubt as to whether one was all that one professed, or was said to be.

For a man to be justified in this sense is for him to be shown a genuine believer, one who will demonstrate his faith by action, which is certainly proper, and which certainly will happen. This justification is, in effect, a manifesting of the justification that concerns Paul.

SHOWN TO BE TRUE

In fact, James quotes Genesis 15:6 for the same purpose as Paul does—to show that it was faith that secured Abraham's acceptance. But now he argues this statement was fulfilled (confirmed, shown to be true, and brought to its appointed completion by events) thirty years later, when Abraham (was) justified by works, when he offered his son Isaac upon the altar (James 2:21).

By that, James goes on to say, his faith was *"made perfect,"* i.e., brought to due expression in appropriate action; thus he was shown to be a true believer.

The case of Rahab is parallel (James 2:25).

James' point in this paragraph is simply that faith, i.e., a bare orthodoxy, such as the devils have (James 2:19), unaccompanied by good works, provides no sufficient grounds for inferring that a man is saved. Paul would have agreed heartily (I Cor. 6:9; Eph. 5:5; Tit. 1:16).

They who know the Savior shall in Him be strong,
Mighty in the conflict of the right against wrong;
This the blessed promise given in God's Word,
Doing wondrous exploits, they who know the Lord.

In the midst of battle be thou not dismayed,
Though the powers of darkness against thee are arrayed;
God, thy strength, is with thee, causing thee to stand,
Heaven's allied armies wait at thy command.

Brave to bear life's testing, strong the foe to meet,
Walking like a hero midst the furnace heat,
Doing wondrous exploits with the Spirit's sword,
Winning souls for Jesus, praise, oh, praise the Lord!

THE NEW COVENANT

CHAPTER 3

TITUS

TITUS

"BUT NEITHER TITUS, who was with me, being a Greek, was compelled to be circumcised" (Gal. 2:3).

Paul's familiar metaphors which are those depict the Christian life as a race (I Cor. 9:24–26; Phil. 2:16). He refers to his life and ministry among the Gentiles as such a race and was concerned *"lest by any means I should run, or had run, in vain"* (Gal. 2:2).

He realized that if the recognized leaders of the Jerusalem church opposed his gospel, all the work he had done would be destroyed by their emissaries and he could not hope to accomplish anything in the future. His certainty of the divine origin of his message did not blind him to the practical fatality of division and divergence in the church.

The phrase, *"But neither Titus, who was with me,"* presents the apostle introducing the case of Titus undoubtedly to show that circumcision was not necessary to salvation. It was a case in point.

He had gone up to Jerusalem with express reference to this question. Here was a man whom he had admitted to the Christian faith without circumcising him. He claimed that he had a right to do so; and that circumcision was not necessary in order to gain salvation.

JERUSALEM

If it were necessary, as the Judaizers were claiming, it would have been proper that Titus would have been compelled to submit to this rite. Paul says this was not demanded; or if demanded by any, the point was yielded, and Titus was not compelled to be circumcised.

It is to be remembered that this was at Jerusalem; that it was a case submitted to the apostles there; and that consequently the determination of this case settled the whole controversy about the obligation of the Mosaic laws on the Gentile converts. It is quite evident from the whole statement here, that Paul did not intend that Titus should be circumcised; that he maintained that it was not necessary; and that he resisted it when it was demanded (Gal. 2:4–5).

TIMOTHY

Yet on another occasion he himself performed the act of circumcision on Timothy (Acts 16:3). There is no inconsistency in his conduct. In the case of Titus it was demanded as a matter of rite and as obligatory on him, and he resisted the principle as wrong.

In the case of Timothy, it was a voluntary compliance on his part with the usual custom of the Jews, where it was not pressed as a matter of obligation, and where it would not be understood as indispensable to salvation.

Considering that Timothy was Jewish, no danger or problem would follow from compliance with the custom, and it might do much to conciliate the favor of the Jews, and he therefore submitted to it. Paul would not have hesitated to have circumcised Titus (a Gentile) in the same circumstances in which it was done to Timothy; but the circumstances now were different; and when it was insisted on as a matter of principle and of obligation, it became a matter of principle and of obligation with him to oppose it, which he did, and which in fact, he had no choice (some of the material on circumcision was given by Dr. Albert Barnes).[1]

A GREEK

The phrase, *"being a Greek,"* means that Titus was a Gentile. It was a bold move on the part of Paul to bring with him to the Jerusalem Council, an uncircumcised Gentile, introducing him as a test case if you please. The dispute over the necessity of Gentile circumcision took place at the Antioch church and was successfully resisted there. Then the church in that city determined to send its decision to the Jerusalem church to see whether it would or would not sustain its action (Acts 15:1–2).

CIRCUMCISION

In Galatians 2:3, the phrase, *"was compelled to be circumcised,"* introduces an instance in which Paul defended the purity of the gospel from the encroachments of those who would have mixed aspects of the Mosaic law with grace as the way of salvation. This incident was the attempt of the Jewish legalists to force the rite of circumcision on Titus, and all Gentile converts for that matter. The outcome of the struggle, as Paul said, was a successful defense of the gospel.

The word *compelled* denies, not the attempt to compel Titus to be circumcised, but the success of the attempt. The context clearly indicates that strong pressure by the Judaizers was brought to bear upon the Jerusalem church to impose circumcision upon Gentile converts. Titus was the figure, the individual if you will, around whom the controversy was raging. The end result was that the Jerusalem Council sustained the decision of the Antioch church to the effect that circumcision was not to be required of Gentile converts.[2]

PAUL'S POSITION

Paul did not reject circumcision as a damnable thing; neither did he by word or deed enforce the Jews to forsake it. In I Corinthians 7:18 he said, *"Is any man called being circumcised? let him not become uncircumcised."*

But he rejected it as a thing not necessary to righteousness, seeing the fathers themselves were not justified thereby (Rom. 4:11), but it was unto them a sign only, or a seal of righteousness, whereby they testified their faith.

As stated, at this conference it was decided that circumcision was not necessary to justification and therefore not to be forced upon the Gentiles; however, the false apostles were not satisfied to leave it at that, but continued to require the same as necessary to salvation, which here Paul is refuting.

The apostle's purpose in relating this entire incident was to show that even there in the Jerusalem church his Greek companion was not compelled to submit to the ceremonial law. This being true, what grounds could his opponents possibly have for insisting on circumcision in the homeland of the Gentiles?

If the reader is not so familiar with Old Testament doctrine, he may wonder as to how in the world that circumcision could play any part in the salvation process.

THE OLD TESTAMENT ACCOUNT

In Genesis 17, God's divine covenant with Abraham is set out first as a series of promises which were personal and were to become national. Circumcision of the males was a sign of that covenant. It was in this symbol of the divine promise which was applied to the divinely-nominated recipients. Consequently, this relationship of circumcision to foregoing promise shows that the rite signifies the gracious movement of God to man. In a sense, circumcision was the token of that work of grace whereby God chooses out and marks men for His own, at least as it was under the old covenant.

The covenant of circumcision operates on the principle of the spiritual union of the household and its head. The covenant is *"between me and thee and thy seed after thee"* (Gen. 17:7).

Thus, those who became members of the covenant were expected to show it outwardly by obedience to God's law, expressed to Abraham in the most general form, *"Walk before me, and be thou perfect"* (Gen. 17:1). Consequently, the relation between circumcision and obedience remains a biblical constant that is under the old covenant (Jer. 4:4; Acts 15:5; Rom. 2:25–29; Gal. 5:3).

In this respect, circumcision involves the idea of consecration to God, but not as its essence. Circumcision embodies and applies covenant promises and summons to a life of covenant obedience. The blood which is shed in circumcision does not express the desperate lengths to which a man must go in self-consecration, but the costly demand which God makes of those whom He calls to Himself and marks with the sign of His covenant.

The Bible candidly allows that it is possible to possess this sign and nothing more, in which case it is spiritually defunct and indeed condemnatory (Rom. 2:27). Actually, the Old Testament plainly teaches it, as it calls for the reality appropriate to the sign (Deut. 10:16; Jer. 4:4), and warns that in the absence of the reality the sign of circumcision is nothing (Jer. 9:25), and foresees the circumcision of the heart by God (Deut. 30:6).

IN THE NEW TESTAMENT

The New Testament is unequivocal: without obedience, circumcision becomes uncircumcision (Rom. 2:25–29); the outward sign fades into insignificance when compared with the realities of keeping the Commandments (I Cor. 7:18–19), faith working by love (Gal. 5:6) and a new creation (Gal. 6:15).

Nevertheless, the Christian is not at liberty to scorn the sign. Although, insofar as it is expressed salvation by works of law, the Christian must shun it (Gal. 5:2), yet in its inner meaning he needs it (Isa. 52:1; Col. 2:13). Consequently, there is a *"circumcision of Christ,"* the *"putting off* (of) *the body* (and not only part) *of the ... flesh,"* a spiritual transaction not made with hands, a relation to Christ in His death and resurrection, sealed by the ordinance of the new covenant (Col. 2:11–12).

Paul says that to Christians who would engage in circumcision, thinking that it pertained to salvation (Phil. 3:3), the enforcement of the outmoded sign is tantamount to a heathenish gashing of the physical body, which of course, is preposterous.

WHAT CIRCUMCISION HAD BECOME
BY THE TIME OF CHRIST

The sign of circumcision was meant to serve as a symbolism of the covenant relationship with God, in other words, that man was separated from the heathen unto God and unto God's ways; however, it was a symbol only, and was not to be looked at as anything more or less. Of course, to flagrantly ignore this command by God would have been spiritually disastrous. But at the same time, the obedience of carrying out the rite of circumcision, did not necessarily mean at all that the person was right with God. In fact, most Israelites were not, for the simple reason that many if not most came to believe, that the mere carrying forth of these particular rites and ceremonies constituted salvation, which it did not.

In fact, the Jews of New Testament times had so associated circumcision with Moses that they had virtually forgotten its more fundamental association with Abraham (Acts 15:1, 5; 21:21; Gal. 5:2–3). Our Lord had to remind them that circumcision antedated Moses (Jn. 7:22).

Paul is emphatic that it was the current understanding of the Mosaic connection which was obnoxious to Christianity (Gal. 5:2–3, 11), and constantly brings his readers back to Abraham (Rom. 4:11; 15:8).

PRESENT SIMILARITIES

As some of the Christian Jews were attempting to force the rite of circumcision into the salvation process, the modern variety attempts to do the same.

When this is done, which is wrong to begin with, the salvation process always degenerates to the sign or symbol. In other words, those who submitted to such, ultimately equated the sign with salvation, with a personal relationship with Christ ignored.

Those presently who attempt to attach water baptism with salvation, or the Lord's Supper, or tongues, or joining particular churches are doing the same identical thing as the Judaizers of old. They are attempting to add works to grace which God can never accept. That's the reason Paul said, *"Christ is become of no effect unto you, whosoever of you are* (attempt to be) *justified by the law; ye are fallen from grace*" (Gal. 5:4). The same must be said presently: Any professing Christian who thinks that his salvation consists of works or ordinances of any nature is fallen from grace, that is, if he ever was in grace. Salvation is in Christ alone, and faith in Him and faith alone secures that salvation (Eph. 2:8–9).

That being the case, are these people who depend on water baptism or anything other than Christ saved? No!

FALSE BRETHREN

"And that because of false brethren unawares brought in, who came in privily to spy out our liberty which we have in Christ Jesus, that they might bring us into bondage" (Gal. 2:4).

The problem here was not just a matter of Gentile or Jewish customs; the truth of the gospel itself was at stake.

As we have already stated, previous to the public meeting Paul privately told the leading apostles what were the doctrines he preached and the effects produced, lest they should think that he had run or was running in vain—he had no such apprehension himself—and in order that they might be able to intelligently guide the public discussion. Their decision was that the Gentile believers were not bound to observe the law of Moses. As to the Hebrew believers, they made no such pronouncement (Acts 15).

Teachers (false teachers) visited the Galatian churches, and taught that all (even Gentiles) must join the Hebrew church, so to speak, and observe the law of Moses if they were to be saved. It was these teachers and their teaching that Paul denounced.

Two principles were in opposition: Salvation by works and salvation by faith. The one principle directed men to great activity in going about to establish their own righteousness (Rom. 10:3; Tit. 3:5); the other forbade all carnal religious effort and commanded faith in a Saviour who had accomplished everything necessary for man's redemption.

The world applauds the first principle, and whatever the world applauds influences and pleases man, for it gives a certain glory to him. But the glory obscures Christ's glory and falsifies the gospel.

THE LOUD DEMAND

In Galatians 2:4, the phrase, *"And that because of false brethren unawares brought in,"* pertains to Satan's efforts to pervert the true gospel of Jesus Christ.

In the Greek, the words *false brethren are pseuda-delphos,* and mean "a spurious brother, pretended associate." It also means "untrue, erroneous, deceitful, wicked, liar."

Also in the Greek, the word *unawares* is *pareisakatos,* and it means "smuggled in, to introduce surreptitiously."

False brethren suggests that they were fellow believers, but their insistence upon the necessity of the law constituted in Paul's eyes a denial of Christ, and I personally think it constituted a denial in the eyes of the Lord as well.

The loud demand—which these false brethren were making, that all Gentile converts should be circumcised—was distinctly rested by them upon the principle that otherwise those converts were not qualified for sonship in God's family or for admission to church fellowship with, at any rate, the believing circumcision. This demand of theirs, made upon this pernicious principle, was that which had raised the present controversy, and had brought Paul and his fellow deputies to Jerusalem. If under such circumstances Titus, with Paul's concurrence, had consented to be circumcised, then whatever the motive of his consent, it would have seemed to those false brethren, and not to them only, but indeed to the church at large that all had agreed in recognizing the soundness of that principle of theirs that circumcision was indispensable for perfect divine acceptance.

It was these false brethren then that made it impossible at the present juncture that those who held fast to the truth of the gospel should accept counsels of compromise or conciliation.

INDIFFERENCE

In matters of indifference, that which did not pertain to salvation, there may well be room for conciliation—this no one could ever be more ready to see and act upon than Paul; but there is also a time for the unbending assertion of truth, and the clamors of the false brethren made the present to be one of the latter kind. In that particular juncture of church development, the doctrine itself of the absolute justification of men through faith in Christ, and faith in Christ alone was at stake.

If Titus was not qualified for Christian fellowship by simply his faith in Christ, then neither was he qualified for acceptance with God by simply his faith.

Considering this matter, which was very important, the apostle's feeling is that men who do not accept the truth that through faith in Christ we are justified, and through faith only, have no proper place in the truth of the gospel. In other words, such who travel that road are not saved.

THREE PARTIES

There were three parties in the Jerusalem controversy:
- Paul and Barnabas, who maintained that Gentile converts were not to be circumcised.
- The false brethren, who demanded that they be circumcised.
- The Jerusalem apostles, who for the sake of expediency were urged by the false brethren to insist that Paul and Barnabas require circumcision of their Gentile converts.

These false brethren desired, as stated, to bring both Jew and Gentile under Mosaic law.

WHY WAS THIS ALLOWED BY THE CHURCH AT JERUSALEM TO COME TO THIS PLACE?

We have to assume that if James, who in fact was responsible, did not totally approve of the action of these false brethren, at least it seems, he did not oppose it. It must be remembered that it is Paul who refers to them as *"false brethren,"* and not James. James had made his decision as it regarded the Gentiles, but nothing was said about the Jews, which later caused tremendous problems.

This matter had arisen, which proved to be of such hurt to the early church, and which caused Paul such great problems, simply because James did not go far enough in his thinking, concerning the excellent decision he rendered about this matter, concerning the Gentiles (Acts 15). He should have included the Jews in this decision as well. Admittedly, such a decision may have caused problems with the nation of Israel as a whole. Nevertheless, the Word of God must be adhered to strictly, irrespective of the cost. As it was, and despite the compromise on the part of James—compromise, incidentally, which was wrong—James suffered martyrdom not many years after the Jerusalem Council (Acts 15).

There are not two kinds of salvation, one for the Jews and one for the Gentiles. There is only one salvation, which applies to all, irrespective as to race, color, nationality, status, place, position, education, or gender.

It was not easy for Paul to stand against what one might call the entirety of the church. However, had he not done so, and been adamant in his demands, the gospel would have been seriously hindered, if not totally destroyed.

It is very clear that these people greatly opposed Paul. They regarded him as a turncoat against Judaism; consequently, they perverted and misstated his gospel; they claimed to have a clearer view of the nature of true salvation than he had. In fact, such adversaries he met everywhere (II Cor. 11:26), and it required all of his tact and skill to meet their plausible representations.

LIBERTY IN CHRIST JESUS

In Galatians 2:4, the phrase, *"who came in privily to spy out our liberty which we have in Christ Jesus,"* indicates that their approach was subtle, smooth, and made to seem very plausible, which characterizes all deception.

Despite their claims, these people were unsaved Jews who in fact, had accepted the Lord Jesus as their Messiah, but who claimed nothing of salvation through His precious shed blood, and who clung to the salvation-by-works system of apostate and legalistic Judaism, which system they were desirous of bringing into the church itself.

In other words, the only difference in them and the Jews who had crucified Christ was that they accepted Jesus as the Messiah, when the other group did not. There was no trust in Him for salvation due to what He did at Calvary and the resurrection, but merely that He was in fact the Messiah. Consequently, that is no more than many in the modern church who think of Jesus as a good man but place little or no stock in what He did at Calvary. These latter, even as the former, are not saved.

TRUTH IS AT STAKE

Therefore, the problem was not just a matter of Gentile or Jewish custom; the truth of the gospel itself was at stake.

Regrettably, even as stated, very few saw through this as Paul and Barnabas. These impostors had come into the church conducting themselves in what looked to be a very spiritual manner, prepared to detect and to regard with the keenest dislike anything, either in doctrine or in church action, which would infringe upon their own legalism, and to wage war upon it. For this notion of hostile intent is strongly suggested by the phrasal verb "to spy out."

The idea is that they were making use of their membership in the church in Jerusalem to promote these false views. As well, their membership in that church gave them legitimacy. In fact, this is Satan's greatest method. He works far better from within than from without.

LIBERTY

This liberty (Gal. 2:4) means the whole spirit of freedom which faith in Christ imparts to the Christian, including, for one thing, the emancipation from the yoke of ceremonialism, from religion, from dead works, etc. This was Satan's way to wage war against gospel liberty, and he continues with the same presently.

LIBERTY AS TAUGHT IN THE BIBLE

What does Paul mean when he uses the word *liberty*? Liberty from what? In fact, this one word defines the Christian experience as possibly few others.

The biblical idea of liberty (freedom) has in its background the thought of imprisonment or slavery. Rulers would imprison those whom they regarded as wrongdoers (Gen. 39:20); a conquered nation might be enslaved by its conqueror, or a prisoner of war by his captors, or an individual might, like Joseph, be sold into slavery.

When the Bible speaks of liberty, a prior bondage or incarceration is always implied. Liberty means the happy state of having been released from servitude for a life of enjoyment and satisfaction that was not possible before.

The idea of liberty appears in Scripture in its ordinary secular application (Ps. 105:20; Acts 26:32); but it also receives a significant theological development. This sprang from Israel's realization that such freedom from subjugation by foreigners as she enjoyed was God's gift to her. In the New Testament, liberty becomes an important theological concept for describing salvation, which we will get to momentarily.

ISRAEL'S LIBERTY

At the exodus, God set Israel free from bondage in Egypt in order that henceforth the nation might serve Him as His covenant people (Ex. 19:3; 20:1; Lev. 25:55; Isa. 43:21). He brought them into the *"land flowing with milk and honey"* (Ex. 3:8; Num. 14:7; Deut. 8:7), settled them there, and undertook to maintain them with political independence and economic prosperity as long as they opposed idolatry and kept His laws (Deut. 28:1–14).

This meant that Israel's freedom would not depend upon her own efforts and either the military or the political realm, but on the quality of her obedience to God. Her freedom was a super-natural blessing, the Lord's gracious gift to His Own Covenant people; unmerited and apart from Him unattainable in the first instance, and now maintained only through His continued favor.

Disobedience, whether in the form of religious impiety or social injustice, would result in the loss of freedom. God would judge His people by national disaster and enslavement (Deut. 28:25, 47; Judg. 2:14; 3:7, 12; 4:1; 6:1). He would raise up hostile powers against them, and would ultimately cause them to be deported into a land where no tokens of His favor could be expected (Deut. 28:64; II Kings 17:6–23; Ps. 137:1–4; Amos 5).

DELIVERANCE

The structure of the theological idea of liberty is here fully evident. Liberty, as the Old Testament conceives it, means on the one hand, deliverance from created forces that would keep men from serving and enjoying their Creator, and on the other hand, the positive happiness of living in fellowship with God under His covenant in the place where He is pleased to manifest Himself and to bless.

Liberty is from slavery to powers that oppose God for the fulfillment of His claims upon one's life. Liberty is not man's own achievement, but a free gift of grace, something which apart from God's action man does not possess at all. In its continuance, liberty is a covenant blessing, something which God has promised to maintain as long as His people are faithful. Liberty does not mean independence of God; it is precisely in God's service that man finds his perfect freedom.

Man can enjoy release from bondage to the created only through bondage to His Creator. Thus, the way that God sets men free from their captors and enemies is to make them in essence, His own slaves. He frees them by bringing them to Himself, but remember, His yoke is easy and His burden is light (Ex. 19:4; Mat. 11:28–30).

THE CHRISTIAN'S LIBERTY

The full development of the idea of liberty appears in the Gospels and especially, the Pauline Epistles where the enemies from whom God through Christ liberates His people are revealed to be sin, Satan, the law, and death.

Christ's public ministry was one of liberation. In Luke 4:18, He opened it by announcing Himself as the fulfillment of Isa. 61:1: *"... the LORD hath anointed me ... to proclaim liberty (release) to the captives."*

Ignoring zealot hankerings after a national liberation from Rome, Christ declared that He had come to set Israelites free from the state of slavery to sin and Satan in which He found them (Jn. 8:34–36, 41–44). He had come, He said, to overthrow *"the prince of this world,"* the *"strong man,"* and to release his prisoners (Mk. 3:27; Lk. 10:17; Jn. 12:31). The casting out of demons (Mk. 3:22) and healings (Lk. 13:16) were part of this work of dispossession.

Christ appealed to these (Mat. 12:28; Lk. 11:20) as proof positive of the coming among men of the kingdom of God (the promised blessings stated in which men effectively receive God's forgiveness and salvation and are effectively made subject to God's will).

BONDAGE

Paul makes much of the thought that Christ liberates believers, here and now, from destructive influences from which they were previously in bondage:

- From sin, the tyrannical overlord whose wages for service rendered is death (Rom. 6:18–23)
- From the law as a system of salvation, which stirred sin up and gave it its strength (Rom. 6:14; 7:5–13; 8:2; I Cor. 15:56; Gal. 4:21; 5:1)
- From the demonic powers of darkness (Col. 1:13)
- From heathenistic superstition (I Cor. 10:29; Gal. 4:8)
- From the burden of Jewish ceremonialism (Gal. 2:4)

To all of this Paul affirms freedom from the remaining bondages to indwelling sin (Rom. 7:14, 23), and from physical corruption and death, which will in due course be added (Rom. 8:18–21).

FREEDOM

This freedom, in all its aspects, is the gift of Christ, who by death bought His people out of bondage (I Cor. 6:20; 7:22).

Present freedom from the law, sin, and death is conveyed to believers by the Spirit, who unites us to Christ through faith (Rom. 8:2; II Cor. 3:17). Liberation brings with it adoption (Gal. 4:5); those set free from guilt become sons of God and receive the Spirit of Christ as a Spirit of adoption, assuring them that they are in truth God's sons and heirs (Rom. 8:15; Gal. 4:6).

THE RESPONSIBLE USE OF LIBERTY

Paul makes a similar contention elsewhere. The Christian is free from the need to work for his salvation, and he is bound neither by Jewish ceremonialism nor by pagan superstition and taboos.

There is a large realm of things indifferent in which *"all things are lawful unto me"* (I Cor. 6:12; 10:23). In this realm the Christian must use his liberty responsibly, with an eye to what is expedient and edifying and with a tender regard for the weaker brother's conscience (Rom. 14:1–15; Rom. 7; I Cor. 8–10).

However, we must remember that all of the moral laws of the Old Testament, mainly the Ten Commandments, are still incumbent upon all believers. The only difference is in the way that these Commandments are kept, which is totally different than before.

The believer is to place his or her faith exclusively in Christ and what Christ has done for us at the cross, which then gives the Holy Spirit, who works exclusively by and through the cross, latitude to work within our lives. With our faith properly placed, the Holy Spirit will then have latitude to work, and will literally keep the Commandments for us, without us becoming involved, with the exception of us continuing to use our faith and continuing to place our faith in the proper position, which is in Christ and the cross.

We might think that is too easy; however, to be sure, it is probably one of the most difficult things that anyone ever attempted to do. Satan will fight this as nothing else, simply because he knows we have found the source of victory. But if we will persevere, place our faith as it should be placed, which is in Christ and the cross, and maintain it accordingly, to be sure, victory will be ours (I Cor. 1:17-18; 2:2; Col. 2:10-15; Gal. 6:14).

FREE WILL

The free will of man is always upheld by God, but with conditions. God will never force a person's will, but Satan most definitely will force an individual's will.

Let me explain: There are millions of alcoholics around the world who would love to stop drinking, but their willpower is not strong enough. They literally drink themselves to death, and the same could be stated regarding many other situations. God has nothing to do with that, but Satan most definitely does. However, even though it may come as a shock to most Christians in reading what I am about to say, Satan can force a believer's will if that believers' faith is in the wrong place.

Let me explain: The apostle Paul said, *"For I know that in me* (that is, in my flesh) *dwelleth no good thing: for to will is present with me; but how to perform that which is good I find not"* (Rom. 7:18).

He plainly tells us here that he tries to overcome by his will-power but is unable to do so, and that remains the same for every believer. Around the world, Satan is forcing the will of untold millions of Christians because their faith is in anything other than Christ and the cross. And that being the case, they have only their willpower, which is never enough. For the believer to have total protection by the Lord, total power of the Holy Spirit, he must place his or her faith exclusively in Christ and the cross, under-standing that it was there that all victory was won. That being the case, as we've already stated, the Holy Spirit—who is God, can do anything, and works exclusively by and through the cross of Christ—will then work mightily on our behalf. That comes as a shock to most Christians, not knowing how the Holy Spirit works.

The Word of God says, *"For the law of the Spirit of life in Christ Jesus hath made me free from the law of sin and death"* (Rom. 8:2).

First of all, this is a law that we are speaking of, however it is not the law of Moses, but rather a law devised by the Godhead in eternity past. It's the way the Holy Spirit works.

The short phrase, *"In Christ Jesus,"* which Paul uses more than one hundred times in his Epistles, speaks of Christ and what He did for us at the cross.

He made me free from the law of sin and death.

The two most powerful laws in the world are the law of the Spirit of life in Christ Jesus and the law of sin and death. The only law that is stronger than the law of sin and death is the law of the Spirit of life in Christ Jesus. We have that law working for us as long as we place our faith exclusively in Christ and the cross. Then Satan cannot override our will.

If every Christian in the world who is reading these words that are in front of your face at this moment, they would nod their heads in agreement. Millions have struggled with problems in their hearts and lives, unable to overcome, even though they have tried their strongest to do what should be done. But once they find Christ as it regards what He has done for them at the cross, and they place their faith there never to move it elsewhere, then the Holy Spirit will work mightily on their behalf. Then the Evil One cannot overcome their will or force them into doing things that they don't want to do.

Now some would say, well if that's the case—that Satan is forcing my will—then I'm not responsible. Oh yes, you are! We are responsible in that we have not placed our faith where it must be placed, which is Christ and the cross. That's where the responsibility comes in. If we fail there, we fail.

The only way the believer can overcome sin, and I mean the only way, is to understand that all victory over sin is in the cross. It's not in anything else. In other words, the believer cannot fast his way to victory. He can fast for three days, twenty days, or a hundred days, but he's not going to fast his way to victory. If that were the case, then the Lord did not have to come down from heaven, assume this mortal coil, and die on the cross. He could have just taught men how to fast. But He didn't do that, did He? No, He didn't. But He did go to the cross, and there the victory was won. And please understand that the cross of Christ is the only place for sin. There is no other. That's why

John the Baptist said: *"Behold the Lamb of God, which taketh away the sin of the world"* (Jn. 1:29).

The material you have just read is some of the most important that you will ever read. Don't take it lightly. This is biblical, and it's God's way, and I speak of the way of the cross. There and there only can we have, find, and continue in victory.

BONDAGE

In Galatians 2:4, the phrase, *"that they might bring us into bondage,"* means "to be reduced to abject slavery." The tense of the sentence structure tells us that it was not merely an intention on the part of the Judaizers, but an attempt which they thought had assured hopes of success.

The bondage spoken of here by Paul is in the first instance that of the Mosaic law; however, it also refers to the believer being thrown into a position of spiritual failure. In other words, the power to stop sinning resides totally in Christ and the cross. The law of Moses or any other law for that matter had no power in this respect whatsoever. Consequently, if the believer begins to rely in any measure on anything else other than the finished work of Christ, bondage to sin is the guaranteed result. This is so important that we need to address it further.

A BRIEF DESCRIPTION

In Romans 7, Paul evinced the fact that he had no victory in his heart and life, and we speak of victory over sin, even though he was saved, baptized with the Holy Spirit, and an apostle. This was at the beginning of his conversion experience. He didn't want to sin, but despite willing not to, the power of sin was stronger than his will, which always resulted in failure of one sort or the other (Rom. 7:18).

He sought the Lord earnestly for an answer to this dilemma and was given the answer which he gave to us in Romans 6. In that chapter, he tells us that not only was the sin debt paid by Jesus at Calvary, but as well, the sin grip was broken. All of this was done through what Jesus did at Calvary and the resurrection.

THE POWER OF THE CROSS

Everything Jesus did at the cross was for sinners. Consequently, when the believing sinner has faith in Christ, in effect, God looks at him as having been baptized into the death of Christ, buried with Him, and raised with Him in newness of life (Rom. 6:1–8).

However, we learn from the words of Jesus in Luke 9:23 that the power and strength of the cross does not end with conversion, but as well applies itself to our everyday walk before God—our sanctification. Jesus said, *"If any man will come after me, let him deny himself, and take up his cross daily, and follow me"* (Lk. 9:23).

This speaks of a daily partaking of the benefits of the cross, which means that it has a bearing on our lives in totality, and will do so until the resurrection. In other words, the believer must understand that everything he has in Christ—his salvation, as well as his overcoming victory—is all in the cross. That's what Jesus meant by one taking up his cross daily and following Him.

Any individual who ceases to depend on what Christ did at Calvary, and begins to trust in his own strength, willpower, or ability, which in effect is a law of his own making, will without question fail, and that person will once again be brought into bondage—sin. In fact, the harder he tries in that capacity, the more he will fail. His personal efforts, which actually constitute the flesh irrespective as to how religious they may be, will not bring him victory but rather the very opposite.

WHY?

The way and manner in which the believer has victory in his everyday walk is because the Holy Spirit helps him to do so. Consequently, what is difficult or even impossible for us is no problem for the Holy Spirit whatsoever. This is what Paul is talking about in Romans 8.

However, the Holy Spirit will function only in the legal confines of Calvary. He will not exert His power or perform His tasks of victory on behalf of the saint unless that saint is trusting in what Jesus did on the cross. The Holy Spirit will not help you to overcome sin by your willpower (Rom. 7:18; 8:1-11). Neither will He help you to overcome sin in any other capacity. He will only work according to the confines of what the Lord Jesus Christ has done, and this is where most believers miss it.

If we fail to take up the cross daily, which means to trust daily in what Jesus did at Calvary as it regards our victory, then we have set ourselves on a road of failure and irrespective as to what we do, failure will be the result. As stated, the reason is simple: the Holy Spirit will not function in any capacity except through the finished work of Christ on the cross.

In fact, this is what Satan was attempting to get believers to do in the early church. If he could get them to depend on works, they were not depending on the cross; consequently, they were doomed to return to bondage. He does the same thing today.

THE CROSS

Satan's current efforts are just as great in this capacity as they were in the early church. Satan knows very well that our salvation and our victory resides in what Jesus did at Calvary. He also knows that it is a finished work, needing nothing added respecting our salvation or our daily walk before God. So he does all within his power to draw us away from that and that alone, which gives us what we need.

PRESENT CIRCUMSTANCES

It is unfortunate that the church today—and I think I can say this without fear of exaggeration—is depending less on the cross of Christ than ever before in its history. In much of the Charismatic church world, the cross and the shed blood of Jesus Christ are belittled and even referred to in some circles as "past miseries."

While they recognize the veracity of the cross, at least to a certain extent regarding one's salvation, these particular teachers see nothing in the cross thereafter. According to them, one's victory depends on proper confession and faith, etc., with the cross playing no part whatsoever.

This is not only wrong, but it borders on blasphemy.

As well, most of the denominational and Pentecostal world have forsaken the cross in favor of humanistic psychology. In effect they are denying the power of God which resides in grace, which comes through the cross and enables the believer to overcome any and all that Satan may seek to use as a snare. You cannot have it both ways—it's is either the cross or humanistic wisdom, which James said is *"not from above,"* and is therefore earthly, sensual, and devilish (James 3:15).

So the modernists deny the cross altogether, while the fundamentalists ignore the cross. But let all and sundry know that everything one has in the Lord is found exclusively in what Jesus did at Calvary. As well, despite the claims of others, there is no other source for victory.

Just as I am, without one plea,
But that Thy blood was shed for me,
And that Thou bidst me come to Thee,
O Lamb of God, I come, I come!

THE NEW COVENANT

CHAPTER 4

THE TRUTH OF THE GOSPEL

THE TRUTH OF THE GOSPEL

"TO WHOM WE GAVE place by subjection, no, not for an hour; that the truth of the gospel might continue with you" (Gal. 2:5).

We see in this Scripture the absolute refusal by Paul to compromise even to the slightest degree. He knew that even the slightest admixture of law and grace would hinder the Galatians from operating in the emancipating gospel of Christ. In fact, it would do more than hinder, it would rob them of all victory and possibly their souls. What was at stake here was far more than a mere church argument, but rather the entirety of what Jesus paid for at Calvary and the resurrection.

It is amazing that God has entrusted so much into the hands of human care. When we consider the magnitude involved, the significance of what is being said and done, and then to realize that possibly one man in the entirety of the world—the Apostle Paul—stood between the salvation of humanity and the total wreckage of the salvation message, we are left speechless. But that's exactly the way it was.

NO SUBJECTION

The phrase, *"To whom we gave place by subjection, no, not for an hour,"* proclaims the fact that Paul would not yield one iota, nor compromise in the slightest.

This strong language shows beyond a doubt that the course followed by the apostle was a firm denial to yield with a submission which was so urgently demanded.

"To whom" refers to the individuals who were demanding the compromise. So this was not merely a matter of philosophy, but rather one between individuals. The idea is that we will not submit to this at all. We will not yield even for the shortest time. We will not waiver in our opposition to their demands, or in the slightest degree become subject to their wishes. We steadily oppose their claims, in order that the great principle might be forever settled that the law of Moses was not to be imposed as obligatory on Gentile converts.

We say the same thing as it regards the message of the cross. We will not bend; we will not give one inch; we will do our very best to do exactly what the Word of God says. Irrespective of the fact that some people will not even mention the word *cross* because they fear that they will be identified with us, and they don't want to do that. I'm sure that there were many in Paul's day who felt the same way and did the same thing. Irrespective, Paul did not give way one inch, and neither will we. Here we are and here we stand, and as the song says, *"I shall not be moved."* It is the cross of Christ which is the gospel, and to ignore the word *cross* thinking that we can embrace other things is a fool's hope. The cross of Christ is the meaning of the new covenant, while Jesus is actually the new covenant. When we examine the cross, we are examining the meaning of the greatest work that God ever gave to man—the new covenant. It must not be compromised; it must not be sidetracked; it must not be ignored. It is the cross, the cross, the cross!

A GREAT PRINCIPLE WAS SETTLED

In the whole passage, Paul means to say, as seems obvious to me, that a great principle was settled. The question came about as to whether the Mosaic rites were to be imposed on Gentile converts. False brethren introduced this spurious teaching and demanded it, but Paul steadily maintained his ground. He did not yield a moment.

As we have previously stated on other occasions, when this situation did not impact the salvation of the soul, he was willing to yield and become all things to all men, yet here he did not court them or temporize with them in the least.

The phrase, *"by subjection"* here means, "that he did not suffer himself to be compelled to yield."

The phrase, *"for an hour"* is equivalent to the shortest period of time. He did not waiver or yield at all.

THE GOSPEL OF JESUS CHRIST

The phrase, *"that the truth of the gospel might continue with you,"* presents in simple but glaring detail the significance of this grave crisis. The entire status of Gentile Christianity was involved in the case of Titus. The question as to whether Christianity was to be merely a modified form of legalistic Judaism or a system of pure grace was at stake.

In fact, justification by faith was on trial. Circumcision, at least in a situation of this nature, would have set it aside. If Paul had yielded, the truth of the gospel would have been compromised, which would have abrogated the great price paid by Jesus at Calvary.

A TRUE AND A FALSE GOSPEL

When Paul speaks of the *"truth of the gospel,"* he shows that there are two gospels, one true and one false. Actually, the true gospel does not change and cannot change simply because there is no need for change—perfection has no such need. However, the false gospel, although presented here in the form of the demand for circumcision, still can take any route, go down any bypath, proceed in any and all directions, and incorporate any and all lies.

The true gospel is of itself simple, true, and sincere; however, Satan sets about to corrupt and deface that gospel, which in fact, he succeeds in doing in many cases.

Therefore, when Paul says *"the truth of the gospel,"* he would have us to understand also the contrary. It is as if he would say, *"the false apostles do also preach a faith and a gospel, but they are both false: therefore have I set myself so constantly against them."*

Regarding the gospel and its presentation, all false teachers claim the name of God, of Christ, and teach that their doctrine is the pure gospel of Christ. So the claims from one to the other will not change.

SO HOW DOES ONE KNOW THE TRUTH?

The true gospel changes lives, whereas the false message changes nothing except that for the worse. Jesus clearly and plainly told us to check the fruit (Mat. 7:15–20). Thank God we can say without fear of contradiction that if the message of the cross changes lives, and in fact it is the only message that will change lives, all sin must be addressed at the cross, as all sin can only be addressed at the cross. It can be addressed in no other way. It is the cross where the price was paid, and where mankind can be redeemed, and the cross alone where mankind can be redeemed.

The truth of the gospel is that our righteousness comes by faith alone, without the works of the law, or any other works for that matter. The corruption or falsehood of this false gospel is that we are justified by faith, but not without the works of the law. In other words, it is Jesus "plus."

At this hour, millions say, "We preach the gospel, but it justifies not, except it be furnished with charity, or membership in certain churches, or submission to certain religious ordinances, etc." This is not the truth of the gospel, but falsehood and dissimulation. The true gospel is that man's works, even as good as they may be, are not the ornament or perfection of faith. Faith itself is God's gift, and it is faith in Christ which claims the gift. Upon faith in Christ and what He did for us at the cross, we are justified, for the simple reason that our dependence is in Christ and Christ alone.

THE WAY MAN REASONS

Man's reason has the law or certain works for its object, thus thinking with itself: This have I done, this I have not done. But faith being in its proper office has no other object but Jesus Christ the Son of God, who was delivered to death for the sins of the whole world. Consequently, those who truly believe on Christ look not to works say not, "What have I done?" "What have I offended?" "What have I deserved?" But what has Christ done? Here the truth of the gospel answers properly.

What has He done? He has redeemed us from sin, from the devil, and from eternal death. Faith, therefore, acknowledges that in this one person, Jesus Christ, we have forgiveness for sins and eternal life. He that turns his eyes from this object has no true faith, but a fantasy and a vain opinion.

If faith in Christ is compromised to the least degree, then the Son of God died in vain. Then it is but a fable that Christ is the Saviour of the world.

Consequently, considering that, our stoutness in this matter is godly and holy, for by it we seek to keep our liberty which we have in Christ Jesus, and thereby to retain the truth of the gospel; which if we lose, then do we also lose God, Christ, all the promises, faith, righteousness, and everlasting life. (Much of the statement on the new covenant was derived from the writings of Martin Luther.[1])

THE OTHER APOSTLES AND PAUL

In these passages the weight of the historical context is impressive. We have the picture of the apostles (some of the Twelve) at Jerusalem, wavering on neutral ground, tending to advise compliance on Paul's part, and then finally coming out for Paul by declaring openly for freedom from the law. This attitude is suggested in the following verses, both in the attitude of reserve Paul seems to have encountered at Jerusalem (Gal. 2:6, 9) and in the related wavering of Peter at Antioch. Moreover, this fits in with the fact of greatest certainty; namely, that the conflict was primarily between the false brethren and Paul and that in the end (whether wavering before that time or not) the apostles stood with Paul and Barnabas.

THE FALSE BRETHREN

Paul's references to the false brethren in Galatians 2:4 entail a military metaphor, used to indicate the subversive and militant nature of the evil that Paul was fighting. The term *false brethren* is used only twice in the New Testament (here and in II Cor. 11:26). In each case Paul uses the term of those who are not in fact Christians, though pretending to be so. They are in fact Satan's ministers, who will subtly introduce destructive heresies to weaken and ruin the church (II Cor. 11:13–15).

Paul speaks of the desire of these legalizers *"to make us slaves,"* in the manner of those who would take a city by stealth or force in order to place the inhabitants in chains.

NO PERSONAL MOTIVE

Paul's defense of the gospel he had received from God was not made for any personal or selfish reasons, but *"so that the truth of the gospel might remain"* with believers.

The word *truth* has a decided emphasis in contrast to the falseness mentioned in the preceding verse. Therefore, it cannot mean only "the truths" of the gospel or even "the true message" of the gospel; it must mean "the true gospel" as opposed to "the false gospel" being taught by the false brethren. There is also a possibility that Paul is thinking of his earlier reference to that other gospel, which is really no gospel at all (Gal. 1:6–7).

ADDED NOTHING TO ME

"But of these who seemed to be somewhat, (whatsoever they were, it maketh no matter to me: God accepteth no man's person) for they who seemed to be somewhat in conference added nothing to me" (Gal. 2:6).

Paul is here dealing with a problem that was rapidly getting out of hand in the early church, especially in the Gentile areas. Those who had been with Jesus during His earthly ministry were given a place of distinction that could have dangerous consequences.

The Jews had a built-in safeguard against idolatry, but Paul's Gentile converts could easily fall into this trap. With their idolatrous background it was only a short step from the veneration of Jesus' earthly disciples to a cult of divinity. In fact, already

Paul's claim to apostleship was being challenged by his enemies at this very point—he had not been one of the original disciples.

Thus, while writing to Gentile converts about his relationship with these leaders, he emphatically points out that with God the outward appearance is not the important thing. Authority in the church comes from God. It comes, not based on one's past outward relationship with Jesus on earth, but in the light of one's present inward experience with Christ. In other words, what a person is, is what they are at that moment in Christ.

This did not mean that Paul had no respect for these leaders, or even that he did not hold them in high esteem. The fact that he was in Jerusalem for a conference demonstrates the opposite. It is instead a reflection of his concern that the true basis of authority be observed.

THE ORIGINAL APOSTLES

The phrase, *"but of these who seemed to be somewhat,"* actually spoke of the original Twelve, or ever how many were present at that time.

The idea is, that not only did Paul successfully maintain his position with regard to the matter of Gentile immunity from the obligation of circumcision at the Jerusalem Council, but the persons of eminence in the church there, imposed no restrictions nor commands upon him relative to the matter.

The expression, *"these who seemed to be somewhat,"* is from the same Greek word translated "reputation" in Galatians 2:2, and refers to the apostolic leaders of the church at Jerusalem. It would have included James the Lord's brother, plus the Twelve, plus others, no doubt also (minus James the brother of John, for he had by now been executed).

Paul speaks in this manner, because the false apostles were attempting to set the dignity and authority of the original Twelve against Paul in order to weaken his authority and bring his ministry into contempt. This Paul might not suffer.

He allowed the apostles their place and position and their authority to be reverenced. Yet his gospel and ministry are not to be overthrown for the name or title of any, whatsoever he be, an apostle or an angel from heaven.

NO RESPECTER OF PERSONS

In Galatians 2:6, the phrase, *"whatsoever they were, it maketh no matter to me: God accepteth no man's person,"* means no disrespect. The apostle is merely asserting his own independence of them, thus by contrast setting off his apostolic authority in the light of theirs.

He says that it made no difference with him what their former position was, referring to their former intercourse with the Lord Jesus. Knowing Christ after the flesh (II Cor. 5:16) gives one no position of preeminence in the church. Furthermore, he says that God is no respecter of persons, literally, "God does not receive the face of a man." He shows no partiality because of a man's natural ability, his position or possessions in the various departments of human society.

The idea is that it made no difference to Paul who these men were, what position they were holding, and what advantages they had had, so far as his receiving at their hands an apostolic commission was concerned. He had received his commission directly from God. In fact, this is the manner in which every divine call is received.

WHY WAS THIS STRONG TERMINOLOGY IMPORTANT?

As we have already stated, Paul's apostleship was being called into question. The thought was, at least among his detractors of which there seemed to be many, "Why would God give to Paul the meaning of the new covenant, seeing that he was not one of the original Twelve, and in fact, had formerly been a persecutor of the church?"

Paul's person was one thing; however, the effort of Satan was directed toward the new covenant given to the apostle Paul. If he could impugn Paul's person enough—cast enough inflection upon him, raise doubts about his character—of necessity his message would be impugned as well. This was the plan of Satan all along, and he used the church of that day to carry it out, even as he does presently.

Paul is holding firm his apostolic commission irrespective of the fact that he was not a part of the original Twelve, had never seen Jesus in the flesh, nor was a part of the early proceedings. He makes the point that these things are of no consequence, at least as far as the call of God is concerned.

THE EARLY CHURCH AND NOW

It is very revealing to read of these situations which took place at that particular time, especially considering that most have the idea that everything in the early church was sweetness and light. And yet, I wonder what the reaction would be if all the parties in question, were transferred to this particular present time?

It is my personal thought that the modern church is much weaker spiritually speaking than the early church. I fear that in this particular climate, the original Twelve would be made into demigods, and Paul would have been castigated. It is almost that bad anyway, so what would it be, if there were men here presently who had personally spent some three and a half years with Jesus Christ?

The idea of all of this is that whatever the real rank of the original apostles and standing was, it did not in the least affect Paul's authority as an apostle, or his argument. While he rejoiced in their concurrence, and while he sought their approbation, he did not admit for a moment that he was inferior to them as an apostle, or depend on them for the justness of his views. What they were, or what they were thought to be was immaterial to his claims as an apostle, and immaterial to the authority of his own views as an apostle.

He had derived his gospel from the Lord Jesus; and he had the fullest assurance that his views were just. Paul makes this remark evidently in keeping with all he had said, that he did not regard himself as in any manner dependent on them for his authority. He did not treat them at all with disrespect; but he did not regard them as having a right to claim any authority over him.[2]

ADDED NOTHING TO ME

In Galatians 2:6, the phrase, *"for they who seemed to be somewhat in conference added nothing to me,"* means that they contributed in no way to his call to the ministry, nor to his ability to preach the gospel of Jesus Christ. Consequently, the Jerusalem apostles imposed on him no burden of doctrine or practice, and imparted to him nothing in addition to what he knew.

PAUL'S THOUGHTS

Paul could very well have had Moses in mind when he said *"God accepteth no man's person."* God had told the lawgiver, *"Thou shalt not respect the person of the poor, nor honour the person of the mighty"* (Lev. 19:15). It is a principle of divinity; God is no respecter of persons. He does not regard the dignity or authority of men. He suffered Judas to fall away, and Saul the first king He rejected, and you will find throughout the Scriptures that God oftentimes rejected those who in outward show seemed to be good men.

If in these examples God seems to be cruel, it was necessary that such fearful examples should be given, and also written, for the simple reason, that God does not judge from the outward but from the heart (I Sam. 16:7).

This vice is naturally grafted in man, to highly esteem the persons and outward state of men, and more regard the same than the Word of God.

Contrariwise God will have us fix our eyes, and to rest wholly upon the Word itself. He will not have us to reverence the apostleship in the persons of Peter or Paul, but rather Christ speaking in them, and the Word that they bring, and preach unto us.

This the natural man cannot see, but the spiritual man only discerns the person from the Word, the veil of God from God Himself. Now this veil of God is every creature.

THE VEILS

Moreover, God here in this life deals not with us face to face, but covers and shadows Himself, so to speak, from us. That is, as Paul said, *"Now we see through a glass, darkly; but then face to face"* (I Cor. 13:12). Therefore, we cannot be without veils (so to speak) in this life.

And here wisdom is required, which can discern the veil from God Himself; and this wisdom the world has not.

The covetous man hears, *"Man shall not live by bread alone, but by every word that proceedeth out of the mouth of God"* (Deut. 8:3; Mat. 4:4). He eats the bread, but sees not God in the bread, for he beholds the veil only. So he does with gold, and other creatures, trusting in them so long as he has them, but when they leave he despairs. Thus, he honors not the Creator, but the creatures, not God, but his own belly.

WE REVERENCE ONLY GOD

We say these things lest any would think that Paul utterly condemns these outward veils, or persons. For he says not that there ought to be no persons, but that there is no respect of persons with God. There must be persons, and outward veils; God has given them, and they are His good creatures; but we must not trust in them. So the prince, the magistrate, the preacher, the schoolmaster, the scholar, the father, the mother, the children, the master, the servant, etc., are persons and outward veils, which God will have us acknowledge, love, and reverence, as His creatures, which we must have in this life, but He will not have us so to reverence them and put our trust in them, so as to forget Him.

And to this end that we should not too much magnify the outward persons, or put too great trust in them, God it seems, leaves in them offenses and sins, yea, great and foul sins at times, in other words the knowledge of such, to teach us what difference there is between persons and God Himself.

David the good king, because he should not seem to be a person upon whom men should trust, fell into horrible sins—adultery and murder.

Peter, that excellent apostle, denied Christ. These, and such examples of which the Scriptures are full, ought to warn us that we repose not trust in persons—an outward veil—nor think that when we have the outward show we have all things, as it is in much of religion, where they judge things according to the outward veil and, therefore, religion is nothing else but a mere respecting of persons and outward show.

NOT TRUST OR GLORY IN THEM

Let us use bread, apparel, possessions, gold, silver, and all other creatures, but let us not trust or glory in them, for we must trust and glory in God alone. He only is to be loved, at least in this manner. He only is to be feared and honored.

Paul here calls the apostleship or office of the apostles (which wrought miracles, converted many to the faith, and were also very familiar with Christ) the person of man. The word *person* includes the whole outward lifestyle of the apostles which was holy and their authority great. Yet, says he, God esteems not these things; not that He esteems them not at all, but in the matter of justification he regards them not, be they ever so great and glorious.

For we must mark this distinction, that in matters of divinity we must speak far otherwise than in matters of policy. In matters of policy, God will have us honor and reverence these outward veils or persons as His instruments by whom He governs the world. But when the question touches salvation, conscience, the fear of God, faith, and the service of God, we must not fear these outward persons, we must put no trust in them, look for no comfort from them, or hope deliverance by them. For this cause God will have no respect of persons in judgment, for judgment is a divine thing.

IN PERSON

Here, since we must need lose the one, let us lose the person, and stick to God. For it is written that we must obey God rather than man (Acts 4:19). So there Paul argues, against the false apostles, the question here is not concerning respect of persons as we think of such, for there is a far weightier matter at hand, a divine matter concerning God and His Word, and whether this Word ought to be preferred above and before the apostle-ship, or no.

And he answers, so that the truth of the gospel may continue, so that the righteousness of faith may be kept pure and incor-rupt, let the apostleship go, let an angel from heaven, let Peter, let Paul, perish altogether.

Martin Luther said: "If the pope will grant unto us, that God alone by His grace through Christ does justify sinners, we will not only carry him in our hand, but will also kiss his feet. But since we cannot obtain this, we in God are against him above measure, and will give no place, no, not one hair's breadth to a hundred emperors, nor a thousand popes, not to the whole world."

(The above material on respect of persons, etc., was derived from the scholarship of Martin Luther, the great reformer.[3])

ANOTHER VIEW

Most commentators are reluctant to admit, even as we have already stated, that Paul may be deprecating in any way those who were apostles before him. Some deny it outright, point-ing out (quite properly) that Paul's obvious intention in these verses is to show his unity with the apostles both in spirit and doctrine. It is argued that it is not likely that Paul would speak poorly of them in the same context.

Other commentators admit the slightly deflating tone of these expressions as used in Galatians 2:2, 6, and 9, but refer them to something other than Paul's own opinion of the original Twelve—that is, either to the exaggerated claims concerning them made by the legalizers or to the exaggerated views entertained by the Galatians or both.

Over against these views need to be placed the fact that a very good case can be made for the existence of a real though balanced note of disparagement on Paul's own part and for this in itself being the best explanation for the grammatical difficulties throughout the passage.

THE ACTUAL PHRASES

While it is true that the phrase, *"those of reputation,"* is not necessarily deprecating, nevertheless it can convey this meaning. More pertinent is the fact that this sense of the word occurs again in Galatians: *"For if a man think himself to be something, when he is nothing, he deceiveth himself."* (Gal. 6:3).

The very repetition of the phrase in the Greek text seems ominous. It is hard to explain exactly why this is so, but the effect of the repetition is much like the effect of Antony's repetition of the word *honorable* concerning Brutus in his eulogy at the funeral of Julius Caesar in Shakespeare's play. The more he speaks the word, the less honorable Brutus and the other conspirators appear.

The expression Paul uses grows fuller and slightly stronger with each repetition. The apostles are at first called "those who seemed to be leaders." Next, they are "those who seemed to be important." Finally, they are "those reputed to be pillars," at which point the veiled reference is dropped and those of reputation are named—James (the Lord's brother), Peter, and John.

One commentator observed that it is as if Paul's rising indignation is finding this studied courtesy of Galatians 2:2 impossible to maintain.

PETER

The story of Peter's conduct at Antioch, which immediately follows this section, lends credence to the feeling that Paul's disappointment with the conduct of those who should have been leaders in this great crisis of faith and doctrine, but who failed to take the lead is increasingly spilling over into the letter as he retells and (to some extent) relives the events of the council.

According to this interpretation, Paul felt that the Jerusalem apostles did not perform on a level commensurate with the reputation they held, either at the council or (in Peter's case) after it. If they had been alert to the issue, the legalizers would not have succeeded even to the degree they did.

THE DELICATE SITUATION

The delicate situation lying behind these verses alone explains the grammatical difficulties. To understand them, one must see Paul as torn between a desire to stress the basic unity that did exist between himself and the Twelve and the need to be honest in indicating that, so far as he was concerned, the apostles did not perform well in the crisis. Thus, his initial allusion to the apostles in Galatians 2:2 seems to him on second thought to be too vague.

He breaks in with the Titus incident, but again not indicating clearly enough that it was the apostles who for the sake of harmony were urging, it seems, that Titus be circumcised. Finally, Paul picks up the matter of the apostles again in Galatians 2:6 and eventually names them (Gal. 2:9), this time indicating that those who were reported to be "pillars" almost failed to do the work of supporting the gospel.

Looked at grammatically, the entire passage from Galatians 2:2-10 is a problem. But if these verses are considered against the historical context just outlined, they not only make sense, but also greatly increase admiration for the apostle Paul. How many men would be able to strike such an emotional balance in as highly charged a situation as this and at the same time make the points they need to make in writing?

WHAT EXACTLY DOES PAUL DO?

Paul has done the following:

- Recognized the position and authority of the Jerusalem apostles without diminishing his own authority in the slightest.
- Indicated, in opposition to the exaggerated claims about them made by the legalizers, that the apostles were men after all and hence, not always perfect in their initial reactions or conduct.

- Decisively separated the gospel and policies of the Twelve, for all their weaknesses, from the Gospel and policies of the legalizers.

- Taken note of the fact that he and the Twelve, rather than the legalizers and the Twelve, stood together. Eventually he will even show that the agreement between himself and the Twelve was cordial both in relation to their respective spheres of ministry (*"James, Peter and John ... gave to me and Barnabas the right hands of fellowship"*) and in regard to the special obligation of the Gentiles toward the Jerusalem poor (*"the very thing I was eager to do"* [New American Standard Bible]).

- As far as the gospel Paul preached was concerned, the Jerusalem Conference had two results. Negatively, the Twelve "added nothing" to Paul. Paul's gospel was complete because it was received by revelation. Positively, the "pillars" extended to Paul the right hand of fellowship—that is, they recognized that all of them had been entrusted with the same gospel and that they differed only in respect to the different fields in which they had been assigned to preach.

THE GOSPEL OF THE UNCIRCUMCISION

"But contrariwise, when they saw that the gospel of the uncircumcision was committed unto me, as the gospel of the circumcision was unto Peter" (Gal. 2:7).

All of this presents Paul's central purpose for relating this incident. In the defense of his authority as having come from God, he here relates that even the leaders of the church did not add anything to his message.

In fact, the decision they made and steps they took presented a positive action based on an important and far-reaching insight. As Peter was the recognized leader of those who were ministering the gospel to the Jewish world, even though he at times also ministered to Gentiles, so they saw that to Paul had been committed a similar ministry to the Gentiles, although he as well often ministered to Jews.

CONTRARIWISE

The phrase, *"But contrariwise, when they saw that the gospel of the uncircumcision was committed unto me,"* presents the Jerusalem apostles championing the cause of Paul after they had heard the issue discussed in private conference.

The words "when they saw," gives the reason for the statement which follows. They imply that what the Jerusalem apostles had learned, had led them to give their endorsement to Paul's message and his stand on the matter of Gentile circumcision. The duty of preaching the gospel to the uncircumcised part of the world, that is, to the Gentiles, had been received by Paul as his peculiar office when he was converted and called to the ministry (Acts 9:15; 22:21). The Jerusalem apostles now perceived that he had been especially entrusted with this office from the remarkable success which had attended his labors.

Evidently, it is not meant here that Paul was to preach only to the Gentiles and Peter only to the Jews, for Paul often preached in the synagogues of the Jews, and Peter was the first to preach to a Gentile (Acts 10). Rather, it is meant that this was the main business of Paul to preach to the Gentiles, or that this was especially entrusted to him.

THE HUMAN EQUATION

Once again, the phrase *"when they saw,"* actually says in the Greek, "When they got to see." This implies the fact that of all of this was somewhat new to them. There is little evidence that the original Twelve had been preaching to Gentiles; consequently, they had not faced these particulars. A few of them, no doubt, were apprised of it previously, Cephas in particular; but the majority of that assemblage of apostles and elders knew Paul chiefly by hearsay, and hearsay that was not always the friendliest to him.

The three names in Galatians 2:9 are to be conceived of as acting as they did in order to give expression to this newly-awakened feeling of the general body, and not merely to their own individual judgment. In other words, the Lord did a great thing that day, and to the credit to the original Twelve, along with James, they yielded to the Holy Spirit, at least in part.

THE DEFEAT OF THE FALSE APOSTLES

With the words of this verse Paul mightily confutes the false apostles, for he assumes to himself the same authority which they had boasted attached only to the original Twelve, and had denied to Paul. He uses here a figure of speech called an inversion, returning their argument against themselves.

Luther said, "The false apostles, says he, do allege against me the authority of the great apostles to maintain their cause; but I do allege the same against them, to wit that the apostles are on my side. For the apostles when they saw the gospel over the uncircumcision to be committed to me, and knew of the grace that was given to me, they stretched out the right hand of fellowship to me and Barnabas, approving my ministry, and giving thanks to God for the gifts I had received."[4]

GOSPEL OF THE UNCIRCUMCISION

Paul speaks of the gospel of the circumcision and the gospel of the uncircumcision. What does he mean by that?

His thought is not that there are two different gospels or two different types of messages adjusted to the needs of the Jews and the Gentiles respectively. He means that to him was committed the responsibility of taking the gospel of grace to the Gentiles, and that to Peter was given the commission of taking it to the Jews.

The word *committed* implies a permanent commission. This word was also a technical word used in the imperial government of Rome.

The apostles were the imperial secretaries of the King of kings, the Lord Jesus, to whom was entrusted the writing and propagation of the New Testament message.[5]

THE GOSPEL OF THE CIRCUMCISION

In Galatians 2:7, the phrase, *"as the gospel of the circumcision was unto Peter,"* speaks of Peter's ministry to the Jews, although, as stated, he also preached at times to the Gentiles.

The way and the manner in which Paul uses this statement tells us that he recognized the authority and leadership of Simon Peter, but at the same time, he places himself on the same level with the elder apostle, and most important of all, the Holy Spirit sanctioned this position. And yet, one is not to think that the apostle is speaking of two different gospels; he isn't. Actually, it is very easy to see how completely the substance of Peter's doctrine was one with that of Paul's, as we read his two epistles (I Pet. 5:12). They preach the same gospel and the same message.

JEW AND GENTILE

The idea of all of this, is not so much to stake out particular claims, but rather that Paul's place and position be recognized by the original Twelve, which would put to silence the contention of these false brethren. As well, it is difficult to feel that Paul would have written as he does here, if he was aware that Peter had been constituted by the Lord Jesus to be His own vicar upon earth, supreme over the whole church and all its ministers, as contended by the Catholic Church.

There was no subordination of Paul to Peter, either in fact, or in the opinion of those who were assembled in Jerusalem on this solemn occasion. And further, as to the division of missionary work between these two apostles, there is often great exaggeration as to the meaning of what is stated here.

On the one hand, we find Paul, after this time, when entering upon new ground, addressing himself first to the Jews (Acts 17:2; 19:8; 28:17). On the other hand, to say nothing of credible tradition, we find traces of Peter's activity at Antioch and possibly Corinth (I Cor. 1:12; Gal. 2:11). Moreover, the earliest churches, almost everywhere, were mixed bodies exactly as they should have been, and we really cannot discriminate between the Jew and Gentile members, and neither should we.

There is only one gospel, one message, one faith. It is for all!

THE ONE WHO COMMISSIONED

"For he who wrought effectually in Peter to the apostleship of the circumcision, the same was mighty in me toward the Gentiles" (Gal. 2:8).

Just as the gospel is one gospel, no matter to whom it is preached, so also is the commissioning and enabling of those who preach it one delegation. The reason is that the one who commissioned and empowered both Peter and Paul is God.

WROUGHT EFFECTUALLY

The phrase, *"For he that wrought effectually in Peter to the apostleship of the circumcision,"* stresses that God was working equally in both Peter and Paul to enable them faithfully and effectively to carry out the mission for which God had chosen them.

Wuest said: "This verse is a parenthetical statement. It confirms the contents of the preceding verse, namely that God delegated to Paul the responsibility of giving the gospel to the Gentiles, and to Peter, the responsibility of giving the same message to the Jews. It is not to be confused here that there were two different messages. The message was one and the same irrespective as to whom it was delivered. The statement pertains to the commission or calling and not the message."[6]

Paul's reasoning is as follows: He recognizes without hesitation Peter's apostleship and its divine source. Then he proves that the recognition of his apostleship given by the Jerusalem apostles was merited, because his experience in preaching the gospel among the Gentiles was equal and like in character to their efforts among the Jews. He says that God, who wrought effectually in Peter's work among the Jews, did the same with reference to his work among the Gentiles. All of which means that both Peter and Paul were recipients of the blessing of God in their work for Him, which is tantamount to saying that He gave recognition to each one as an apostle by divine appointment.

THE WORK OF GOD

The word *wrought* is from the Greek word *energeo*. The fact that this word is not used in connection with the words Peter and me, tells us that this verse is not describing the work of grace in the hearts of Peter and Paul, but the work of God for them in owning and blessing their preaching with the result that souls were saved in each case. This is in line with the context, for it speaks of God's seal of approval resting upon the work of both Peter and Paul, and thus upon their apostleship. In other words, God anointed the preaching and teaching of both of these apostles simply because both were teaching and preaching the truth. God will not anoint error. This would as well have to do with the signs, wonders, and miracles, which the Lord wrought by their hands.

THE RECOGNITION OF LEADERSHIP

It should be understood in the reading of these passages that Peter and Paul, and all others for that matter, who were truly of God, were not called or given their commission by men, but rather by God. The emphasis laid upon this by the Holy Spirit is ample to say the least. There is a total absence of any type of hierarchy in these meetings. Such simply did not exist. The recognition of leadership, which Paul calls an apostleship, was based upon the clear evidence of the same divine activity registered in these particular individuals.

The evidence furnished which should be the case now as well as then, was the working of God Himself in these particular ministries. In effect, the Holy Spirit supplied His own witness, even as He continues to do.

MIGHTY IN ME

The phrase, *"the same was mighty in me toward the Gentiles,"* presents the word *mighty* in the Greek as being the same as "wrought effectually," as it pertained to Peter.

This tells us that the church is one, meaning that there is no such thing as a Western gospel, or an Eastern gospel. As well, there is no such thing as a "white man's gospel," or a "black man's gospel," etc. It is one gospel for one world, which is presented by one church, which is one body of Christ.

If it is to be noticed, and it certainly should be insomuch as it is glaringly obvious, that the proof of these ministries was not the recognition of men, but the moving and operation of the Holy Spirit. That's the way it was then and that's the way it should be now, but such is little the case presently, with the recognition of men being paramount, which God cannot bless, inspire, or anoint.

In fact, whether men believe it or not, the true operation and moving of the Holy Spirit is frowned upon by most. In other words, souls being saved, lives being changed, bondages of darkness being broken, with believers being baptized with the Holy Spirit, sadly and regrettably, count for little in this present climate. In fact, by the powers that be, which incidentally are man-placed powers and not those of God, for the most part are ignored. Of course there are a few exceptions to that rule, but not many.

I stand beside the crimson stream,
That flows from Calvary's mount,
And long to wash away all sin,
Within its cleaning fount.

The blood of Christ alone will save,
From guilt, and fear, and care;
His blood will sweetly purify,
When sought in earnest prayer.

I claim the promised blessing now,
Freedom from every sin:
The power to lead a holy life,
With Christ and God, shut in.

I sink into the crimson stream,
Christ's blood is now applied;
I rise again, redeemed by Him,
And wholly purified.

THE NEW COVENANT

CHAPTER 5

GRACE

GRACE

"AND WHEN JAMES, CEPHAS, AND JOHN, who seemed to be pillars, perceived grace that was given unto me, they gave to me and Barnabas the right hands of fellowship; that we should go unto the heathen and they unto the circumcision" (Gal. 2:9).

The exact use and order of the names of the leading apostles in this verse should not escape notice. First, the order obviously corresponds to the relative positions and work of James and Peter as recorded in Acts. Peter was the great missionary, hence, when Paul is speaking of the ministry to the Jews, Peter is prominent and James is not mentioned (Gal. 2:7–8).

In dealing with a particular and official act of the Jerusalem church, however, James (who apparently presided at the council) is mentioned in the first position with the names of Peter and John following.

Lightfoot points out, rightly so, the fact that James is first called *"James, the Lord's brother"* (Gal. 1:19) but here only "James" is explained clearly by the Acts narrative.[1] At the earlier visit to Jerusalem by Paul there were two prominent Jameses in the city—James, the Lord's brother, and James, the brother of John, both being sons of Zebedee. So, in describing that visit, Paul identifies the proper James. By the time of this visit (which is supposed to be that of Acts 15), James the son of Zebedee had been put to death by Herod (Acts 12:1–2).

JAMES, CEPHAS, AND JOHN

The phrase, *"and when James, Cephas, and John,"* presents the apostle for the first time identifying the leader of the Jerusalem church, who was James. Even though Peter and John definitely were leaders, even to a far greater extent than James, still, it seems that the Twelve had no distinctive official connection with this particular church more than with other churches; and therefore in meetings held at Jerusalem, the presidential position would naturally be conceded, not to any one of the apostles, but to the man who was stately recognized as the superior "elder" of this particular community.

It has been argued for centuries whether this meeting of which Paul now speaks is the Acts 11:30 meeting or the Acts 15:4 meeting, with most scholars coming down on the side of the latter. In fact, that seems to be the case here, with James the brother of John not being mentioned, for the simple reason that if, in fact, it was the Acts 15:4 meeting, James had by now been martyred, which would not have been the case with the Acts 11:30 meeting. And yet, it is certainly possible if, in fact, it was the Acts 11:30 meeting, that James the brother of John simply was not in Jerusalem at this particular time.

In reference to the name Cephas (Peter), it may be observed that Paul finds occasion to name this apostle nine times. In seven of these he writes, according to the best manuscripts, *"Cephas"* (I Cor. 1:12; 3:22; 9:5; 15:5; Gal. 1:18; 2:9, 14); in two, *"Peter"* (Gal. 2:7–8).

The Judaizers in the church, whether at Corinth or in Galatia, in their hankering after whatever was distinctively Jewish, were sure to effect the use of the Hebrew form; on which account, probably, Paul in dealing with these men, is seen so frequently using the form himself.

PILLARS

The phrase, *"who seemed to be pillars,"* presents a metaphor (a figure of speech in which a word or phrase literally suggests a likeness). The word *pillars* is from the Greek *stulos,* which was used to speak of literal pillars or columns of buildings.

The church is looked upon as a temple of God, and these men, among others, were looked upon as supporters of the church, men of distinction and prominence.

The word *seemed,* as used here by Paul, does not cast any doubt nor present an assumption, but means here "to repute." That is, these three men were reputed to be pillars of the church, and we speak of the church in general.

Peter was the most aged of the apostles and regarded as the head of the Twelve. John was the beloved disciple, and his influence in the church must have been great (of necessity). Paul felt that if he had the countenance of these men, it would be an important proof to the churches of Galatia that he had a right to regard himself as an apostle. Their countenance was expressed in the most full and decisive manner. (Actually, Jesus had said in His letter to the church in Philadelphia, *"Him that overcometh will I make a pillar in the temple of my God"* [Rev. 3:12].)

GRACE

In Galatians 2:9, the phrase, *"perceived the grace that was given unto me,"* presents the apostle here referring to grace as pertaining to everything he had received of God. Possibly, the reason for him using this word as he did was because the Lord had taken him from being a persecutor and waster of the church and made him an apostle, appeared to him several times, and enriched him with spiritual gifts. One could attribute such to no less than the grace of God.

As well, the word *grace,* which is here so carefully employed, should be noted as involving the assertion of a great principle characteristic of this epistle. Actually, the meeting in Jerusalem was all about salvation by grace alone through faith in Jesus Christ. This action shows that the Judaizers were totally wrong. Neither Jewish nor Gentile Christians had to be circumcised and live as Jews in order to be saved.

THE RIGHT HANDS OF FELLOWSHIP

The phrase, *"they gave to me and Barnabas the right hands of fellowship,"* presents this act as a pledge of friendship and agreement. This showed that they were wholly with Paul and not against him.

"The right hands of fellowship" expressed agreement between the chief apostles and Paul, as if to say, "In doctrine we are companions and have fellowship together therein, for we preach one gospel, one baptism, one Christ, one faith. And we conclude that neither uncircumcision nor circumcision ought to hinder our society and fellowship, since it is but one gospel which we preach.[2] In effect, it is very similar to a covenant.

As well, the reader is not to regard this act as a reconciliation, meaning that they had previously been separate in doctrine, for such is not the case. This handclasp simply ratified by a palpable gesture the formal assurance between the two parties that they regarded each other as friendly partners in a common undertaking.

In the case now under consideration there was no "strife" between James, Peter, and John, and Paul and Barnabas, which needed to be "ended" by "an oath." Regarding the manner of meeting it was this was the perfect gesture.

FELLOWSHIP

The word *fellowship* is from the Greek *koinonia*. It defines the compact recognized and sealed by the right hands of fellowship as a partnership, in this case, a partnership in the preaching of the same gospel. It was a mutual alliance for Paul and Barnabas to grasp the proffered hands of James, Peter, and John.[3]

In fact, this symbol of "fellowship," characterized the early church regarding its structure and government more so than anything else. The churches of that time, and made so by the Holy Spirit, were actually a fellowship, and not a denomination. They were a fellowship as it respects doctrine and community. Yet each church was an independent entity within itself, controlled by no outside force.

This is the way the Holy Spirit set up that particular structure, and this is the way and manner in which He intended for it to continue. Unfortunately, men have attempted to change this order for that which is man-devised, and because of the desire for control.

A DENOMINATION

It is not wrong to form and have a religious denomination and neither is it wrong to be associated with such. Ideally, a denomination should be a tool which can be very helpful for the work of God. The wrong comes in when men make more of such than it actually is, in effect, taking it into denominationalism. If that is done, spiritual significance is attached to the denomination. In other words, one is spiritually improved by belonging to such, or so it is claimed, and as well, the man-devised offices in these particular denominations are looked at as spiritual offices.

Of course, none of that is biblical, as should be obvious; nevertheless, many denominations have a tendency to go that route.

The Word of God should be the basis, the foundation, the pattern, and the example for all we do. If it is not solidly backed up by the Word, we simply should not go in such direction.

THE SCOPE OF THIS JERUSALEM MEETING

The issue at hand respecting the Jerusalem meeting can be summed up in the following: Is the Spirit of God going to be recognized as the symbol or sign of salvation, or will ceremony and ritual be added?

Whenever a person comes to Christ— is born again—the Spirit of God at that time comes into his heart and life. This is what we mean by the "divine nature," coming into the believer. Immediately a change takes place in that person's life, with the change actually continuing for the length of life (Rom. 8:29; I Cor. 15:49; II Cor. 3:18; Col. 3:10). The indwelling of the Holy Spirit is the sign that the person has been born again (Jn. 3:5–8).

Satan attempted to change this sign from the Holy Spirit to that of ceremonies and rituals, which he continues to do unto this present hour. In fact, untold millions of people think they are saved simply because they belong to a certain church, practice certain religious rituals, or engage in religious ordinances. While in fact it may be religious, still, it is not regeneration. Consequently, those people are not saved. Instead of the indwelling Holy Spirit within their hearts and lives, which is the sign of true conversion, they are instead depending upon "works," which is exactly what circumcision was. In fact, this is the great dividing line of the church presently, and in fact, always has been.

GOD'S WAY OR MAN'S WAY

As we've already stated, the call of God is to be recognized in a person's life by the working, moving, and operation of the Holy Spirit within his life and ministry. Instead, great segments of the church ignore that, actually not even believing in that of which we have said, rather looking to that which is appointed by men. In other words, the seal of approval is not the moving of the Holy Spirit, but rather the approval of men, i.e., so-called religious leaders.

Likewise, untold millions think they are saved simply because some man, be he preacher or priest, has told them so. There is no change within their lives, and in fact, there can be no change. The reason? They are not born again.

The Scripture plainly says, *"The Spirit itself* (Himself) *beareth witness with our spirit, that we are the children of God"* (Rom. 8:16). If He is present, He definitely will witness to our spirit; consequently, we won't have to have some man or woman to tell us so.

In actuality, that's what the meeting in Jerusalem was all about and why it was so very, very important. Would it be faith or works? Faith in Christ guarantees relationship with God, while works guarantee nothing. In fact, the doing of religion, which constitutes works of all descriptions, is the greatest narcotic there is. Untold millions are lulled into a deep spiritual sleep—a sleep of death—thinking they are saved simply because they are religious, when in fact they aren't saved! Consequently, and I will say it as bluntly as I can, there is nothing worse than a false way of salvation.

THE HEATHEN AND THE CIRCUMCISION

In Galatians 2:9, the phrase, *"that we should go unto the heathen, and they unto the circumcision,"* in effect says that both groups were to take the same gospel to both directions. Paul and Barnabas would go to the Gentiles, and the Jerusalem apostles would go to the Jews; however, there would be overlap in both directions. However, the agreement was more than this, much more.

It was an acknowledgment of apostolic equality. Paul would not be content with the mere approbation of the Twelve upon his missionary labors. He needed to show the Galatians, and all others for that matter, that he was an apostle equal in rank to the apostles at Jerusalem. In addition to that, he deemed it necessary to show them that his contention for Gentile freedom from the obligation of circumcision was sustained in the Jerusalem Council.

However, this mutual understanding did not forbid Paul to minister to the Jews on occasion or prevent Peter from ministering to the Gentiles should the opportunity arise. In fact, Paul generally began his ministry in each new place by preaching to the Jews. Peter as well ministered at the Gentile church in Syrian Antioch.

THE CALLING OF APOSTLES

As well, Paul being given the same rank, or rather recognized as such by Peter who headed up the Twelve, proclaimed the veracity of all other apostles who would be called by God from then until now. While there certainly could not be any more like the original Twelve—and for all the obvious reasons—still, the office of the apostle stands unto this hour and carries the same rank, at least if one desires to use that term, as the first apostles (Eph. 4:11). In fact, it is through the office of the apostle that spiritual guidance is given to the church. This began on the day of Pentecost and has continued unto this hour (Eph. 2:20).

Again, please allow us to acknowledge the following facts:

- God is still setting apostles in the church presently (I Cor. 12:28-29; Eph. 4:11).
- It is to apostles that the Holy Spirit gives the leading and guidance of the church. The Holy Spirit knows the message that is needed, and ordains apostles to carry out that message.
- All who are apostles are called by God. They are not called or appointed at all by man.
- The apostle is known by the message that God has given him to give to the church. As stated, the Holy Spirit knows what is needed, and uses the apostle to give that message to the church.
- For instance, in the 1950s and 1960s, the Lord moved greatly upon certain men and women and gave them the message of divine healing, which was used to greatly strengthen the Pentecostal church.
- Presently, the message the Holy Spirit is endeavoring to attend to the church is the message of the cross.

That's why Jesus plainly and bluntly told us, *"He that hath an ear, let him hear what the Spirit saith unto the churches"* (Rev. 2:7, 17, 29; 6:13, 22).

THE OUTCOME OF THIS MEETING

As a result of being led of the Spirit, that which could have been very grievous turned out to be a delightful harmony between Paul and the apostles at Jerusalem. The result showed the wisdom of the course which he had adopted. There had been no harsh contention or strife. No jealousies had been suffered to arise. Paul had sought an opportunity of a presentation of a full statement of his views to them in private, and they had been entirely satisfied that God had called him and Barnabas to the work of making known the gospel among the heathen.

Instead of being jealous at their success, the apostles had rejoiced in it; and instead of throwing any obstacle in their way, they cordially gave them the right hand of fellowship.

How much we should learn from this excellent example provided by the Holy Spirit. How easy it would be to prevent jealousies and strife in the same way. If there was, on the one hand, the same readiness for a full and frank explanation, and if, on the other, the same freedom from envy at remarkable success, how many strifes that have disgraced the church might have been avoided?

The true way to avoid strife is just that which is proposed here: Let there be on both sides perfect frankness; let there be a willingness to explain and state things just as they are; and let there be a disposition to rejoice in the working of the Holy Spirit in the hearts and lives of others, even though it should far outstrip our own. In this manner, contention in the church would cease, and every devoted and dedicated minister of the gospel would receive the right hand of fellowship from all—however venerable by age or authority—who love the cause of the gospel of Jesus Christ.

(Most of the above material was taken from the scholarship of Dr. Albert Barnes.[4])

WHICH I ALSO WAS FORWARD TO DO

"Only they would that we should remember the poor; the same which I also was forward to do" (Gal. 2:10). This verse is not a mere postscript, but rather that which is meant to be taken very seriously.

To show how seriously that Paul took this particular promise, we need only look at the space devoted to the subject of giving (Acts 24:17; Rom. 15:26–27; I Cor. 16:3; II Cor. 8–9). In fact, Paul gave the greatest dissertation on giving found in the entirety of the Bible in the chapters of II Corinthians.

Martin Luther, the great Reformer, made mention of the fact that after the preaching of the gospel, the office and charge of a true and faithful pastor is to be mindful of the poor.

Where the church is, there must need be poor, for Christ said we should have the poor with us always, and the poor must have the gospel preached to them (Mat. 11:5).

Luther said it, and he is right—the world and the devil at times persecute the church; consequently, many are brought to poverty, even as were many in Jerusalem. If it is to be noticed that where the true gospel is preached, there are few who will take care of the work of God, while false worship, superstition, and idolatry, go forward with no cost spared, and every man ready to give.

Luther went on to say, "Herein came so many monasteries, cathedrals, and bishoprics in the pope's church, where all impiety reigned, with so large revenues for their sustentation." He went on to say, "Whereas now, where the true gospel is preached, a whole city thinks much to find one or two preachers of the gospel, which before, while the pope reigned, did sustain monasteries of monks, nuns, and friars with whole swarms of massing priests."[5]

REMEMBER THE POOR

In Galatians 2:10, the phrase, *"Only they would that we should remember the poor,"* presents not merely a request added to the agreement, but a part of the agreement itself.

In the Greek, the word *remember* is *mnemoneuo,* and it means "benefit or care for." In fact, this is the only instance in the New Testament where this word is used in this manner. It means, "We should keep on remembering the poor."

I think James had in mind the mother church in Jerusalem, and for a specific reason. Understanding that all the money given—and there were quite large sums taken up by Paul—and that these sums were taken to Jerusalem causes us to understand that the need was greatest there.

THE NEED

The situation with the mother church at Jerusalem was no doubt unique during that time. Almost instantly many thousands of Jews gave their hearts and lives to the Lord Jesus Christ beginning on the day of Pentecost, and proceeding forward.

When these people came to Christ, the far greater majority of them were excommunicated from the synagogue. To be sure, this was of far greater significance than the mere the denial of fellowship. There was no such thing as a separation of church and state in Israel of that day—they were one and the same. In fact, religion ruled Israel in every capacity. As well, much of the activity was handled in the many synagogues in each city in Israel. The children attended school in the synagogues. Much of the social activity was carried on in the synagogues, as well as most trials for criminal cases. As a matter of necessity, the synagogues also served somewhat as employment offices.

When anyone was excommunicated—at least in the worst form, which pertained to all Christians—in many cases these people lost their jobs, were evicted from their homes (if they did not own their homes), and were banned and blackballed from every aspect of life and living. Their families actually disowned them, and they were treated as though they were dead.

A VERY DIFFICULT SITUATION

Considering that thousands, almost instantly, were thrown into this situation—a situation that continued throughout the entirety of the time of the early church until Jerusalem was destroyed in AD 70—one can well understand the difficulties involved.

In effect, thousands of people were literally out on the street with nowhere to go, and no way to provide for themselves. However, the Lord did provide, but it took some doing. The Scripture says, *"Neither was there any among them that lacked: for as many as were possessors of lands or houses sold them, and brought the prices of the things that were sold, and laid them down at the apostles' feet: and distribution was made unto every man according as he had need"* (Acts 4:34–35).

Those who had a surplus sold everything they didn't absolutely need to help provide for this situation. In fact, the problem continued for years, hence Paul constantly received money to help as it regarded this situation.

How acute this problem was in the other churches in Judea, we are not told. It is doubtful that it persisted to the extent of that in Jerusalem. This city housed the Sanhedrin, the very ones who crucified Christ; consequently, their hatred for the followers of Christ knew no bounds. As far as they were concerned, any Jew who would accept Christ was to be treated with all disdain, hence the excommunication.

Knowing of this great difficulty, the churches raised up by Paul all over the Roman Empire felt an obligation to the mother church in Jerusalem, which was right and proper. Consequently, at the instigation of Paul, it seems that great help was given respecting this need. In fact, all of the effort of which we are made aware in the Word of God was tendered toward the church

at Jerusalem. There is no record of efforts being made outside
of that particular situation.

WHICH I WAS FORWARD TO DO

The phrase, *"the same which I also was forward to do,"* casts
a light in several directions.

First of all, anyone who loves God will always give. As it
regarded the prince of apostles, if one studies his writings to
any degree at all, it becomes obvious as to the large heart of the
apostle Paul. So this was not something that had to be imposed
upon him, but rather that which he desired to do. I personally feel
that Paul saw this not only as an opportunity to be of help as it
regarded a critical need, but that the sustenance provided by the
Gentile churches would help ameliorate some of the problems
which we have been addressing for the entirety of this epistle.

By the Gentile churches helping in this matter, Paul knew
that this portrayed a great truth to the mother church in Jerusalem, that these Gentiles considered themselves as a part of
the church, the same as the Jews, and that they were not to be
looked at as anything less. In other words, these offerings helped
bridge the gap, at least Paul hoped they would.

As a result, how perseveringly and how earnestly the apostle
strove to aid the poor of the Jewish churches both before and
after the conference spoken of here. In fact, in Paul's first epistle
to the Corinthians, he tells them that he had given order to the
churches of Galatia respecting the manner in which they should
collect the offerings for this need (I Cor. 16:1).

RESPONSIBILITY

Every believer should be *"forward to do,"* exactly as Paul, as it regards the work of God. Our giving should be commensurate with the blessings given to us by the Lord. It is not a question of buying anything from the Lord, for He has nothing for sale. It is a matter of showing the *"sincerity of your love"* (II Cor. 8:8).

Paul is speaking here of giving to the work of God in this case toward the destitution of the saints in Jerusalem, which of necessity must include tithing.

GIVING THE TENTH

I feel the following article by the great holiness preacher of a century past, G.D. Watson, would be appropriate and a blessing to you:

It is no small perversion of Scripture that the passage of Malachi 3:10, about bringing the tithe into the storehouse, should always be applied to a spiritual consecration. If all Christians would only take it just as it reads, and begin at once to give God a tenth, even beside our offerings, of all that we receive, it would prove to be the keystone to the arch of a full consecration, and one of the greatest blessings of our lives, both spiritual and material.

Some may say that the giving of a tenth was only a Mosaic law; but this is a gross mistake; tithing was in practice by the saints of God some 500 years before the giving of the law. Abraham gave a tenth of his spoils to the priest of God (Heb. 7:4), with this particular priest, incidentally, being a type of Christ, and considering that all believers whether Jews or Gentiles, have come in under the Abrahamic covenant, the Holy Spirit meant for this to serve as an example for the entirety of all believers for all time. In other words, tithing was intended by God to be the undergirding foundation of His work respecting economics.

As well, Jacob gave a tenth of his income to the Lord, showing that this was meant not only for Abraham, but for all who would follow thereafter. When the Holy Spirit gets possession of a soul, He writes this principle of giving a tenth on the heart, showing it not merely a Mosaic, but a Holy Spirit law. As stated, the Holy Spirit gave the example through Abraham, and we are to follow.[6]

THE ABRAHAMIC COVENANT

The Abrahamic covenant is eternal, meaning that it is still in force today, and in fact, ever will be. It consists of several particulars, with justification by faith being the bedrock. The covenant consists of the following:

- Justification by faith. As stated, this is the foundation of the entirety of this covenant. It is the sum total of God's dealings with man, and that which was effected at Calvary. It is instituted by faith (Gen. 15:6; Rom. 5:1).

- Anyone who will aid and abet the child of God, considering that all believers are children of Abraham, will be blessed (Gal. 3:7). Consequently, everyone who hinders the child of God is cursed (Gal. 6:2; Gen. 12:3).

- The Abrahamic covenant includes everything that was paid for at the cross. Jesus said of Abraham, *"Your father Abraham rejoiced to see my day: sand he saw it, and was glad"* (Jn. 8:56).

- Tithing is included in the Abrahamic covenant. In fact, there is no mention of tithing before Abraham. The first record of tithing is found in Genesis when Abraham paid tithe to Melchisedec (Gen. 14:18-20).

Abraham paid tithe to Melchisedec who was a type of Christ. We are children of Abraham, and therefore we are to pay tithe to the work of God, which guarantees blessing. Incidentally, Abraham paid tithe to Melchisedec some 400 years before the law was given.

Malachi said, *"Will a man rob God? Yet ye have robbed me. But ye say, wherein have we robbed thee? In tithes and offerings ... Bring ye all the tithes into the storehouse, that there may be meat in mine house, and prove me now herewith, saith the LORD of hosts, if I will not open you the windows of heaven, and pour you out a blessing, that there shall not be room enough to receive it"* (Mal. 3:8-10).

Now, if the Lord said that He would open up the windows of heaven and pour us out a blessing that there would not be room enough to receive, and if that was said under the old law—and it was—He will do much more under the new covenant, which is now based on better promises (Heb. 8:6).

BLESSINGS

There are marvelous spiritual blessings connected with giving a tenth to the Lord; it is a wonderful stimulant to faith; it strengthens obedience on all other lines; it brings light into the mind on other subjects; it is as a safeguard against greed and stinginess; it makes benevolence a fixed affection in the soul, and not a spasmodic action; it makes us appreciate our nine-tenths far more; it makes God's special providence more real to us; it makes the conscience tender, and gives sweet access to God in prayer.

As well, it is a great blessing financially to constantly give a tenth of all we receive to the Lord. The living God keeps His financial promises just as absolutely as He does His salvation promises.

"Honor the LORD with thy substance, and with the firstfruits of all thine increase: so shall your barns be filled with plenty" (Prov. 3:9-10). How few Christians positively believe this Word and steadily act on it. I have never met a person yet who has given a tenth to the Lord regularly and ever regretted it. Uniformly, they testify that since they have done so, they have prospered far better in all of their temporal affairs. I am absolutely sure that God does not want any of His to be destitute. If all of us who are in debt would repent of the sin of getting into debt, promise God never to go into debt again, give Him one-tenth of all that we receive, and stick to the covenant with a loving heart, then God will begin to work financial mercies for us and soon have us free from debt (Rom. 13:8).

(When we speak of debt, we are not speaking of a house note or a car note, but rather the running up of debt for incidentals which we cannot afford.)

PARTIAL OBEDIENCE

God will not do wonders for us until we get away from our slipshod faith and partial obedience. A great many will say they keep no regular account; they *think* they give about a tenth—that is the way of partial obedience. If the truth be known, many people do not keep much account simply because they want to try to squeeze God out.

It will please God to give Him the tenth, and not "a guess" about the tenth.

Some people aim to give a tenth at the end of the month, or at the end of the year. This is degrading our Lord by putting self first and Him last. Honor God always by putting Him and His kingdom first, and then He will honor you. Just as soon as you receive any money, be it ever so small, take out the tenth for the Lord; do not wait until you spend the nine-tenths—don't use it all up, and promise to pay the Lord's tenth out of the next money you get. That is a slovenly, shabby way of dealing with God.

Treat your Lord in all these matters with the respect and honor as if He stood visibly by your side; don't' be mean and stingy in your treatments of Him, but generous, prompt, and free-hearted, and God will treat you like a prince, and ever and anon He will astonish you with great favor.

Be you ever so poor, old or young, married or single, parent or child, even if you have only an occasional dollar to call your own, give ten cents of it to God; and do it lovingly, rigidly, and as sure as you live, omnipotence will find some way to bless you in your temporal affairs. I believe that Frances and I have paid tithe on every dollar that we have made since we married many, many years ago. Actually, at one time, I was giving nearly fifty percent. And to be sure, God has rewarded me greatly, and I give Him all the praise and all the glory.

BELIEVE IT!

Will you believe this? Will you begin at once to do it? Ask the Holy Spirit to help you keep it as a holy covenant. Ask for divine guidance just where you should give the tenth; don't bestow it according to your preference, but keep your mind impartial, and the Spirit will lead you where to give it.

I constantly have people asking me where they should pay their tithes. To be frank, that question is very easy to answer: You should pay your tithe—and you must pay your tithe or God will not honor it—to where you are fed. It is just that simple. That which feeds you deserves your support.

If the church you are attending does not feed you, then you need to try to find one that does, and to be sure, you should not continue to support such an effort. If they aren't preaching the gospel, they do not need support.

Let us say it again: you should support that which feeds your soul and helps you to understand the Word of God to a

greater degree. If you follow that rule, you will be perfectly surprised by how much you can give away in a year and never miss it.

The Word says, *"Give, and it shall be given you."* God's Word
is true; obey it, prove it, and see for yourself.

WHAT WAS PETER'S REAL SIN?

*"But when Peter was come to Antioch, I withstood him to the
face, because he was to be blamed"* (Gal. 2:11).

Before we go into some depth regarding this particular passage, I think it would be helpful to look at Simon Peter a little
more closely concerning his former days. I speak of his denial
of Christ, for in some way this has a bearing on Peter's action
at this particular time as it regarded Paul. And yet, whatever we
say is only meant for instruction that we may learn from the
great apostle's personal experiences.

No man is perfect, even the greatest have had great problems,
but they overcame these things and that's what made them great.
Whatever we might say about this man as we attempt to learn
from his mistakes, which the Holy Spirit intends for us to do,
the fact remains, that Simon Peter was one of the greatest men
of God who ever lived. Nothing can change that.

THE REAL SIN

Recently a prominent religious leader implied that Peter's
sin of denying Christ was only an impulsive act spawned by
fear while he was temporarily backslidden. What does the Bible

reveal about Peter's problem? It is, after all, the final authority on this and all other matters.

We obviously cannot draw a conclusion about this issue by just taking a few verses out of context. The Scriptures reveal a rather consistent pattern in Peter's life. We view this pattern during the approximately three years that he physically walked with Jesus. So it is safe to assume that the same basic way of life existed before he became a disciple.

PETER'S PERSONALITY

He lived up to the name Jesus ascribed to him (Jn. 1:42). Both the Aramaic *Cephas* and the Greek *Peter* mean "rock." It does not take much reading about this fisherman to realize that he was an extremely self-confident individual. Because of this pride in his own ability, he constantly made rash statements and performed impetuous acts that revealed his overconfidence.

Peter, for example, was the only one of the disciples that asked to be allowed by Jesus to walk on the water; however, he soon began to sink and the Lord had to rescue him and rebuke him for his lack of faith (Mat. 14:28–31). However, despite the sinking, it must as well be remembered that he did walk on the water—*twice*.

In one breath, this same man could announce his spectacular confession of Jesus as the Messiah, even as the Son of God, yet in another breath acquiesce as a mouthpiece of Satan who adamantly opposed the concept of Jesus suffering for the sins of mankind (Mat. 16:13–23).

Peter could reject the Lord's offer to wash His feet, then suddenly leap to the opposite extreme and ask Jesus to wash his feet, his hands, and his head (Jn. 13:6–10). He could rashly endeavor to rescue the Lord by attempting to decapitate the high priest's servant (Mat. 26:50–51), yet shortly after cringe in terror when asked by a servant girl if he was one of the Lord's disciples (Mat. 26:69–75). It does not take very much imagination to realize that his denial of Christ was the culmination of a consistent and longstanding pattern of pride.

CHRIST'S DEALINGS WITH PETER

The Lord obviously attempted at different times and in a variety of ways to get Peter to recognize his problem. To illustrate, the interesting story in Luke 5:1–11, definitely contains a far more important message than just the fact that Peter, James, and John caught a draught of fish. After fishing all night and catching nothing, these disciples were instructed by Christ to cast their nets once more. Peter obeyed, and as a result of their great catch, fell before the Lord acknowledging his own utter sinfulness.

Another step in the Lord's patient dealing with Peter can be seen in conjunction with the disciple's boastful proclamation of his willingness to go with Christ to prison and even to death (Lk. 22:33). Just before this haughty pronouncement, Jesus told Peter that Satan desired (literally, "begged earnestly") permission to sift him as wheat. He also assured Peter that He had prayed for him, and that he should strengthen his brethren after his predicted return (Lk. 22:31–32). The Greek word Jesus used for "converted," or "return," is in the Greek *epistrepsas*. It means "a change in the course of action," so it does not in itself imply that Peter backslid.

Among other things, this incident shows that the devil must obtain permission from God before he can try a believer. More importantly, it points us to the fact that God many times accomplishes His purpose by actually using the devil as His instrument in sifting Christians.

In other words, the devil probably thought he had gained the upper hand in this situation, while all the time the Lord was using him to awaken Peter to his underlying problem. He may never have recognized his own pride if he had not failed in such a dramatic fashion.

DEPENDING ON THE GRACE OF GOD

We know that this event caused Peter to change from a man who depended on his own ability to a man who depended on God's grace. This is evident from his dialogue with Jesus after the Lord's resurrection (Jn. 21:15–19). When Jesus asked Peter if he loved Him more than "these," He could have been referring to the fishing implements or to the other disciples. I believe He was talking about the latter to remind Peter of his former boast that the others might desert the Lord, but he would not (Mk. 14:29).

More importantly, Jesus used the verb *agapao,* which refers to unconditional love, or the love that God Himself is (I Jn. 4:16). Peter, however, responded with the Greek verb for a less lofty type of love—*phileo*—which means "the love of friends."

Jesus, in the second question, again used the Greek *agapas,* and Peter again used *phileo.* In the third question, Jesus shifted to *phileis,* and Peter responded with the same basic word. Why?

Some people might say these two words are used interchangeably. It is true in some cases, but it is not likely that Jesus would use the two different terms in the same context to mean the same thing, especially in the configuration in this passage.

Is this just a play on words? No. I sincerely believe it indicates Peter's refusal now to manifest the former confidence in his own ability. He had fallen into that trap once. He was determined not to do it again.

Furthermore, it indicates that his entire life has turned to a total dependence on God's grace. That fact was evidenced a few days later when God miraculously used him on the day of Pentecost. He finally was truly qualified to be God's instrument. And so should it be with all of us.

DESIRE AND SINCERITY

Peter had the willingness before, and he manifested that desire many times and in a multitude of ways. It was he who exclaimed that there was no one else to whom they could go because Jesus had the words of eternal life. This transpired after many disciples ceased to follow the Lord (Jn. 6:68).

Despite his pride, Peter possessed a sincere desire to do God's will; therefore, the Lord did not cast him aside but lovingly worked in his life until he finally came to that place of humility and dependence on God's grace. Perhaps Peter's desire was one reason the Lord accorded him the privilege of participating in events that only two other Disciples, James and John, were allowed to share (Matt. 17:1; 26:37; Mk. 5:37).

In conclusion, it seems quite obvious from the total picture that Peter's betrayal was not just the result of one rash act. More importantly, the entire scenario of Peter's life in the Gospels clearly indicates the way the Lord patiently worked with him until he finally came to that place of throwing himself utterly on the grace of God. The book of Acts reveals the glorious results!

Are you allowing the Lord to conquer self in you so that He truly can manifest Himself through you?

(The above material on Simon Peter was derived from the work of Dr. H. Rossier.[7])

Lord Jesus, I long to be perfectly whole;
I want Thee forever to live in my soul;
Break down every idol, cast out every foe—
Now wash me, and I shall be whiter than snow.

Lord Jesus, look down from Thy throne in the skies,
And help me to make a complete sacrifice;
I give up myself and whatever I know—
Now wash me, and I shall be whiter than snow.

Lord Jesus, for this I most humbly entreat;
I wait, blessed Lord, at Thy crucified feet,
By faith, for my cleansing I see Thy blood flow;
Now wash me, and I shall be whiter than snow.

Lord Jesus, Thou seest I patiently wait:
Come now, and within me a new heart create;
For those who have sought Thee, Thou never saidst No!
Now wash me, and I shall be whiter than snow.

THE NEW COVENANT

CHAPTER 6

ANTIOCH

ANTIOCH

"BUT WHEN PETER WAS come to Antioch, I withstood him to the face, because he was to be blamed" (Gal. 2:11).

The phrase, *"But when Peter was come to Antioch,"* presents this city as the one used by God to spearhead world evangelism. In fact, the spiritual emphasis had shifted from Jerusalem to Antioch, and possibly because of the insistence of the Christian Jews in Jerusalem to continue in the law of Moses, which of course was an untenable situation, considering that Jesus had already fulfilled the types and symbolisms of the law.

There were several cities named Antioch, but this city was situated on the river Orontes, and was long the capital of Syria. Hence, it was known as Antioch, Syria. Built by Seleucus Nicanor, it was called Antioch in honor of his father Antiochus. It was founded about 300 years before Christ. It was long the most powerful city of the East, and was inferior only to Seleucia and Alexandria.

It was famous for the fact that the rite of citizenship was conferred by Seleucus to the Jews, as well as the Greeks and

Macedonians, so that here they had the privilege of worship in their own way without molestation. It is probable that the Christians were regarded merely as a sect of Jews, even though it seems that most in the church were Gentiles, and would be here suffered to celebrate their worship without interruption.

The city was honored as a Roman colony, a metropolis, and an asylum. It was large; was almost square; had many gates; was adorned with fountains; and was a city of great opulence.

THE JEWS AND THE MOSAIC LAW

In Galatians 2:11, Paul opens the question as to whether the Jew himself is still bound by the Mosaic law, which of course they were not. In the Jerusalem Council, the question was as to whether the rite of circumcision should be required of the Gentiles. The particular Mosaic legislation to which Paul had referenced here, and which he presented as a test case before the Galatians, had to do with the Levitical legislation regarding the eating of certain foods. While one purpose of the giving of the legislation prevented the eating of certain foods and the prohibition regarding other foods was a dietary one to promote the physical well-being of the Jews, yet another was that of keeping the Jews a separate people from the Gentiles, thus preserving clean the channel which God was using to bring salvation to the earth. The forbidden foods were found on the tables of the Gentiles. Hence, a Jew could never accept the dinner invitation of a Gentile. This was one of the factors which kept the nation of Israel apart from the Gentile world.

THE CROSS

God had made clear to Peter that this legislation was set aside at the cross, by the vision He gave him while he was on the housetop of Simon the tanner, with the result that Peter was willing to go to the home of the Gentile Cornelius (Acts 10). This occurred before the incident to which Paul refers in these verses.

When Peter came to Antioch, he saw Jews and Gentiles eating together, enjoying their fellowship. Then, when certain Jews from the Jerusalem Church came as representatives of James, and saw Peter eating with the Gentiles, they contended that he was going against Levitical legislation. They brought pressure to bear upon Peter, and he discontinued his fellowship in this manner.

This caused the Jews in the church at Antioch to cease eating with the Gentiles and brought about a division in the church. Thus Paul, in resisting Peter, showed that he not only refused to take orders from the Jerusalem apostles, but on the other hand felt that his apostolic position gave him the right to stand openly against them in matters which he considered to be wrong conduct. In no way could he have better demonstrated his independence as an apostle than this which he did regarding Peter at Antioch.[1]

THE DESIGN

The design for which Paul introduces this statement here is evident. It is to show that he regarded himself as on a level with the chief apostles, and that he did not acknowledge his inferiority to any of them. Peter was the eldest, and no doubt the most honored of the apostles. Yet Paul says that he did not hesitate to resist him in a case where Peter was manifestly wrong and thus showed that he was an apostle of the same standing as the others.

Besides, what he said to Peter on that occasion was exactly pertinent to the strain of the argument which he was pursuing with the Galatians, and he therefore introduces it (Gal. 2:14–21) to show that he had held the same doctrine all along, and that he had defended it in the presence of peter, and with Peter not contradicting Paul.

The time of this journey of Peter to Antioch cannot be ascertained; nor the occasion on which it occurred. Some feel this incident took place before the council in Jerusalem, and others after. Personally, I believe it occurred before that council, but there is no proof, I think, either way.

THE GALATIANS

In this narrative which Paul gives, several points here were definitely meant by him to be directed toward the Galatians.

He shows to these Gentile Galatians who were wavering in their attachment to him and to the gospel which he had preached to them, how he had successfully asserted their rights and their equal standing with Jewish believers when the Gentiles were assailed by *"certain who came from James"* (Gal. 2:12).

In contrast with his own unflinching championship of their cause, were here seen vacillation and inconsistency on the part of Peter. Were, then, any justified in exalting these "pillars"—James and Peter—as certain were disposed to do, for the sake of disparaging him (Paul)?

In fact, this experience at Antioch should lead them to regard with suspicion the Jewish brethren, who were setting themselves to tamper with the truth of the gospel. Crooked conduct was sure to accompany such darkening of the truth, as on that occasion was most palpably evinced in the case of even Barnabas, and was in open encounter before the whole church exposed and rebuked.

The Pulpit Commentary says, "And especially, there was the grand principle that the law of Moses was for the Christian believer annihilated through the crucifixion of Christ; which principle Paul had then held aloft in the view of the church, and here takes occasion to enlarge upon, because it was so directly relevant and helpful in respect to the trouble now springing up in Galatia."[2]

PETER IN ANTIOCH

The manner in which Peter's coming to Antioch is introduced seems to proclaim that his coming was not felt to have been at all an extraordinary circumstance. In other words, it seems to be obvious, that he had possibly visited the church at Antioch several times. It is even thought that he traveled often, taking his wife with him (I Cor. 9:5).

Actually, there is a tradition, which gained early acceptance in the church (Eusebius), that Peter ultimately became the bishop (pastor) of the church at Antioch. There is little proof as to whether or not this is true.

WITHSTOOD HIM TO THE FACE

The phrase, *"I withstood him to the face,"* means that Paul openly opposed and reproved him. Thus, Paul showed that he was equal with Peter in his apostolic authority and dignity. The instance before us is one of faithful public reproof; and every circumstance in it is worthy of special attention, as it furnishes a most important illustration that at times there must be reproof, and the manner in which such reproof should be conducted:

- Peter allowed the opinions of others to influence him, and by his action overturned the truth. Paul lived in the light and power of the gospel of which a glorified Christ is the center, and being both firm and ardent as well as clear-sighted, he did not spare Peter, but rebuked him in the presence of all.
- Paul did this openly. It was reproof addressed to the offender himself. Paul did not go to others and whisper his suspicion; he did not seek to undermine the influence and authority of another by slander; he did not vilify Peter, and then attempt to justify himself on the ground that what he had said was no more than true: he went to him at once, and evidently before others, frankly stating his views, and reproved him in a case where he was manifestly wrong.

The word *but,* as it introduces Galatians 2:11, presents the contrast between the fellowship of Paul with the Jerusalem apostles and his attitude against them respecting that which he thought was wrong.

The word *withstood* means "to set oneself against, to withstand, resist, oppose." This verb implies that the initial attack came from the other side.

It was Peter in Paul's mind, who was the aggressor. Although not intentional, yet in effect, it was an attack on the position which Paul was maintaining at Antioch. Actually, what Peter did, undercut Paul in all that he had taught, even as we shall see.

ONE OF THE MOST IMPORTANT
EVENTS IN CHURCH HISTORY

We see Peter and Paul here in open antagonism: The rebuke coming from Paul, and the blame resting unequivocally on Peter, and this on a question very seriously affecting Christian faith and conduct in all future ages.

THE DEFENSE OF THE TRUTH

Here we have no trifling matter at hand, but the chief article of all Christian doctrine. We are speaking of justification by faith, or otherwise, when in reality, there is no otherwise.

The utility and majesty of this of which we speak, and which Paul addressed, is of such significance, that it beggars description.

Who is Peter?

Who is Paul?

Who is and what is an angel from heaven?

What are all the creatures together, to the article of justification, which Paul saw here in danger by the conduct of Peter? Wherefore he is obliged to put aside the dignity of Peter for the truth's sake.

Wherefore we must not be ashamed for the defense of the truth, to pay whatever price must be paid, be we called proud, obstinate, or what they will, we must hear none of this. We must give place to none when it comes to the truth. Only here are we allowed to be obstinate and inflexible.

For this cause we offend man, that is if we have to do so, even tread down the majesty of his person, or the entirety of the world for that matter, simply because the only avenue of the soul—justification by faith—must never be hindered, weakened, or compromised.

When it says that Paul withstood Peter to his face, he makes points against the apostles of Satan, who slander those who are absent, and in their presence dare not open their mouths. Paul did not do that, he frankly and openly withstood him to his face, not for any ambition or other carnal affection, but because he was to be blamed.

THE INFALLIBILITY OF THE APOSTLE?

I think it is here obvious that apostles, even though their calling is from God, and even though it is the highest rank there can be under the New Testament economy, are not infallible. It is possible for an apostle to be wrong, even as Peter here was. In fact, the prophets themselves have sometimes erred, and been deceived.

Nathan said unto David that he should build a house unto the Lord (II Sam. 7:3). But this prophecy was shortly corrected by revelation from God. So did the original Twelve err also, for they imagined that the kingdom of Christ should be carnal and of this world, saying, *"Lord, wilt thou at this time restore again the kingdom to Israel?"* (Acts 1:6).

And again Peter, although he heard the command of Christ, *"Go ye into all the world, and preach the gospel to every creature"* (Mk. 16:15), still, had not gone, and would not go to Cornelius, if he had not been admonished and compelled by a vision (Acts 10).

And in this matter of Paul's rebuke, Peter did not only err in judgment, but committed a great sin; and if Paul had not resisted him, all the Gentiles which did believe would have been constrained to receive circumcision and to keep the law of Moses, which would have destroyed their salvation.

The believing Jews would have been confirmed that these things were necessary to salvation, and by this means would have received again the law instead of the gospel, Moses instead of Christ. And of all this great enormity, Peter, by his dissimulation, had been the occasion. Therefore, we may not attribute to the saints such perfection, as though they could not sin.

THE WORD IS THE STANDARD, NOT MEN

In this entire scenario it is plainly obvious that the Word of God is to be the standard, the foundation, the guiding light of all that is done, and not men.

However, the Catholic Church would proclaim the opposite, demanding that the people heed the pope, bishops, and priests, with the Word of God given no place at all.

All too often, even in Protestant circles, men demand obedience even at the expense of the Word of God, men incidentally who refer to themselves as spiritual leaders, but in fact have been given that position by elective ballot, and not by God. In other words, they occupy a man-devised position.

Even though all preachers of the gospel have some spiritual authority, still, the only binding "spiritual authority" so-called, is the Word of God. It is infallible, unchangeable, and is to be the rule of conduct, thought, decision, and direction respecting all things.

HOW IMPORTANT IS THE TRUTH?

I think we should see from this scenario given by Paul, actually prompted by the Holy Spirit, as to how significant all of this is. In fact, had it been allowed to continue, quite possibly the new covenant would have been destroyed. As we've already stated, we are speaking here of the single most important thing there is: the salvation of the soul. Satan would love to compromise that message. In fact, he does all within his power to compromise it, and has succeeded in many if not most religious circles in doing so.

I do not at all enjoy taking the stands that I feel we must take respecting my own personal ministry. I have suffered much for that stand.

I have watched the church drift into humanistic psychology, into what has actually ceased to be a drift, but rather a speedy slide downward, and I have lifted my voice as strongly as possible against this direction. It has not endeared me to the leadership of the Assemblies of God, the Church of God, the charismatics, or others.

Personally, I consider this problem—the "psychological way" versus the biblical way—to be little less significant, if any at all, than the law/grace issue of Paul's day. As believers could not have both law and grace then, they cannot have the psychological way and the biblical way at the same time now.

THE CROSS OF CHRIST

It is the same with the message of the cross. One cannot have the cross and psychology in the same capacity. One or the other must go simply because either one cancels out the other. So that leads the modern church in a very perilous situation considering that the cross in most circles is rejected in favor of humanistic psychology.

As well, it has not endeared us regarding many to take a stand against the "money gospel," which in fact, is no prosperity at all. The same can be said for the music of the world brought into the church, which affects worship, and above all, substitutes an ungodly direction for the Holy Spirit respecting the winning of people to God.

The list could go on. It is not pleasant to be looked at as a pariah, to have every type of lie that Satan can devise told about one's person, and even have so-called religious leaders aid and abet the Evil One in the spreading of these lies.

Irrespective, as a minister of the gospel, I have but one duty, one obligation, one responsibility, and that is to hear from heaven and deliver to the people exactly that which I have heard. Consequently, I lay on my face before God day after day, asking Him to give me leading and guidance, that I may be anointed to proclaim His Word, and which He has done. By His grace, He has helped us to see untold thousands brought to a saving knowledge of Jesus Christ, and I exaggerate not. We give Him all the praise and all the glory.

Yes, the truth is worth defending at whatever price.

BLAME

The phrase, *"because he was to be blamed,"* indicates that Peter's action had aroused the indignation of the Antioch Christians. The intrigue of the Jerusalem Jews who had come to Antioch, their purpose of which was to affix the stigma of uncleanness on the uncircumcised Gentile Christians, was countenanced by Peter and Barnabas.

Consequently, the public judgment had turned against Peter. Paul could not, therefore, keep silent, but was forced to rebuke Peter.

Here the argument for Paul's apostolic independence has come to the highest level yet attained. In Jerusalem Paul faced Peter as an equal in rank and in the gospel ministry. At Antioch he faced him as his superior in character and courage.

JAMES

"For before that certain came from James, he did eat with the Gentiles: But when they were come, he withdrew and separated himself, fearing them which were of the circumcision" (Gal. 2:12).

It is clear that these men were sent by James, and not that they merely claimed such. They were men of importance as is shown by the deference with which Peter treated them, and the manner with which he bowed to their request (or demands).

As well, they were not from the ranks of the Judaizers who Paul had castigated. James would not send men of that stamp, but rather Jewish Christians of Jerusalem who like James were still most scrupulous in their obedience to the Mosaic law. James, even after the decision of the council at Jerusalem regarding the relation of the law to Gentile converts to Christianity, still held to the view that the Jewish converts were under the law.

So, we have here Paul's statement as it regarded the lapse of James regarding the Jews, when he gave his decision concerning Gentiles and the law recorded in Acts 15:19–29.

Whereas James lapsed there, which caused great difficulties, some scholars believe that Paul himself lapsed in faith, when the apostle at the request of James took upon himself a Jewish vow to show the Jews in Jerusalem that he was still a strict Jew (Acts 21:18–26). Actually, I have taken the position that Paul did not at that time lapse, with commentary on that particular chapter in Acts, hopefully explaining the situation to a greater degree.

And here we have the occasion of Peter's lapse when James sent this mission to Antioch with the purpose of enforcing the

Mosaic law so far as the Jewish Christians were concerned. News had reached Jerusalem that Jewish and Gentile Christians were mixing together and even eating together, hence the mission from James.

CERTAIN CAME FROM JAMES

The phrase, *"For before that certain came from James,"* gives us all too well another example as to why apostles or anyone else for that matter, are not to be the final word, but rather the Word of God itself. As we've already stated, this is one of Satan's greatest efforts, to demand that men follow man instead of God. While apostles and all others as well, are to be loved, respected and appreciated, as it regards the call of God upon their lives, with the believer gleaning all that is possible from the ministries of these particular individuals, still, it is always the Word of God which is the final authority on all things.

As we have said a number of times, if James had included the Jews in his decision respecting Acts 15, it would have been a tremendous boon to the work of God. It should be obvious to the reader that the Lord did not and does not have one salvation for Gentiles and another for Jews.

WHY DID NOT PAUL RAISE THAT QUESTION AT THE COUNCIL IN JERUSALEM?

I think it is obvious as to why he said nothing at that time. He was very thankful to the Lord, considering this decision by

James respecting the Gentiles as a tremendous victory. In fact, Paul held very little status in that particular council; consequently, his position of authority would have counted for little at that particular time. However, if Peter had come out strongly for this cause, that the ruling should apply to Jews as well, it would have carried great weight, no doubt carrying the day; however, even though Peter did stand strongly for the Gentiles not having to abide by Mosaic law, he said nothing respecting Jews (Acts 15:7–11). Considering the great vision the Lord had given him concerning this very problem, even as recorded in Acts 10, it should have been sufficient ground on which he could have stood respecting this issue. Nevertheless, he took no stand except for the Gentiles, for which Paul regarding that much, was no doubt, extremely thankful.

EAT WITH THE GENTILES

In Galatians 2:12, the phrase, *"he did eat with the Gentiles,"* shows that Peter knew the right way, especially considering the remarkable vision which he had as recorded in Acts 10. He had learned that God designed to break down the wall of partition between the Jews and the Gentiles, and he, consequently, familiarly associated with them, and partook with them of their food.

This means that he evidently disregarded the peculiar laws of the Jews about meats and drinks and partook of the common food which was in use among the Gentiles, whatever that may have been. Thus, he showed his belief that all the race was henceforward to be regarded as on the same level, and that the peculiar institutions of the Jews, which were now fulfilled in Christ anyway, were not to be considered as binding, or to be imposed on others.

The words *eat with* in the Greek implies close fellowship or cooperation. In the Greek, this tells us that it was a practice of Peter to eat with the Gentiles. In other words, he held not at all with the old Jewish rituals.

The preposition speaks of the fact that in the act of joining in their meals, not only in the Christian love feasts which were connected with the worship program of the local church, but also held the same in their homes. Peter was on terms of the greatest intimacy with these Gentiles. In fact, at that particular time, the love feasts were recognized as the bond of fellowship in the infant church.

ANTIOCH AND THE COUNCIL AT JERUSALEM

Some hold that this council of Acts 15 was held after the situation at Antioch of which Paul speaks; I personally share that opinion.

RELIGION OR RELATIONSHIP?

The reader may be somewhat confused regarding this great to-do concerning food. We have already explained in previous commentary the dietary laws contained in Mosaic legislation. As stated, all of this was given by God for a particular purpose, which in effect, pertained to the coming of the Messiah, which were all fulfilled when Jesus came. These things were no longer necessary when Jesus came and died on the Cross, such having fulfilled its purpose.

However, the Jews desired to continue these laws and regulations of old, some of them even claiming that one had to do these things in order to be saved. In fact, eating or not eating certain foods did not make any difference, unless one construed that it had something to do with one's salvation, which is exactly what was happening.

It is the same presently. Let's use jewelry for instance: One particular Pentecostal denomination for years forbade the wearing of any type of jewelry by women in that particular church. Now, the wearing or not wearing of jewelry had nothing to do with anything for that matter; however, if they claimed, which some did, that such had to do with one's salvation, then it falls under the same category of this of which we are discussing here.

People are saved by faith in Christ, not because they do or don't do certain things of this nature, which in fact, have no moral bearing on anything, just as the food or circumcision of which Paul spoke. When these type of things are done, religion is the result and not relationship with Christ. As a result, all of this contains some very important lessons for us about the difference between religion and relationship.

THE ENCOUNTER BETWEEN PETER AND PAUL

Even though we will discuss this further, please notice a few facts presently about this incident:

- It was such a serious issue that Paul "opposed" Peter against, or to, his face.
- Paul twice labeled Peter's conduct "hypocrisy" and added that the remaining Jews and even Barnabas were led away by it.
- Peter apparently knew he was wrong because he did not attempt to defend his action. At least we have no record of any defense.

What makes this encounter so serious? The key is in Galatians 2:14, which begins with a very strong, "But." Paul followed this contrasting term with *"when I saw that they walked not uprightly according to the truth of the gospel."* "Walking straight with" or "conforming to" the truth of the gospel was paramount in Paul's life, and thank God it was, or salvation in Christ may have at that time been destroyed, which was Satan's intention.

The simple but profound fact that Jesus died for our sins according to the Scriptures, that He was buried, and that He was raised on the third day according to the Scriptures was the message that Paul gave first priority (I Cor. 15:3–4).

PETER'S PROBLEM

Peter knew that acceptance of the sacrifice of Christ on the cross was the only thing that would bring salvation to a life and soul (Acts 2:38; 4:12). Why then did he temporarily fail to act in conformity to the truth of the gospel?

When he segregated himself from the Gentile believers in Antioch and fellowshipped only with Jewish believers, he was turning his back on the gospel by showing his preference for the religion in which he participated before his conversion to Christ. However, as we shall see, he did this out of fear instead of conviction.

PAUL'S LESSON

Paul learned about religion the hard way. Before his conversion to Christ (Acts 9:1–19), his entire life was absorbed in religion, yet he did not have a relationship with Jesus. Some people do not seem to realize that he was not converted until he was in his thirties, or at least in his late twenties. In fact, he lived nearly half of his earthly life as a zealous self-righteous Pharisee (Phil. 3:4–6).

At a particular time, though, God allowed him to hear the testimony of a person, Stephen, who did have a living relationship with Jesus (Acts 7:54–60). The attitude and words of Stephen while being martyred must have had a profound impact on Saul of Tarsus.

Anyhow, the time arrived when he exchanged those twenty-five or thirty years of empty religion for a personal relationship with Jesus Christ (Phil. 3:7–14), and actually the same kind of relationship that Stephen enjoyed.

Is it any wonder that he was so disturbed when he viewed the hypocrisy of Peter, Barnabas, and the other Jews in Antioch? This matter was serious because their action was implying that justification could come from practicing religion. I know that is why he stated unequivocally *"that a person is not justified by works of law but through faith in Christ Jesus"* (Gal. 2:16).

DOING AND BEING

Religion deals with *doing,* but relationship is concerned with *being.* Religion attempts to gain merit with God by doing good things. On the other hand, a person with a genuine relationship with Christ will also perform good works, but those deeds will emanate from the relationship (James 2:18–26).

We are facing a battle between what is *good,* and what is *best.* Religion constantly involves itself in doing good things. This is commendable, but it is not best. God's way is the only best way because it emphasizes a living relationship with Christ, and out of this relationship will come good works.

Paul was distressed with any theosophy that even suggested salvation could result from good works. He had tried that approach for approximately half of his earthly life, and he knew it did not work.

Why did it not work? Because God willed that salvation would be granted to people by grace through faith (Eph. 2:8) and not by works (Eph. 2:9).

WHY DID THE LORD DESIGN THE RECEIVING OF SALVATION IN THIS MANNER?

In brief, God's justice could never have been satisfied by man's works, inasmuch as the sin debt was so great that man could never hope to settle the account in this manner. Consequently, the only way for people to be saved was for Jesus Christ to settle that account, which He did at Calvary's cross, and the believing sinner having faith in that—what Christ did at Calvary—instantly, wondrously, even miraculously, insures salvation (Jn. 3:16).

Once Paul realized these things of which we have just said, which were actually given to him by Jesus Christ through revelation, Paul died to the law in order to live to God (Gal. 2:19). This is a way of saying that he rejected the religion of trying to gain merit with God by performing good works. Instead, he accepted Christ and was thereby granted a living relationship with God. And, by the way, his good works was killing Christians. No wonder the apostle demands faith even as he does under the leading of the Holy Spirit.

A CONTINUOUS LIFE OF VICTORY

This great truth does not end there, though. You see, God does not just want us to experience the initial victory over sin that comes at conversion. He has provided a continuous life of victory for us, as we appropriate on a daily basis the benefits of the cross. That's what Jesus was talking about, respecting the taking up of the cross daily and following Him (Lk. 9:23).

It is because of this that Paul's discourse on relationship contains three definite aspects:

- The historical basis, or the sacrifice of Christ on the cross.
- The initial experience of conversion that occurs when a person accepts Christ as Saviour.
- The continuous aspect of living the overcoming Christian life.

All three are based on God's grace, and come through the cross of Christ.

We continue to enjoy a constant relationship with Christ because of the process described in Galatians 2:20, which we will arrive at momentarily. Unfortunately, some people fail to live overcoming Christian lives because they shift from relationship to religion after they become Christians, which in fact, is a problem I think for every believer. In other words, they seem to think they are living proper Christian lives because of their works. The Bible teaches no such thing!

If we are "trying" to live overcoming Christian lives by practicing good works, then we need to stop trying and start allowing Christ to live through us. The good works will be present, but they will result from relationship as previously stated, and not from religion.

THE PROCESS

According to Galatians 2:20, which we will address to a greater degree momentarily, this is the way the process works: *"I am crucified with Christ"* comes from a perfect tense verb in the Greek, so it relates to the process that begins at conversion and continues throughout this earthly life. The sinful Adamic nature is constantly being put to death by our constant trust in what Jesus did for us at Calvary and the resurrection. Our victorious overcoming is not a onetime affair, but rather a continuing, daily process. We must exhibit faith daily in Christ and the cross.

In addition, *"Nevertheless I live, yet not I"* shows that the human nature or sin nature is no longer in control. *"But Christ liveth in me"* indicates a new source of control.

How does the life of Christ operate through us?

The phrase, *"I live by the faith of the Son of God,"* shows that faith must not only be exercised at conversion but throughout our lives.

But faith in what? Faith in what Jesus did for us at Calvary and the resurrection. There He paid the terrible sin debt and as well, He broke the grip of sin within our hearts and lives. However, even as we have stated, it takes a continuous faith, which means continuous believing even on a daily basis, which is what Jesus referred to in taking up the cross daily and following Him, in order for us to maintain this victory.

MAINTAIN

To be frank, the key is in the word *maintain*.

In fact, every single believer is already an overcomer and victorious in Christ, through his faith in Christ. There is nothing the believer can do in the form of works to make himself victorious or an overcomer that already having been done in Christ. Jesus defeated Satan on our behalf, consequently becoming victorious. As well, He overcame every rudiment of Satan, sin, and darkness, and He did such on our behalf. Our faith in Him and what He did grants us the status of "victory" and "overcomer."

However, Satan does all within his power to shove us away from that position we have in Christ. He makes us believe that we have to do something—perform good works, become very religious—in order to be an overcomer, which he knows will never work, and in fact is an insult to Christ. Such action portrays, whether we realize it or not, that Jesus did not finish the work at Calvary and consequently needs our help.

THE TRAP

In fact, I think I can say that most every Christian has fallen into this trap in one way or the other. We should understand, that it makes no difference as to how sincere we are or how hard we try, if we're trying to gain victory outside the legal confines of Calvary—what Jesus there did for us—we will fail every time.

That which makes this process work is the grace of God. The Holy Spirit works on our behalf, which He will do only within the legal confines of Calvary and the resurrection, which alone will gain us victory through the grace of God. We did not earn such as we cannot earn such, it being given to us freely by the Lord upon our faith.

That is why Paul closed the passage with the affirmation, "I do not set aside the grace of God." The truth is, if we do not permit the grace of God to operate in us, we will not be overcoming Christians.

Religion says, "I can do it." Relationship says, "Christ can do it through me." Take your pick: do you want religion that operates by works, or a relationship that operates by grace? Religion guarantees failure, while the grace of God, which all of us desperately need and can have through Christ, guarantees victory.

HE WITHDREW

In Galatians 2:12, the phrase, *"but when they were come, he withdrew and separated himself,"* suggests a retreat on the part of Peter from motives of caution. The Greek text indicates that Peter did not start his withdrawal from the Gentile tables at once, but gradually, under the pressure of the criticism of those sent from James. It gives a graphic picture of Peter's irresolute and tentative efforts to withdraw from an intercourse that gave offense to these visitors.

The word *withdrew* also was used of furling the sails of a boat. Peter, the former fisherman, was expert at that. Now, he was trimming his sails in a controversy that involved Jewish freedom from the Mosaic law which had been set aside at the cross.

The word *separated* also speaks of a gradual separation. The whole incident is characteristic of Peter. It seems he was always the first to recognize great truths and the first to draw back from these truths. Witness his great confession of the deity of the Lord Jesus, and so soon after, his repudiation of the prediction of our Lord to the effect that He would die at Jerusalem and be raised again (Mat. 16:13–23); also his call to preach (Mat. 4:18–20), and his action of returning to his fishing business instead of fulfilling his commission of preaching the gospel (Jn. 21:3). And of course the greatest failure of all, in his proclamation of faithfulness to the Lord, and then a few hours later his denial (Lk. 22:31–34).

It is much to be marvelled that Peter, being so excellent an apostle, should fall into this error, for at the council in Jerusalem, he was very bold in defense of this very article, when the

Pharisees which believed, held that it was necessary to circumcise the Gentile converts, and command them to keep the law of Moses. Peter then protested vehemently against putting a yoke upon the Gentiles, *"which neither our fathers nor we were able to bear"* (Acts 15:5–11).

"Let him who thinketh he standeth take heed lest he fall" (I Cor. 10:12). No one would think what danger there is in traditions and ceremonies. Of the law and good works comes a trust in such, and where that is, there can be no proper trust in Christ.

Peter knew the article of justification better than we do, and yet how easily he gave great occasion of offense, that is, if Paul had not withstood him.

BEFORE MEN

Peter allowed the opinions of others to influence him, and by his action overturned the truth. Consequently, the weakness and poverty of man are seen in Peter's conduct. A man is weak in proportion to his importance before men.

When he accepts the position of being nothing, he is independent of public opinion and can do everything. The Christian exercises an evil influence over the world to the degree in which it influences him; and the potential for evil is increased if the Christian has a reputation for godliness. In fact, it is a great snare for the heart to seek to maintain a reputation among men; and when this is a motive, the esteem, even though just in itself, becomes an agency for evil. So Peter drew away all the Hebrew Christians, and even Barnabas with him, into his dissimulation (hypocrisy).

THE FEAR OF MAN

It must be noted that Peter did not simply make an honest mistake. The Peter who had received the vision prior to going to the house of Cornelius and who defended Paul at the council was not fooled by the arguments of the legalizers.

The difficulty was that he gradually gave in to pressure exerted by the legalizers, even though he knew what was right. In other words, Peter played the hypocrite. The same Peter who had denied his Lord for fear of a maidservant now denied Him again for fear of the circumcision party. As this problem was acute, it is acute now. Most preachers, and I think I speak without exaggeration, are not free in their own spirits to preach what they know in their hearts to be true. They fear what certain people in the church will say, or what denominational heads may say or think, or others of their peers in some way.

As well, there is something in all men that desires to be accepted, or even applauded by other men. So, when fear is coupled with self-will, there are very few who will preach "thus saith the Lord," irrespective as to what others think. To be sure, there will be adverse results from some quarters.

A PERSONAL EXAMPLE

In the early 1980s, we had the largest television audience in the world relative to gospel. In prayer one particular morning, the Lord spoke to my heart with a great moving of the Holy Spirit, telling me certain things He desired that I address: the Catholics and their gospel of works, the denominational world and their denial of the Holy Spirit, the Pentecostals and their abandoning the Holy Spirit, and the charismatics and their false doctrine.

This was something which went on for many weeks regarding the moving of the Holy Spirit upon my heart. The Holy Spirit was perfectly open with me, telling me exactly what would happen: "Your own will turn against you," He said.

Even though I understood that readily, I am glad that at the time I did not fully understand the implications of what was being said. If so, I am not certain I would have been strong enough to have obeyed.

THE CATHOLICS FIRST

To be frank, I knew absolutely nothing about Catholic doctrine at that particular time. Besides that, Catholic charismatics were giving to our ministry millions of dollars each year in donations. However, when I began to study Catholic doctrine, I realized what the Holy Spirit was saying to me.

The conventional wisdom at that particular time among Pentecostals and charismatics was that Catholics who had truly been saved, with many being baptized with the Holy Spirit, were to stay in the Catholic Church. That was the message that was being propagated. To be frank, I knew very readily as to what was being preached about this particular situation, but I thought little about its direction.

When I began to study Catholic doctrine, I realized that there was no way the Holy Spirit could condone Catholics who had truly been saved staying in this error; such was not scripturally or spiritually possible (Jn. 16:13–15). If they were truly saved, they had to come out of this false way.

I BEGAN TO PREACH THIS WHICH
I KNEW TO BE TRUE

I little dreamed the furor that would erupt upon my first message. Having the ear at that time of most of the church world, my message came across like a bombshell.

To be sure, I did everything to be diplomatic and kind, but I unequivocally stated, at least as it regarded Catholics, that if they were truly saved, they were going to have to come out of the Catholic Church. I made no bones about it, I pulled no punches, and I stated it just like I believed it to be.

Almost instantly, the giving from Catholic charismatics dried up, with my Pentecostal and charismatic friends castigating me in no uncertain terms for my particular stand. I mean that my message aroused an anger from those quarters which I little expected, at least to that degree.

Whether it was true or not, I had no way to prove, but I was told that the leader of a major Pentecostal denomination stated that he wished he could publicly apologize to the Catholics for my stand. He was greatly displeased at my message. Whether this man actually said this or not I am not sure, but I do know that the policy of the leadership of that particular denomination, at least for the most part, was definitely opposed to my message; there was no doubt about that!

By the way, and I think I can say without fear of exaggeration, we saw many Catholics brought to a saving knowledge of Jesus Christ all over the world.

ANGER!

One particular pastor of a very large Pentecostal church was very angry about my stand and confronted me about it in the presence of other preachers. I quietly asked him, "How many Catholics you seen saved under your ministry?"

He sat there for a few moments, and then finally said, "None, of which I am aware."

I answered, "By the grace of God, I have seen many brought to Christ."

His ridiculous reply was, "If you had not told them to come out of the Catholic Church, you would have seen many more saved."

In other words, he was saying that if we preached a lie, that would get people saved. To be frank, I really did not know how to answer such stupidity. I guess I would have to say with Jesus, *"Can the blind lead the blind? Shall they not both fall into the ditch?"* (Lk. 6:39).

The man fear which Peter experienced, and which millions of other preachers have experienced down through the centuries, has been one of Satan's greatest weapons against the truth.

Most are not willing to pay the price demanded in order to take a proper stand. It is much easier to compromise the message, and thereby gain the plaudits of the crowd. Of course when this happens, the preacher then becomes a hireling.

There is every evidence that Peter repented regarding this thing, but the facts are, most never do repent.

I can see far down the mountain,
Where I wandered weary years,
Often hindered in my journey
By the ghosts of doubt and fears;
Broken vows and disappointments
Thickly scattered all the way;
But the Spirit led, unerring,
To the land I hold today.

THE NEW COVENANT

CHAPTER 7

BARNABAS

BARNABAS

"AND THE OTHER JEWS *dissembled likewise with him; insomuch that Barnabas also was carried away with their dissimulation*" (Gal. 2:13).

Unfortunately, conduct such as that of Peter is not inconsequential, neither in his day nor now. So one is not surprised to read that other Jews, including Barnabas, were led away by his dissimulation.

If Peter had been a lesser man or less prominent, the defection might have been less serious. Of course, I speak of influence and not of the individual. It is always serious with the individual, irrespective as to whom he may be.

But this was Peter—the pillar apostle—the companion of the Lord during His earthly ministry!

What Peter did moved others.

It is obvious that any Christian must give heed to his actions; the greater the position or responsibility, then the more important those actions become.

DISSEMBLED

The phrase, *"And the other Jews dissembled likewise with him,"* gives the result of Peter's action in the church at Antioch.

The Jewish Christians there refused to eat anymore with their Gentile brethren in the Lord. In fact, the church was split wide open on the issue.

The love feast—the bond of fellowship expressive of Christian love amongst the brethren—was now divided into two groups. The friendly groups of Jews and Gentiles in the fellowship of the homes were discontinued. The fact that the Jews of the Antioch church followed Peter in his withdrawal from the Gentiles, shows that the entire group had previously eaten with the latter. In other words, they had all been one, which is what was intended by the Holy Spirit.

In the Greek the word *dissembled* is *hupokrinomai,* and it speaks "of the act of concealing one's real character under the guise of conduct implying something different." Literally, the word means, *"to answer from under,"* as an actor who speaks from under a mask. Our word, *hypocrite,* comes from this Greek word.

In this present case, the knowledge, judgment, and feelings which were concealed were worse only from the viewpoint of those who had come from Jerusalem of whom Peter and the Antioch Jews were afraid. From Paul's viewpoint, it was their better knowledge which they covered up by their misconduct, the usual type of hypocrisy that proceeds from fear.

Paul, by characterizing their actions as hypocrisy, implied that there had been no real change of conviction on the part of

Peter and the rest of the Jews, but only conduct that misrepresented their true convictions.

In other words, Peter and the other Jews at Antioch did not really believe in what they were doing, but succumbed to this false position because of fear of the Jews who had come from James in Jerusalem.

PAUL'S POSITION

Although Peter's concern about his visit to the home of Cornelius was expressed in terms of that which was "unclean," it involved more than the actual eating of food. Certainly the central issue was fellowship which was typified in Semitic culture by the common table.

There is no evidence, however, that the Jerusalem church understood the incident (Peter's vision) as a new general policy of Jewish-Gentile fellowship. Instead, there is every indication that its significance was simply the recognition that the gospel had been given to the Gentiles as well as the Jews. In fact, the decision of the Jerusalem Council further indicates that the two groups would continue to be separate, with the Jews continuing under the law.

This presented a critical problem for Paul, as should be obvious, because his churches in Macedonia and Achaia, as well as Asia Minor, were in great part made up of both groups. How was Christian fellowship possible if the Jewish believers were separated from their Gentile brethren because of the restrictions of their law? So it becomes obvious here as to what Paul had done.

ANTIOCH

In Antioch, as no doubt was the case elsewhere as well, Paul had taught the Jewish believers to place the unity of their Christian fellowship above the limitations of the law. All were one, which meant that the Jews were to ignore the restrictions of the law, which were fulfilled in Christ and set aside anyway.

Considering the tremendous influence of the Antioch church, it seems that James had sent a delegation to that city to check on the proceedings respecting the mingling of Jews and Gentiles. Every indication is, that this delegation made a serious consequence out of this matter. So serious in fact, that Peter along with Barnabas and the other Jews defected.

As we have repeatedly stated, if James had included the Jews in his decision of Acts 15, this problem would never have arisen. As well, any error if not corrected, always leads to greater error, until it finally engulfs the whole. How could there be one gospel, if Jews were not free to have fellowship with Gentiles? In fact, what kind of gospel would that be?

Paul completely ignored the law keeping demands of the Jewish leadership in Jerusalem as it referred to Jews, which is what he should have done. However, it did not endear him with that particular leadership, as should be obvious.

HYPOCRISY

The problem was one of basic insincerity—either while participating in the table fellowship or by separation from that fellowship in the interests of the Law. Paul concludes that at one time or the other the action was a sham.

It will be seen, as the apostle proceeds, that it was this duplicity that was the great wrong—not simply the refusal of Jews to share table fellowship with the Gentiles.

In the strictest Scriptural sense hypocrisy is the direct opposite of sincerity. Hypocrisy is duplicity, and insincerity in purity or singleness of motive. Thus, such profession is hypocritical only to the degree that it reflects insincerity. But to the extent that one's words or actions are not sincere he is being hypocritical.

BARNABAS

The phrase, *"insomuch that Barnabas also was carried away with their dissimulation,"* once again uses the word *hypocrisy*, i.e., *dissimulation*.

But now regarding Barnabas, and the fact that he was swept off his feet and carried away with their hypocrisy. It was hard enough for Paul, the apostle to the Gentiles and the champion of Gentile liberty from the law, to have Peter act as he did. But the hypocrisy of Barnabas was the cruel blow.

With the single exception of Paul, Barnabas had been the most effective minister of the gospel in the conversion of the Gentiles. He had been deputed with Paul by the Antioch church to the council at Jerusalem as its representative. He had come back with the news that the position held by Paul and himself with regard to Gentile freedom from circumcision had been sustained by the Jerusalem apostles.

Now, his withdrawal from social fellowship with the Gentiles came with the force of a betrayal to Paul and the church at Antioch. The defection of Barnabas was of a far more serious nature with regard to Gentile freedom even than the vacillation of Peter.

CHIEF COLLEAGUE

Barnabas was Paul's chief colleague in the evangelization of the Gentiles, and now to have him play the hypocrite and deserter, was a bitter blow to the great apostle. This may well have prepared the way for the dissention between them which shortly afterwards led to their separation (Acts 15:39). Barnabas, the foremost champion of Gentile liberty next to Paul, had in a sense, become a turncoat.

THE CHARGE MADE BY PAUL

Peter knew the truth. So, we know that hypocrisy, at least as it is entertained in this capacity, is not a sin of ignorance, but rather the very opposite. Considering the defection of all the other Jews, even Barnabas, we begin to get the picture as to how serious the situation actually was.

It is a wonderful matter to consider that God preserved the church being yet young, and the gospel itself one might say, by one person only. Paul alone stood, it seems, for the truth.

Paul then reproved Peter for no small matter, but for the chiefest article of all Christian doctrine, which by Peter's dissimulation (hypocrisy) was in great danger. Certainly it is much to be marvelled that such excellent men as Peter, Barnabas, and others, should so suddenly and so lightly fail, especially in that thing which they had before held, and taught unto others. It is a perilous thing to trust to our own strength, for in that we think ourselves most sure, we may err and fail, and bring ourselves and others into great danger.

Luther said:

> Thus, we see that we are nothing with all our gifts be they ever so great, except God assist us. When he leaves us to ourselves, our wisdom and knowledge are nothing. For, in the hour of temptation, it may suddenly come to pass, that by the subtlety of the devil, all the comfortable places of the Scriptures shall be taken away out of our sight, and such places only as contain threatenings, shall be set before our eyes, which shall oppress us, and utterly confound us. Consequently, let no man glory of his own righteousness, wisdom, and other gifts; but let him humble himself, and pray with the apostles, 'Lord, increase our faith' (Lk. 17:5).[1]

ACCORDING TO THE TRUTH OF THE GOSPEL

"But when I saw that they walked not uprightly according to the truth of the gospel, I said unto Peter before them all, If thou, being a Jew, livest after the manner of Gentiles, and not as do the Jews, why compellest thou the Gentiles to live as do the Jews?" (Gal. 2:14).

Paul has already shown that he opposed Peter to his face because he was wrong, but we are not to think that he did this because he loved exposing error or, even less, because he loved an argument or desired to enhance his own prestige. To be frank, there was nothing of that in this. Paul's real concern was for the truth of the gospel. It was not a matter of personalities.

To the Corinthians he wrote, "Who then is Paul, and who is Apollos" (I Cor. 3:5). As well, it is not a matter of trivial forms or ceremonies. What was at stake was the gospel itself. Hence, Paul acted out of the very concern that Peter lacked.

This is the second time that Paul has spoken of *"the truth of the gospel"* (Gal. 2:5, 14)—the good news that men and women do not become accepted with God because of anything they have done, or can do, but solely on the basis of God's grace shown in the death and resurrection of Jesus Christ. Moreover, on the basis of this death all who believe become fully accepted by God and are accepted equally. Peter's conduct compromised this principle for it implied that there could be a superiority in some Christians based on race or traditions.

It is not enough merely to understand and accept the gospel, as Peter did, nor even to defend it, as he amply did at Jerusalem. Christians must also practice the gospel consistently, allowing it to regulate all areas of our conduct.

WALK NOT UPRIGHTLY

The phrase, *"But when I saw that they walked not uprightly according to the truth of the gospel,"* presents the idea that Paul may not have been present when all of this began. Could he have been present in Antioch and yet have failed to see what was happening before such tragic consequences developed?

Is it possible that, even though seeing it, Paul hesitated to take drastic action? But this hardly fits his personality. Thus, it has been suggested that he was absent from Antioch when the situation was developing and saw it only when he returned.

So Paul confronted Peter before them all. His primary concern was to defend the truth of the gospel, but he was also convinced that the hypocrisy should be clearly revealed. To accomplish this it was necessary for him to publicly rebuke Peter, the recognized and highly respected leader of the church. Such action was indeed a bold step, but Paul was convinced that the enormity of the error justified it. Now, at this later time, he could refer back to it as evidence that he had divine authority for the gospel which he preached.

A STRAIGHT COURSE

In the Greek, the word *uprightly* is *orthopodeo,* and it means "to walk with straight feet," thus, "to walk a straight course." It speaks of straightforward, unwavering, sincere conduct in contrast to a crooked, wavering, and more or less insincere course such as Paul had said Peter and the other Jews were guilty of.

Wuest said:

> The words 'according to' are from the Greek 'pros,' and put definite limitations upon the words 'walked uprightly.'

The sense here is not that Peter failed to walk in conformity to the precepts of Evangelical truth, but that his attitude towards the truth of the gospel was not straightforward. The idea is, 'Peter did not pursue a straight course in relation to the truth of the gospel.' He did not deal honestly and consistently with it. His was an attitude that led him to juggle with its sacred truth, to warp it, to misrepresent it, to deal crookedly with it. What an indictment of Peter.[2]

JUSTIFICATION BY FAITH

The *"truth of the gospel"* is the truth which the gospel embodies, with special reference to the doctrine of justification by faith. Peter and Barnabas were acting in a manner which both were inconsistent with their holding of that great truth, and thusly by their actions contravened its advancement in the world.

Peter knew that acceptance of the sacrifice of Christ on the cross was the only thing that would bring salvation to a life (Acts 2:38; 4:12). So, Satan would use some of the greatest men in the church to hinder the great avenue of salvation, which is justification by faith, even though it is certain that they did not intend to do that. Nevertheless, that's exactly what they did.

Was this constituted as sin on their part by God?

The Scripture plainly says, *"For whatsoever is not of faith is sin"* (Rom. 14:23).

It also says, *"Therefore to him that knoweth to do good, and doeth it not, to him it is sin"* (James 4:17).

Yes, what they did was sin, and a very grievous sin at that.

This matter was so serious because their action was implying that justification could come from practicing religion, and Peter knew better!

Called by the ascended Christ Himself, Paul never forgot the great meaning of this call and its implications for his total life as Christ's apostle to the Gentiles. He never compromised the truth of the gospel and its tremendous possibilities for faith and life. This becomes very apparent when studying his fourteen Epistles.

In fact, his firm refusal to compromise the truth of God's Word can be seen in his reactions to this very disturbing situation.

BEFORE THEM ALL

The phrase, *"I said unto Peter before them all,"* means that Paul's rebuke was in the presence of everybody, the whole Antioch church.

This means that the rebuke was not given before the officers of the church only, or before a specially convened and restricted number of people, but right in open church meeting and before all the members of the Antioch church who were present.

Evidently, Paul felt he had no choice in this matter, and was no doubt led by the Holy Spirit. The situation had become the discussion throughout the entirety of the church, therefore, if Paul confronted it at all, he had to confront it publicly, which he did.

This case was of such significance, that it was necessary to establish fixed and just principles; consequently, Paul took occasion to do exactly that.

In fact, if the situation had not been corrected at Antioch, it would soon have spread to all the other churches as well.

THE CONTENDING FOR TRUTH

The fact that Paul reproved Peter before *"them all,"* proves that he regarded himself, and was so regarded by the church at Antioch, as an equal with Peter and as having equal authority with him.

Public reproof is right when an offense has been public, and when the church at large is interested, or is in danger of being led into error.

It is a duty to reprove those who err. It is a painful duty, and one much neglected for that very reason; still it is a duty often enjoined in the Scriptures, and one that is of the deepest importance to the church. He does a favor to another man, who in a kind and gracious spirit, admonishes him of his error, and reclaims him from a course of sin.

He does another the deepest injury, who suffers sin unrebuked to lie upon him, and who sees him injuring himself and others, and who is at no pains to admonish him for these faults.

It is the duty of one Christian to admonish another who is an offender, and to do it in a kind spirit. It is also the duty of him who has offended to receive the admonition in a gracious spirit and with thankfulness.

Excitable was Peter by nature, yet there is no evidence that he became angry here, or that he did not receive the admonition of his brother, Paul, with perfect good temper, and with an acknowledgement that Paul was right and that he was wrong.

Indeed, the case was so plain—as it usually is, if men would be honest—that he seems to have felt that it was right, and to have received the rebuke as became a Christian. In fact, Peter at heart, was too good a man to be offended when he was admonished that he had done wrong.

A good man is willing to be reproved when he has erred, and it is usually proof that there is much that is wrong when we become excited and irritable if another admonishes us of our faults.

As well, it may quickly be added here, that nothing should be inferred from this in regard to the inspiration or apostolic authority of Peter. The fault was not that he taught error of doctrine, but that he sinned by his actions.

WHAT ABOUT PETER'S POSITION AS AN APOSTLE?

Even though we ask this question, actually it should not even be necessary. However, due to the erroneous thoughts of many, it is best that it be addressed.

None of the apostles, or patriarchs, or prophets, were perfect. Paul himself said, *"Brethren, I count not myself to have apprehended: but this one thing I do, forgetting those things which are behind, and reaching forth unto those things which are before, I press toward the mark for the prize of the high calling of God in Christ Jesus"* (Phil. 3:13–14).

The calling and apostleship of these brethren were not affected as it could not be affected. Of course, this predisposes repentance and correction of the situation.

The Word plainly says that the *"gifts and calling of God are without repentance"* (Rom. 11:29). If God calls an individual, that calling remains irrespective as to what happens in the future. While it may be true that the individual might fail, with some even ceasing to function in that which the Lord has called them to do; still, they will answer to God for that calling when they stand before Him.

The situation for apostles who do wrong, at least as far as God is concerned, is the same as it is with anyone else: they have to repent of the situation, put it behind them, and then function as God has called them. This is what Peter and Barnabas did, and which all apostles must do should such a situation occur.

There has never been a perfect human being other than Christ. All have had to go before the Lord, asking for mercy and grace, which He always gives without reservation. There is no such thing, at least in Scripture, of someone forfeiting his calling, that is, if he will humble himself before the Lord, seeking to follow Him in all of His ways. Sinless perfection does not exist in any, even apostles, and such is not the idea as taught in Scripture. However, a broken and contrite spirit is that which the Lord demands of all (Ps. 51; Lk. 18:9–14; I Jn. 1:9).

ONE REQUIREMENT FOR ALL

God does not have one requirement for laypersons and another for apostles. The penalty for sin is the same for all, and the solution for sin is the same for all, as should be obvious.

As well, when God forgives, it is total and complete. There is no such thing as a partial justification.

The moment that Peter and Barnabas repented of this situation, at that moment they were fully restored and in every capacity.

As well, all sin is put in the same category. The Lord does not have one type of repentance for one type of sin and another type of repentance for other types of sin. Such thinking is silly. When Jesus died on Calvary, paying the price for man's redemption, that price sufficed for all.

Preachers who run around claiming that certain ones are not qualified because of something that happened in the past, which has been duly and scripturally repented of, simply don't know what they are talking about. They should understand that if they attempt to apply such to others, they have at the same time applied such to themselves, which means they have automatically condemned themselves (James 4:11–12).

WHY?

The question, *"If thou, being a Jew, livest after the manner of Gentiles, and not as do the Jews, why do compellest thou the Gentiles to live as do the Jews?"* points out, graphically so, the apostasy of the apostle (apostasy is a departure from truth).

Here, the word *compel* means "moral compulsion or persuasion." The idea is that the conduct of Peter was such as to lead the Gentiles to the belief that it was necessary for them to be circumcised in order to be saved. So this tells us, that Peter's defection went much further than the mere dietary laws, but included the basic content of Mosaic legislation.

LIVE

The word *live* as Paul used it here does not refer to the moral living according to Gentile or Jewish fashion, but to the shaping of the life with reference to the external social observances in the Christian fellowship, such as Levitical restrictions on eating.

The present tense of the word *live* must not be pressed to the point of teaching that Peter at the time of this rebuke, was living as the Gentiles do, for he was not. It describes a mental attitude or habit which had in times past shown itself in outward actions, and which was still enforced, but which was being hypocritically covered up by his action of withdrawing from fellowship with the Gentiles. Peter, though continuing to live as a Jew, knew in his heart that all of these things—Levitical law, circumcision, Sabbath keeping—had been fulfilled in Christ. He now placed no spiritual attachment to these things.

So, what he did here was to trim his sails according to the sudden change of wind that came from Jerusalem, so to speak, while not abandoning in principle his convictions.

In his rebuke, Paul forcibly sets forth Peter's inconsistency, for that's what it was, in compelling the Gentiles to obey the Levitical legislation regarding foods, for the Gentiles had only one of two choices in this matter: refuse to obey the law in this respect and cause a split in the Christian church, or preserve harmony by coming under the law.

Worse yet, Peter did all of this with a full understanding of the vision God had given him, which clearly taught him that the Levitical Legislation for the Jew was now a thing of the past (Acts 10:28), and that the line of separation had been broken down between Jew and Gentile by the cross.

WHAT SATAN INTENDED

Peter's action of refusing to eat with the Gentiles did not merely have the effect of maintaining the validity of the law maintained for Jewish Christians, but it involved the forcing of that law upon the Gentile Christians, that, or creating a wide-open division in the church. This latter was what concerned the apostle Paul.

Wuest said:

> He deemed it of utmost importance to maintain the unity of the Christian church as against any division into Jewish and Gentile groups. At the Jerusalem Council he had agreed to a territorial division of the missionary field into Gentile and Jewish divisions, but to create a division respecting doctrine between Jew and Gentile in a Gentile community and church, was out of the question and was something not to be done. In effect, at the Jerusalem Council, it was agreed that the Jewish Christians should continue to keep the law, which of course was wrong, and that the Gentile Christians were to be free from the law, which was right. But, as is obvious, this arrangement left the question undecided

as to which decision of the council should take precedence when an issue arose such as we see at Antioch where Peter's action brought pressure to bear upon the Gentiles. Paul insists that in such an instance, the Jews were not obligated to keep the law.[3]

COMPELLED

This shows us the problems which arise, when the right thing is not done to begin with. When James made his decision in Acts 15 concerning this matter, scripturally the Jews should have been included with the Gentiles. In fact, the failure to do this ultimately destroyed the Jewish segment of the church.

In Galatians 2:14, going back to the word *compellest,* then adding the word *thou,* i.e., "you compel" means, "setting yourself to compel." The "compulsion" applied by Peter was a moral compulsion. In effect, he was withholding from the Gentiles Christian fellowship unless they Judaized.

Put into words, his conduct said this: "If you will Judaize, I will have fellowship with you; if you will not, you are not qualified for full fraternal recognition from me."

According to Pulpit Commentary: "This was an outrage upon what Paul here refers to as 'the truth of the gospel.' It is at our peril that we grieve, by a cold or unbrotherly bearing towards him, one whom we have reason to believe God has 'received' (Rom. 14:3; 15:7). If God in Christ owns and loves him as a son, we ought to frankly own and love him as a brother."[4]

THE TRUTH OF THE GOSPEL

Martin Luther said, "Many have the gospel, but not the truth of the gospel."[5]

So Paul says here of Peter, Barnabas, and other Jews, they "went not the right way of the gospel," that is to say, they had the gospel, but they walked not uprightly according to the gospel. They preach the gospel, but through their hypocrisy (dissimulation), they establish the law, but the establishing of the law is the abolishing of the gospel.

Is it any wonder that Paul was so disturbed when he viewed the hypocrisy of Peter, Barnabas, and the other Jews at Antioch?

This matter was serious because their action was implying that justification could come from practicing religion.

Neither Peter nor Barnabas had changed their views about the fact that God did not require Gentile believers to become Jewish proselytes. That can be seen from Paul's use of the Greek word for hypocrisy.

The problem was that they had been following Gentile customs, in other words, there was no discrimination between Jews and Gentiles, until they gradually retreated because of the presence of certain Jews who had come from James in Jerusalem, who emphasized legalism.

As stated, Peter and Barnabas were suggesting by their actions that Gentile believers had "to Judaize" or become Jewish proselytes. Consequently, it is easy to see the seriousness of their offense.

SINNERS OF THE GENTILES

"We who are Jews by nature, and not sinners of the Gentiles" (Gal. 2:15).

The verses that conclude this chapter contain capsule statements of some of the most significant truths of Christianity. In particular, Paul clearly states the doctrine of justification by grace through faith and defends it over against the traditional objection that justification by faith leads to lawlessness. Actually, the words *justify* and *justification* occur in these verses for the first time, at least as it respects this great issue. Consequently, Paul now begins to develop the message that is central to this epistle, to his gospel, and indeed to Christianity in general. This statement flows out of the situation at Antioch and anticipates the fuller argument of the same doctrine occurring in Galatians 3 and 4.

Sir William Mitchell Ramsay states, "After working through the rest of the epistle, one turns back to these verses and finds in them the whole truth in embryo."[6]

JEWS BY NATURE

Wuest said:

The phrase, 'We who are Jews by nature,' presents Paul here speaking to Peter on the common ground of their former Judaism and in an ironical fashion using the language of Judaism. In using the word *we*, Paul includes himself,

Peter, and the Jewish Christians at Antioch in contrast to the Gentile Christians. In effect, he is saying that he and they are Jews by birth, not only not Gentiles, but not even Gentile proselytes. He implies that as such, the Jews have special privileges and prerogatives. It has been argued as to whether verses 15–21 are part of Paul's words to Peter in the hearing of the Antioch church, or whether Paul's words in verse 14 are all that is reported of what he said to him on that occasion, and that verses 15–21 are specially written to the Galatians as an answer to the question of Paul. The matter is not that important, but most probably, the entirety of the balance of the chapter was spoken to Peter. In fact, in Galatians 3:1, Paul resumes his direct words to the Galatians in the expression 'O foolish Galatians.'[7]

The idea of Paul's statement concerning *"Jews by nature,"* is that both (Peter and Paul) have felt the force of hereditary prejudice. Both had overcome this prejudice. Both had upheld Christian freedom, alike in theory and in practice.

GENTILES

The phrase, *"and not sinners of the Gentiles,"* means that the Jews were not born under the disadvantages of the Gentiles in regard to the true knowledge of the way of salvation. Paul does not mean that he does not regard the Jews as sinners, for his views on that subject were fully expressed in Romans 2 and 3. However, whereas the Jews did have the knowledge of God, the Gentiles had none at all. In fact, the Jews, even from their very beginning as it regarded the Abrahamic covenant, knew about justification by faith as it pertained to salvation (Gen. 15:6). That they veered from this was not through ignorance, but rather because of their own obstinacy and self-will; however, the Gentiles, as stated, had no knowledge of God whatsoever.

By using this phraseology as he did, Paul puts himself for the moment in the position of the most prejudiced Jew, uses his language, and thus makes his argument as strong as possible.

Admitting to the full of all the religious advantages of Judaism, and all the moral degradation of the Gentiles, yet, "even we" have renounced this hope of being justified through Judaism. Actually, this manner of speaking of the heathen was customary and proverbial among the Jews. We may even refer to the language of the Sermon on the Mount (Mat. 6:7, 32).

THE LAW OF MOSES

In Galatians 2:15 and those that follow in this chapter, Paul brings out the fact that for all the privileges of the Jew, it was found that there was no justification whatsoever from the law; and this sent them to Christ, or rather was intended to.

In effect, Paul says:

We thus abdicated our privileged position; we put ourselves on the same level as the Gentiles, and became 'in the eye of the law' sinners like them. Sinners? Must we then admit that all Christ has done for us is to make us sinners? Far be so irreverent a thought. Our sin consists not in quitting the law, but in returning to that which has been abandoned. The function of the law was preparatory and transitional. The law itself taught me to expect its own abrogation. It was a stage on the way to Christ. To Him have I given in a complete adhesion. In His death I am severed from ancient ties. In His death I cease to have any life of my own. All the life I have, man as I am, I owe to Christ, my Saviour. Thus, I accept and do not reject and frustrate the gift so freely offered me: Whereas, by going back to the law for justification, I should be practically declaring the death of Christ useless and unprofitable.

I remember long ago,
The old story sweet and true,
How that Jesus left His Father's home above,
How He all things did forsake,
And the lowly way did take,
And became the meek and lowly Nazarene.

I will follow in the steps,
Of this lowly Nazarene,
Where He leads me I will gladly follow Him,
The forsaken and despised
By the proud and worldly wise,
I will take the cross and gladly follow Him.

If you want to follow Him,
Just forsake your life of sin;
He'll forgive you, and He'll save you through and through;
He will turn your heart from sin,
And will give you peace within,
For He is the meek and lowly Nazarene.

If you want to shout and sing,
As you follow on with Him,
And have constant victory over all your foes,
Seek the cleansing from above,
And be filled with perfect love,
Then you'll love to take the cross and follow Him.

THE
NEW
COVENANT

THE FAITH OF
JESUS CHRIST

THE FAITH OF JESUS CHRIST

"KNOWING THAT A MAN is not justified by the works of the law, but by the faith of Jesus Christ, even we have believed in Jesus Christ, that we might be justified by the faith of Christ, and not by the works of the law: for by the works of the law shall no flesh be justified" (Gal. 2:16).

This is one of the most important verses in the Epistle, as already noted; it contains the first mention of the words *justify* or *justification*. The word *law* is also mentioned for the first time. And, this is the first place in the letter where faith is brought forward as the indispensable channel of salvation.

The word *justify* is a forensic term borrowed from the law courts. It means "to declare righteous or innocent." The opposite of "to justify" is "to condemn" or "to pronounce guilty." Such a term involves an objective standard, and since righteousness is understood to be the unique characteristic of God, that standard must be the divine standard. In ourselves, all persons fall short of this standard: *"For all have sinned, and come short of the glory of God"* (Rom. 3:23).

In Christ, God declares all righteous who believe—that is believe in Christ and what He did at Calvary and the resurrection—imputing divine righteousness to them.

In this sense, justification does not express an ethical change or influence (though ethical changes follow); rather, it expresses the judicial action of God apart from human merit according to which the guilty are pardoned, acquitted, and then reinstated as God's children and as fellow heirs with Jesus Christ, all on the basis of faith in Christ and His atonement carried out at the cross.

THE CHANNEL OF HUMAN FAITH

This experience does not happen automatically. It is true that God justifies, but He does so only as He unites a man or woman to Christ—a union that takes place only through the channel of human faith.

In other words, faith in Christ and what He did is a requirement, an absolute requirement. Faith is the means, not the source, of justification, that being Jesus.

Faith is trust. It begins with knowledge, so it is not blind. It builds on facts, so it is not speculation. It stakes its life on the outcome, so it is not impractical. Faith is trusting Christ and proving His promises. The expression in the middle of Galatians 2:16, *"we have believed in Jesus Christ,"* implies an act of personal commitment, not just assenting to the facts concerning Christ, but actually running to Him for refuge and seeking mercy.

WORKS ARE OUT

It is also implied in this commitment that a person will turn his back on the only other apparent possibility—the attempt to be justified by works done in obedience to formal statutes from whatever source. It is important to note that the Greek article is not present in the phrases "observing law" or "works of law." This means that Paul's emphasis is not really on the Jewish law, the law of Moses, though it includes it, "but rather on any system of attempting to please God by good deeds of any nature."

"Works of law" are literally "deeds of men," and of whatever nature.

So, the introduction of the Greek article *the* as "*the* works of the law," should not have been included in the translation, because it is not in the original.

GREAT SIGNIFICANCE

The threefold repetition of the doctrine of justification by faith in this one verse is important because it shows the importance the Holy Spirit through the apostle gives to the doctrine.

Besides, the three phrases increase in emphasis:

- Paul says, "*A man is not justified by observing … law, but by faith in Jesus Christ.*" "*A man*" is any man, anyone.
- The second phrase is particular and personal: "*We, too, have put our faith in Christ Jesus that we may be justified by faith in Christ and not by observing the law.*" This phrase

involves Paul himself, as well as all who stand with him in the faith.

- The final statement is universal: *"By observing the law no one will be justified."* The words are literally "all flesh," i.e., mankind without exception.

This universal application of the teaching is heightened by the fact that Paul apparently quotes from Psalm 143:2 (as he also does in Rom. 3:20), thereby, adding the stamp of a more general, biblical principle to his statements.[1]

FAITH IN CHRIST

The phrase, *"Knowing that a man is not justified by the works of the law, but by the faith of Jesus Christ,"* is speaking in effect of himself and Peter. This is what rendered the conduct of Peter and the other Jews who *"dissembled"* with him, so entirely inexcusable. Peter knew better and so did Barnabas, and for that matter, so did all the other Jews in the church at Antioch, who had been beneficiaries of the teaching of Paul. They could not plead ignorance on this vital subject, and yet they were pursuing a course the tendency of which was to lead the Gentile converts to believe that it was necessary to observe the law of Moses, or any other laws for that matter, in order to be justified and saved. In other words, a salvation of works.

The apostle plainly intends here to make the categorical affirmation that no man gains justification save through faith in Christ. In fact, the way he states the case, works of the law (any law) can never have any part whatsoever in procuring justification. In fact, *"works of the law"* in attempting to gain justification, actually has the opposite effect, succeeding only in nullifying one's salvation (Gal. 5:4).

As we have already stated, however, faith is, strictly speaking, only the means, not the source of justification—that being Jesus Christ—and more specifically, that which He did at Calvary and the resurrection.

BELIEVED IN JESUS CHRIST

The phrase, *"Even we have believed in Jesus Christ,"* refers to taking upon oneself all the qualities, attributes, and life of the one in whom is believed, in this case Christ. So, it is far more than mere mental affirmation. It concerns giving one's heart and life in totality to Christ, in essence, making Him the Lord of one's life.

Even though the *"believing"* refers to all things about Jesus, His person as the Son of God, His virgin birth, His sinless, perfect life, but more than all it refers to what He did for sinful humanity at Calvary, which included the entirety of the human race and for all time. In effect, He became our substitute, and identification with Him—which comes by faith, simply believing in Him and what He did—guarantees salvation (Jn. 3:16).

In essence, Paul is saying here, "We—you and I, Peter—who are Jews by natural birth, even we—you and I—have believed in Christ Jesus in order that we might be declared righteous upon the principle of faith in Him and not on the principle of legal works."

Even as we have already stated, the literal translation is, "We have believed into Christ," which implies an act of personal commitment, not just assenting to the facts concerning Christ, but actually running to Him for refuge and seeking mercy.

JUSTIFIED

The phrase, *"that we might be justified by the faith of Christ,"* presents the act of God in justifying a believing sinner which consists of taking away his guilt and its penalty, since Christ bore both on the cross, which also includes the imputation of righteousness, even Christ Jesus Himself, in whom the believer stands not only guiltless and uncondemned for time and eternity, but also positively righteous in the sight of the eternal laws of God.[2]

The word *by* as it speaks of the *"faith of Christ,"* means "through," and indicates the channel through which one secures salvation, namely Christ.

THE WORKS OF THE LAW

The phrase, *"And not by the works of the law: for by the works of the law shall no flesh be justified,"* makes the statement as emphatic as is possible for a statement to be made.

As we have already stated, the word *the* should not have been included in any of the three cases where the word *law* is used. While the Holy Spirit through Paul is definitely referring to the law of Moses, He is not referring just to the law of Moses, but actually to any type of law devised by men, in order to achieve justification by God. This is very important!

While the Jews of Paul's day and previous, attempted to gain salvation by merit or works of the law as it pertained to Moses, this is not the problem with most Gentiles. In fact, most of the Gentiles who came to Christ during the time of Paul (and even thereafter) knew almost nothing about the law of Moses.

TO EARN

The idea is this: The concept of trying to earn one's salvation, or sanctification for that matter, or approval by God, had its origin in the thought and practice of man all down through the ages since its inception in the heart of Cain. The whole world in one way or another thinks it can earn salvation by a system of good works. In fact, the world, at least for the most part, whatever it is they believe about life after death, or eternity, etc., pretty well judges everything on the basis of a brownie point system. If their good deeds outweigh their bad deeds, which they always do in their own eyes, this constitutes salvation, etc.

Actually, just last night over television, I heard a movie actor say, "I know when I die that I will go to heaven."

He was asked by the man interviewing him as to how he knew that.

He replied, "Because I am good."

I have no idea what he constituted as being good, but whatever it was, it, nor any of our efforts will ever be recognized by

God as a way to earn or merit righteousness. Such cannot be brought about in that fashion.

Righteousness is a free gift given to all who place their faith and trust in Christ and what He did for us at the cross. It is freely given if we come on the basis of faith and faith alone. But when we try to insert works into the situation, this closes the door to God, for He cannot accept such. He can only accept faith in Christ and what He did at the cross, whether for salvation or sanctification.

GOOD WORKS

This phrase, *"works of the law,"* reaches far; it extends to all that is contrary to grace. Whatsoever is not grace is the law, whether it be judicial, ceremonial, the Ten Commandments, or any type of law of one's own making that constitutes works.

In fact, the entirety of the Catholic religion bases its so-called salvation, upon works. Martin Luther called it "the divinity of the anti-Christian kingdom."

He went on to say, "And moreover, that all men may see how far from the truth these blind guides, and leaders of the blind, have wandered, and how by this wicked and blasphemous doctrine they have not only darkened the gospel, but have taken it clean away, and buried Christ utterly."[3]

The truth is, if anyone can earn salvation by good works of any nature, why did Christ have to come down to this Earth and die on a cruel cross? The facts are, a person can have one or the other— works or Christ—but he cannot have both. An attempt to comingle the two automatically nullifies Christ.

WORKS CAN CAUSE SPIRITUAL BLINDNESS

Please allow us to plainly define what a deadly sinner actually is. Martin Luther went on to say:

> He is such an unholy and bloody hypocrite as Paul was, when he was on the way to Damascus, to persecute Jesus of Nazareth, to stamp out the doctrine of the gospel, to murder the faithful, and utterly to overthrow the church of Christ. And who will not say, but that these were horrible sins? Yet Paul could not see them. He was blinded by a perverse zeal for God, so that he thought these things were perfect righteousness, and high service unto God. Wherefore with Paul, we utterly deny the merit of self-worthiness, and affirm that these speculations are nothing else but mere deceits of Satan. For God never gave to any man grace and everlasting life for the merit of self-righteousness or personal worthiness. Dependence on these things, rather than drawing men toward God, have a tendency to have the opposite effect.[4]

THE TREE OF THE KNOWLEDGE OF GOOD AND EVIL

These good works fool people simply because they are good. Inasmuch as they are good surely, at least as human nature thinks, this will earn or merit something with God. This feeling and spirit which affects all men everywhere and for all time comes from the good side of the tree of the knowledge of good and evil (Gen. 2:17).

The evil part of that tree is obvious and opposed by all the world. I speak of stealing, murder, hatred, racism, etc. However, the good part fools people and deceives them.

That's the reason that the doing of religion is the most powerful narcotic there is. Notice what I said: the *doing* of religion. I speak of good works and the involvement with religious ceremonies and rituals.

The doing of these things somewhat assuages the guilt of man, thereby making him believe that all is well spiritually when in fact nothing is well spiritually, that is if he trusts in such.

THE WAY OF BIBLICAL CHRISTIANITY

The way to true Christianity is this: that a man first acknowledge himself by the law to be a sinner and that it is impossible for him to do any good work. For the law says that man is a corrupt tree (Mat. 7:17), and a corrupt tree cannot bring forth good fruit. In fact, all that one does in this category, despite the efforts otherwise, thinks and speaks against God, whether he realizes such or not. There is no way a person can deserve grace by works. In fact, if one thinks he deserves grace, this great attribute of God is instantly nullified. Grace can only go to one who is undeserving and who knows it.

The trouble with the human race is that it doubles its offense. First of all, it is an evil tree; second, it tries to deserve grace by works or merit, which does the very opposite, actually heaping sin upon sin, which mocks God and guarantees His wrath.

So the first part of Christianity is the preaching of repentance, and the knowledge of ourselves—what we are, namely sinners.

The second part: if one is to be saved, he must forsake salvation by works and understand that God has sent His only-begotten Son into the world, that we might live through Him. He was crucified and died for us, actually offering up Himself as a sin offering. The wrath of God, which should have been poured out upon us who rightly deserved it, was instead was poured out upon Him as He took our place.

So the whole thing of salvation is wrapped up in Jesus and what He did at Calvary and our faith in Him. We simply believe what He did and salvation is instantly given to the believing sinner. By this means we are delivered from sin, justified, and made inheritors of everlasting life, not by our own works and deserts, but for our faith, whereby we lay hold upon Christ.

WHO IS CHRIST?

Christ, according to His true definition, is no law giver, but a forgiver of sins and a Saviour. And yet many in the church look at Him as though He were a law giver.

That's the reason when He came that He did not condemn, for that is what law givers do. Instead, He redeemed sinful men— that' what a Saviour does.

Jesus had to pay for our sins; God could accept nothing less. He paid for them by the shedding of His own life's blood, for the life of the flesh is in the blood. That's the reason the cross is so very, very important.

The shedding of His innocent blood—blood incidentally that was never tainted by sin and not a product of Adam's fall—was an absolute necessity as it regards our salvation. The price had to be paid, and the price was steep, and that was the price—the offering up of a spotless, pure, sinless body and life. That He did, and it was done at the cross.

When we speak of justification, there is no time or place to speak of the law, but the question is, what Christ is, and what benefit He has brought unto us? Christ is not the law; He is not my work, or the work of the law; He is not my charity, my obedience, my poverty; but He is the Lord of life, a mediator, a Saviour, a Redeemer of those who are under the law and sin. In Him we are by faith, and He in us.

We must learn to discern all laws, even the law of God, and all works from the promise of the gospel and from faith, that we may define Christ rightly.

That's the problem with the world, and even the problem with the church, we do not know how to properly define Christ. For Christ is not law and, therefore, He is no exacter of the law and works, but He is *"the Lamb of God, which taketh away the sin of the world"* (Jn. 1:29).

THE FLESH

In the last part of Galatians 2:16, Paul uses the word *flesh*. What does he mean?

Flesh does not signify here manifest and gross sins, for these Paul calls by their proper names—adultery, fornication, uncleanness and the like. By flesh, he means as Christ said, *"That which is born of the flesh is flesh"* (Jn. 3:6)

Flesh, therefore, signifies the whole nature of man, with reason and all other powers whatsoever that belong to man. According to Paul, flesh signifies all the righteousness, wisdom, devotion, religion, understanding, and will that is possible to be in a natural man. He is saying that all of this can never be justified according to works, merits, devotion, or religion.

The idea is this: if no flesh can be justified by the works of the law of Moses, or by any other law, which is the true law of God, how much less shall it be justified by puny laws made up by religious men or even by an individual? (And we speak of laws devised out of our own efforts and abilities.)

THE LAW OF MOSES

In commentary on this verse, we have mentioned two types of laws: the law of Moses, and all other laws—irrespective as to what they might be or who originates them—laws devised in order to secure righteousness in one way or another.

Inasmuch as the law of Moses is the only true law of God, and considering if it cannot justify—and it can't—then how in the world does anyone think he can be justified by laws or works of his own making? Inasmuch as the law of Moses sets the standard, let us look at this more closely, which will hopefully help us to understand moreso what Paul is saying.

THE DEFINITION OF LAW

Is the believer under the law, grace, or both?

This is a question which was settled almost two thousand years ago, and yet millions of Christians are still confused, and they fail to understand the clear distinction between the ministry of the law (the law of Moses) and the ministry of Grace.

However, the Bible leaves no question about the matter. The law was never given to save anyone. Not one single sinner in the history of the human race, Israelite or otherwise, has ever been saved by keeping the law of God.

In fact, God never gave the law to bring about salvation. He knew, before He ever gave Israel the law and commanded them to obey it, that no one (except the Lord Jesus Himself) would ever keep the law of God perfectly; yea, more, He never expected anyone to keep it perfectly for the simple reason that He gave no power in order for men to keep the law, without which they were helpless.

We might multiply Scriptures by the score to prove that the Bible teaches the absolute inability of the law to save a single sinner or keep a single saint saved. However, we do not wish to weary the reader with the recitation of scriptural passages, and feel that Galatians 2:16 is sufficient. However, if desired, the reader may peruse the following: (Rom. 3:19–20, 28; Gal. 2:21; 3:10–11, 13). If these verses mean anything at all, they teach the utter hopelessness of attempting to be saved by human works or keeping the law of God. To be saved by the law, the law must be kept perfectly and continuously without interruption, and it applies to everyone. The Bible says, *"Cursed is every one that continueth not in all things which are written in the book of the law to do them"* (Gal. 3:10).

EVERYONE?

There are no exceptions; it says, *"every one."* There must be unbroken obedience. One single transgression places man under the law's curse. There must be obedience in all things, without one single interruption or failure. The Bible is crystal clear—the law was never given to save a person, justify the sinner, or sanctify the saint. We repeat, therefore: God never expected a single sinner to keep the law; He knew when He gave the law that this was impossible.

We come, therefore, to this question: if it couldn't save man, make him better, or change his heart, why did God give the law?

First, we must clear up some misunderstanding about the word, *law*. What are we to understand by the expressions, "the law of God," or "the law of Moses"? There are many people who think only of the Decalogue—the Ten Commandments— whenever they read the word *law* in the Bible. But the Bible uses the word *law* to describe different things.

Sometimes the word *law* refers to the whole Word of God. Sometimes the word *law* is used to distinguish the books of Moses—Genesis through Deuteronomy—from the rest of the Scriptures. Jesus speaks of *"the law and the prophets"* (Mat. 7:12).

THREE DIVISIONS

The Jews of Jesus' day divided the Old Testament this way:

- The law
- The psalms
- The prophets

The law thus referred to, consists of the five books of Moses. In a general sense, the first five books of the Old Testament are referred to as "the law," as distinguished from the prophetic books of the Old Testament.

In a more narrow sense, the instructions God gave to Israel through Moses on Mount Sinai are also referred to as "the law." This law which God gave to Israel at Mount Sinai after their deliverance from Egypt was a "unit," yet consisted of different commandments. Most people imagine that the only law Moses brought down from the mountain was the tables of stone—the Ten Commandments—but this was not all. God also gave to Moses the laws concerning the feast days, holy days, sacrifices, offerings, dietary laws, civil laws, and the pattern of the tabernacle.

This law, consisting of all these different commandments and ordinances, which Moses received on the mountain was given at the same time that he received the Ten Commandments, and is described in detail in Exodus 20 through 34. All of these laws—civil, dietary, sacrificial, and moral—together constitute the books of the law. And this law of God is a unit. There are many commandments, but they are all a part of the book of the law.

NOT TWO LAWS

There are also those who, because they do not understand the grace of God and the purpose of the law, make a distinction between the law of Moses and the law of the Lord, or the law of God. They seem to think that the Ten Commandments are the law of the Lord, while the laws concerning ordinances, offerings, feast days, and the dietary laws are the law of Moses.

They tell us that Christ fulfilled the law of Moses, consisting of ordinances, but His finished work did not include the Ten Commandments. However, the law of Moses and the law of God are one and the same, and to state that the law of Moses was fulfilled and abolished at Calvary, and not the law of the Lord is a complete misunderstanding of the Bible. The expressions in the Bible, "law of Moses" and "law of the Lord" are used interchangeably.

THREE BODIES OF COMMANDMENTS

In this very connection we could say that the law is divided into two parts: the moral and the ceremonial. However, to divide it into three areas would probably make it more understandable:

- The commandments: the moral law (Ex. 20:1-26).
- The judgments: civil laws (Ex. 21:1-24).
- The ordinances: the sacrifices and feast days (Ex. 24-31).

The law of commandments dealt with Israel's moral conduct, and is set forth in the Ten Commandments. The second area (the judgments) dealt with the social conduct of the people, the civil laws for the nation. The third area (the ordinances) dealt with the ceremonial and religious obligations of the nation of Israel. These included the holy days, the offerings, and sacrifices.

But all of these are part of "the one law" given by the one same God, at one and the same place, at one and the same time, to one and the same nation, by one and the same Moses, and for one and the same purpose.

To show the error of making a difference between the laws of Moses and the law of the Lord contained in the Ten Commandments, we would point out a most convincing fact: The Bible makes no distinction but uses the terms *law of Moses* and *law of God* interchangeably. As an example, let me quote from Luke 2:22, which records the observance of the law by Mary, the mother of Jesus: *"And when the days of her (Mary's) purification according to the law of Moses were accomplished, they brought him to Jerusalem to present him to the Lord; (As it is written in the law of the Lord, every male that openeth the womb shall be called holy to the Lord;) And to offer a sacrifice according to that which is said in the law of the Lord"* (Lk. 2:22–24).

THE LAW OF MOSES AND THE LAW OF THE LORD ARE ONE AND THE SAME

Notice in this passage that Mary is said to have taken the baby Jesus to the temple to present Him to the Lord, in obedience to the law of the Lord and to offer a sacrifice according to the law of the Lord. Where, I ask you, does it say in the Ten

Commandments that she was to bring a sacrifice? That is found in the ceremonial law of Moses, but it is called the *"law of the Lord."*

Again, in Luke 2:39 we read, *"And when they had performed all things according to the law of the Lord, they returned into Galilee."*

To make a distinction, therefore, between the law of Moses and the law of God or the Lord, for our own convenience and to prove our own point, is man-made and artificial and is a violation of the Scriptures. If Christ fulfilled part of the law, then He fulfilled all of the law, and now the believer is not under the law but under grace (Rom. 6:14). We are delivered from the law (Rom. 7:6), free from the law (Rom. 8:2), and dead to the law (Gal. 2:19).

(Actually, even as we've just stated, the law is not dead, but we are dead to the law. In brief, this means that Jesus fulfilled all the ceremonial law, thereby with it not anymore needed, and as well, kept perfectly the moral law, which He in turn keeps through us. So the moral law is still binding on Christians, for moral law cannot change. And yet it is all kept in Christ, which is a work of the Holy Spirit within our lives [Rom. 8].)

WHY DID GOD GIVE THE LAW?

Now an important question arises which I am sure has been suggested by the statement that the law cannot justify, sanctify, or satisfy: why did God give a law which no man could keep, but instead only condemned the sinner?

Paul, the great exponent of grace, anticipated that question and says in Galatians 3:19, *"Wherefore then serveth the law?"* Or in today's language, "What good is the law?"

It was an inevitable question, for Paul proved in the previous chapters that the law was helpless to save a man or change a man. Again we could ask, "Then why did God give the law? What good is it? What purpose does it serve?"

Paul immediately gives the answer in one of the most condense, concise, yet comprehensive statements in the Word of God. Read carefully the inspired answer: *"It was added* (necessary) *because of transgressions* (to explain sin), *till the seed* (Jesus) *should come to whom* (Israel) *the promise was made; and it* (the law) *was ordained by angels in the hand of a mediator* (Moses)" (Gal. 3:19).

THREE THINGS STATED

Notice three things which are clearly stated in this answer through Paul, *"It was added because of transgressions, till the seed should come"*:

1. *The beginning of the law.* It was added—added, of course, to something which must have existed before, which was sin. The law explained what sin was, the transgression of a commandment, and explained the different types of sin— stealing, adultery, lying, etc.

2. *The end of the law.* It was added (necessary) till the seed (Jesus) should come. The law had not only a beginning, but its ministry was until the seed should come. It was for a period of time beginning when it was added and lasting till the seed should come. Now Paul tells us what he means by the seed: *"Now to Abraham and his seed*

were the promises made. He saith not, And to seeds, as of many; but as of one, And to thy seed, which is Christ" (Gal. 3:16). The *"seed"* in our verse is Christ, and so we may substitute the name Christ for the seed and thus we read that the law *"was added … till Christ should come to whom the promise was made."* The ministry of the law was dispensational, meaning that it was to exist only for a period of time. John the Baptist clears up the question as to the length of this dispensation of law. In his introduction of Jesus he says, *"For the law was given by Moses, but grace and truth came by Jesus Christ"* (Jn. 1:17).

3. *The purpose of the law.* It was added because of transgressions. Literally we may read this: *"in order to reveal sin as a transgression."* Before the law was given, there was no transgression of the law. There was sin and there was rebellion, but it was not a "transgression" of the law which had not yet even been given. Clearly and plainly Paul asserts this in Romans 4:15: *"Because the law worketh wrath: for where no law is, there is no transgression."*

A TRANSGRESSION OF THE LAW

The statement is clear, "Before the law came, there was no transgression." We then ask the question: was there no sin before the law came in?

Yes, there was sin before the law, and it was just as wicked and wrong then as it is now; however, Paul also says, *"For until the law sin was in the world: but sin is not imputed* (as a transgression) *when there is no law"* (Rom. 5:13).

What did Paul mean by that statement? Does it mean that God did not hold people accountable for sin before the law was given to Moses? No. As stated, sin and rebellion were the same then as now. The people then were guilty of the fact of sin, even though sin was not specified or then properly identified.

When the law came, it gave to sin a new meaning—it specified what sin was and differentiated between types of sin. Then sin became a transgression of the law.

The idea is this: if there is no speed limit posted on a road, and a man is driving his car at a hundred miles per hour, while he might not be breaking a law (or no law exists respecting this situation), the man is still speeding, and if he continues in that capacity, he will ultimately be engaged in a wreck. In other words, not having a speed limit does not lessen the responsibility of the driver or the danger of speeding.

Likewise, even though there was no specific law of God against sin before the law of Moses was given, men were still sinners and answered to its wages, which was death.

The purpose of the law then was to reveal sin as rebellion against God, as a transgression against better light, for by the law is the knowledge of sin. There is not one verse in the Bible that says by the law is salvation from sin.

This is the first thing a sinner must learn: no man can be saved by trying to keep the law. The only remedy for sin is to plead guilty before the law and flee to the Lord Jesus Christ for salvation by the grace of God.

Not the labors of my hands,
Can fulfill Thy law's demands;
All for sin could not atone;
Thou must save, and Thou alone.

(The statement on the definition of the law was provided by the material of M. R. De Haan, M.D.[5])

Inasmuch as this subject is so weighty, so necessary as it regards understanding on the part of believers, I personally feel the following also given by Dr. De Haan, would be a blessing. I would encourage you to study it carefully. Some questions I think will be answered for you. As well, the same problems the early church had prevail presently.

THE EARLY CHURCH

The first church council in the city of Jerusalem, as recorded in Acts 15, was necessitated by a question concerning the relationship of the believer to the law of Moses.

Paul the Apostle had on his first missionary journey preached the gospel of the grace of God, which referred to salvation without the works of the law. Upon his return, he had rehearsed to the church at Antioch, *"all that God had done with them, and how he had opened the door of faith unto the Gentiles"* (Acts 14:27).

Paul reported to the church how Gentiles had been saved, without becoming Jewish proselytes, or submitting to circumcision, or Sabbath keeping, or any part of the law of Moses for that matter. Actually, these Gentiles did not even know anything about the law of Moses. The Christians at Antioch rejoiced at the good news of the free grace of God.

These reports of Gentiles being saved by grace without the law reached Jerusalem where a group of legalistic Jews insisted that salvation necessitated placing these believers under the law. They were teaching that these Gentiles, in order to be saved, had to become proselyte Jews. These legalists came to Antioch and began to teach the believers, *"Except ye be circumcised after the manner of Moses, ye cannot be saved"* (Acts 15:1).

THE COUNCIL AT JERUSALEM

This started a real dispute between Paul and Barnabas on the one hand, and this group of "law preachers" on the other. A real row broke out. Luke reported, *"Paul and Barnabas had no small dissension and disputation with them"* (Acts 15:2).

These legalists were Jews who did believe in Christ and believed in accepting Him as Saviour; however, they also believed that you had to keep the law of Moses as well in order to be saved, which of course is wrong.

Unable to settle the question, they decided to submit the problem to the apostles and elders at Jerusalem. A committee, including Paul and Barnabas, was appointed to go to Jerusalem. Upon their arrival in the city they were welcomed by the church, to whom they reported all that the gospel of God's grace had accomplished among the Gentiles.

However, they were immediately opposed by the legalistic Pharisees who insisted, *"That it was needful to circumcise them* (the Gentiles), *and to command them to keep the law of Moses"* (Acts 15:5).

The apostles called the church together and tried to settle the controversy, but instead disorder broke out and the meeting resulted in a heated debate. There was much disputing between the two factions which we might well designate as the "Grace Party" and the "Law Party." Peter is the first to testify of his experience, and rehearses his visit to the Gentile household of Cornelius, saying that God *"put no difference between us* (Jews) *and them* (Gentiles), *purifying their hearts by faith* (faith only and not by any type of works)*"* (Acts 15:9).

Peter calls the law of Moses a yoke which they themselves (the Jews) were unable to bear (couldn't live up to) (Acts 15:10) and then concludes with his judgment of the matter: *"But we believe that through the grace of our Lord Jesus Christ we* (Jews) *shall be saved* (saved by faith only), *even as they* (the Gentiles) (Acts 15:11).

JAMES

Peter's speech came somewhat as a surprise to the legalists, the champions of the law; and without any more disputing, the assembly listened quietly to the testimony of Paul, and Barnabas, corroborating the views of Peter. It was now time for James (the Lord's brother) and the senior pastor at the church at Jerusalem (apparently the chairman of the meeting) to speak. The silence which followed the testimonies of Peter, Paul, and Barnabas left the opposition speechless. However, it raised a serious question:

If the Lord was now building a church, the body of Christ consisting of both Jews and Gentiles, while Jesus was in heaven, then what about the promises of the Scriptures concerning the kingdom and the reign of the Messiah on earth?

All the prophets had clearly foretold that when the Messiah should come, He would restore the kingdom of Israel, deliver them from the Gentile yoke of bondage, and Israel as a nation would dwell in her repossessed land.

Were all these prophecies to be cast aside? Must we spiritualize these promises and apply them now to the church? If God is now calling out a church, a body from among the Gentiles, does that mean that God is through with national Israel? These were the questions which needed to be answered, and James rises to the occasion.

SIMPLICITY

The explanation James gives is the essence of simplicity, yet it seems that scholars have been little able to grasp it.

James says that all the promises to Israel concerning the kingdom will be literally fulfilled, but not at that time. First, the Lord is going to carry out a part of His plan, which until now had been a mystery, and then after that, the kingdom promises to Israel shall be realized. The words of James are clear: "*Simeon* (Peter) *hath declared how God at the first did visit the Gentiles, to take out of them a people for his name*" (Acts 15:14).

This is what God was now doing. The kingdom (respecting Israel) had been set aside, and God is now "calling out" from among the Gentiles a people for His name—the body of Christ—the church. This, says James, was in full agreement with the prophecies concerning the kingdom: *"… as it is written, After this* (after the church) *I will return, and will build again the tabernacle of David, which is fallen down* (which it had been and fell completely in AD 70); *and I will build again the ruins thereof* (the second coming), *and I will set it up"* (Acts 15:15–16; Amos 9:11; James was quoting Amos).

"After this I will return"—after what? After He has gathered out from among the Gentiles a people for His name. After this body of the church is complete and the fullness of the Gentiles be come in, then the Lord will return and restore the nation of Israel and will set up the kingdom here on earth, and all the prophecies of the Messiah's reign will be fulfilled to the letter.

TO WHAT ARE MODERN BELIEVERS SUBJECT?

Now comes the answer to the question which had brought them together: are the believers of this church age under the law of the kingdom? Is the believer in this dispensation of grace subject to the laws laid down by Moses for the nation of Israel?

James gives his sentence in the following words: *"Wherefore my sentence is, that we trouble not them, which from among the Gentiles are turned to God: But that we write unto them, that they abstain from pollutions of idols, and from fornication, and from things strangled, and from blood"* (Acts 15:19–20).

Not a word about keeping the law of Moses; not a word about circumcision, but they were advised against four things:

- Idolatry
- Fornication
- Things strangled
- Eating of blood

The first two are obvious as to their meaning, but the last two which pertain to blood, also have a deep spiritual meaning, which we will not explain at this time. Abstinence from these things was advised, not on the basis of law, but grace. These Gentiles had been idolaters; fornication was rampant; and they not at all respected the sanctity of blood. Because these things, which were so common among the Gentiles and so abhorrent to the Jews, were to be especially guarded against; they are warned about them.

THE LETTER

A letter is addressed to the Gentiles at Antioch and sent by the hand of Paul, Barnabas, and a company of others. The letter is in answer to the question, "Are the believers (especially of the Gentiles) under the law of Moses?"

Here is a copy of the letter sent by the Jerusalem elders to Antioch: *"Forasmuch as we have heard, that certain which went out from us have troubled you with words, subverting your souls, saying, Ye must be circumcised, and keep the law ... "* (Acts 15:24).

Notice again the problem: the legalists from Jerusalem had claimed that the Gentile Christians at Antioch must become Jews by submitting to circumcision and to keep the Law.

Now notice the decision: *"... to whom we gave no such commandment"* (Acts 15:24).

Those who teach that Christians are under the law are perverters of the grace of God. "We never gave any such commandments," wrote the apostles and elders to the church at Antioch. The legalistic Sabbatarians were unauthorized, and we now repudiate their demand for *"we gave no such commandment."* This was the message relayed to Antioch: "The Gentile believers are not under the law of Moses."

THE THREE ERRORS

The letter was delivered to the church, *"Which when they had read, they rejoiced for the consolation"* (Acts 15:31). The matter should have been settled, but the law teachers continued their practice of following Paul everywhere he went, trying to undo the grace preached by the apostle.

Everywhere he traveled he was opposed. No less than three books of the New Testament were written to combat errors concerning the law, with other epistles dealing somewhat with these subjects.

There were three errors present from the very beginning of the apostolic age, which in fact, continue with us unto this hour:

1. *Legalism.* Legalism teaches that men must be saved by keeping the law, whether the law of Moses, or a law of one's own making. This error is answered in Paul's epistle to the Romans.

2. *Antinomianism.* This word actually means "conflicting laws." This second error is the exact opposite of the first, teaching that it makes no difference how one lives, for it

is all of grace. After one is saved, it really doesn't matter how much one sins, for it is all covered by the grace of God. This error is answered in the epistle of James. Of course, Paul addresses it in Romans as well and also in his other epistles.

3. *Galatianism.* This third and the most subtle of the errors is the teaching that we are saved by grace, and then we are kept in victory by obeying the law perfectly—a law of our own making. It teaches that we are saved by faith alone, but then our ultimate salvation depends on our works. This error is called Galatianism because it was so prevalent in the Galatian churches, and Paul wrote the entirety of this epistle to refute this error—the epistle to the Galatians.

These three errors are still with us today. Nevertheless, the Word continues to say, *"Where the Spirit of the Lord is, there is liberty"* (II Cor. 3:17).

I heard my loving Saviour say,
There's room at the fountain for me,
Come wash the stains of sin away,
There's room at the fountain for thee.

I came to Him my sins confessed,
There's room at the fountain for me,
When I gave up my heart was blest,
There's room at the fountain for thee.

I plung'd beneath the crimson tide,
There's room at the fountain for me,
And now by faith I am sanctified,
There's room at the fountain for thee.

I found the crimson stream I know,
There's room at the fountain for me,
His blood has washed me white as snow,
There's room at the fountain for thee.

THE NEW COVENANT

JUSTIFIED BY CHRIST

JUSTIFIED BY CHRIST

"BUT IF WHILE WE seek to be justified by Christ, we ourselves also are found sinners, is therefore Christ the minister of sin? God forbid" (Gal. 2:17).

In Paul's day, as today, arguments were directed against this way of salvation, i.e., justification by faith. So in this verse and the ones following, Paul begins to answer these objections, first noting the main argument of his opponents and then revealing the argument by which he refutes theirs.

Paul refers to the standard objection to the doctrine of justification by faith, which he also deals with elsewhere. He is answering the objection that to eliminate the law entirely, as he is doing, is to encourage godless living. The argument would go in this fashion: "Your doctrine of justification by faith is dangerous (as the Judaizers would say), for by eliminating the law, you also eliminate a man's sense of moral responsibility. If a person can be accounted righteous simply by believing that Christ died for him, why then should he bother to keep the law, or for that matter, why should he bother to live by any standard of morality? There is no need to be good. The result of your doctrine is that men will believe in Christ, but thereafter do as they desire."

Paul's reply to this charge is abrupt. His expression suggests that he was aware of the possibility that a Christian can in fact sin, and, on occasion, all Christians do. But this is not the result of the doctrine of justification by faith, and therefore Christ is not responsible for it. Such a thought is abhorrent: "Absolutely not! God forbid!"

If there is sin, as Paul acknowledges indirectly in the next verse, man himself is responsible, and not God.

A MISUNDERSTANDING OF
JUSTIFICATION BY FAITH

Why is it that Paul can reply so vigorously to the objection that his gospel promotes antinomianism—Christians can sin all they desire because grace covers it—especially since he seems to admit that those who have been justified by faith do, at times, sin?

The answer is that the objection totally misunderstands the nature of man's justification. In the eyes of legalizers, justification by faith is nothing more than a legal fiction by which men and women are accounted righteous, when in fact they are not. But justification is *not* a legal fiction.

It is true that men are accepted by God as righteous when in actuality they are not, but this takes place only because God has first joined them to Christ, which was carried out by faith on their part, and this in turn implies a real transformation. We are *"in Christ"* says Paul.

Consequently, we are *"a new creation"* (II Cor. 5:17; Gal. 6:15). Obviously, in return to the old way of life after such a charge is inconceivable.

JUSTIFIED BY CHRIST

In Galatians 2:17, the phrase, *"But if, while we seek to be justified by Christ,"* means that the Jews needed justification exactly as the Gentiles, because they all were sinners.

In fact, when they (the Jews) sought justification in Christ and thus by grace, it was an admission on their part that there is no justification by works, that the seeker is not justified by such and is therefore a sinner. He would not be seeking justification were he not a sinner.

The attempt to be justified in Christ awakened the consciousness of sin, which of course is why justification is sought in the first place. This compels the Jew to put himself on the plain of the Gentiles. The Jew who calls the Gentile a sinner and is seeking to be justified by faith is forced to admit that he is a sinner also. He has found that the law of Moses had failed him as a justifying agency, which in fact it was never designed to do to begin with.

The whole contention was that Jews were better than Gentiles, which Paul refutes. His argument is, if we Jews need justification, which we certainly do, then that means we are no better than the Gentiles. All are on the same level—sinners without God—and all must come to Christ, whether Jew or Gentile, in order to be saved. Many Jews had a problem with that simply because they had the law of Moses which was the Word of God, and the Gentiles had no such thing and in fact were idolaters. Nevertheless, the Holy Spirit puts all on the same level.

THE FALSE ASSUMPTION OF THE JUDAIZERS

Paul repudiates the false assumption of the Judaizers who charged that Christ is the promoter and encourager of sin in that He causes the Jew to abandon the law as a justifying agency, and in doing so causes himself to be put on the same plain of a Gentile whom the Judaizers call sinners and dogs.

The Judaizers argue that in view of the fact that violation of the law is sin, therefore abandonment of the law in an effort to be justified in Christ is also a sin. Thus Christ, they deduced, is the promoter of sin.

It is amazing at the lengths that men will go to in order to promote their erroneous doctrines.

SINNERS

The phrase, *"we ourselves also are found sinners,"* refers to the fact that Jews also were sinners, even though this they did not like to admit, and therefore, needed justification. The Jews would quickly admit that Gentiles were sinners, and even grievous sinners, but they did not want to place themselves in the same category. However, Paul is saying that the Jews are sinners like the Gentiles and are in desperate need of justification, which they can only receive by faith in Christ, which they will loathe to admit.

In Romans 3:9 Paul puts all on the same level: *"What then, are we (Jews) better than they (Gentiles)? No, in no wise: for we have before proved both Jews and Gentiles, that they are all under sin."*

THE MINISTER OF SIN

The question, *"Is therefore Christ the minister of sin?"* refers to Christ being totally unlike the law. The law of Moses was designed to be a *"minister of sin,"* in that it defined sin and specified different types of sin. Speaking of the law, Paul said, *"But if the ministration of death..."* (II Cor. 3:7). He also said and continuing to speak of the law, *"For if the ministration of condemnation..."* (II Cor. 3:9).

Christ is not the minister of sin but rather salvation. He does not deal in death but rather life. He is not the minister of condemnation but rather justification.

Paul is actually stating the fact that if anyone attempts to force the law into justification by faith, they are actually making Christ a *"minister of sin,"* because that's all the law can do. In effect, that's what Paul was doing along with Barnabas, in dragging the law into the great gospel of grace, which had brought salvation to the Jews and Gentiles alike at Antioch.

GOD FORBID

Christ did not come to define sin, to specify different types of sin, even as the law did, but rather to get rid of sin. He came to cleanse people from sin, to set the captive free from sin, to break its strangle hold upon the human heart and life, and He succeeded in doing exactly what He set out to do. Mixing law with grace, irrespective as to whether it's the Mosaic law or a law of one's own devising, presents a tragedy of the highest order. It is like attempting to mix oil with water, or light with darkness, or salt with sugar. To understate the case dramatically so: it won't work!

When Paul said, *"Is therefore Christ the minister of sin?"* he used a type of terminology which was known to the Jews. For instance, in II Corinthians 3:6, he spoke of two ministers—the letter and the Spirit—of which the former kills, while the latter gives life. That is the law kills, which it was designed to do, but the gospel gives life. Paul is accustomed to giving reproachful names to the law, and for the simple reason that the Jews were attempting to make something out of the law that God never intended. Consequently, it is necessary that we understand his manner of speech.

A SHOCK!

It is impossible for the nature of man to keep the law, for it is simply not in him to do such, and that because of the fall.

Yes, even in those who are justified and baptized with the Holy Spirit, even they cannot keep the law. Paul found this out himself, incidentally the hard way, and gives us the account in Romans 7. The question is, if those who are truly justified cannot do this, how in the world can the wicked do it, who do not have the Holy Spirit? Wherefore he who teaches that righteousness comes by law keeping, which much of the church world believes presently, whether they understand such or not, doesn't actually understand what he is saying, or what he is affirming. If he will be honest, he will admit that he cannot even keep the law himself, much less trying to impose it upon others.

The right use and end of the law is to accuse and condemn as guilty, in order to show man what he actually is. That man may see himself to be in danger of sin, wrath, and death, thereby to be brought to trembling desperation. The law requires perfect obedience under God and condemns all who do not accomplish that, which in fact includes everyone. In fact, there is no man living or who has lived, except Jesus Christ, who accomplished this which God requires of us.

So, when Paul used the words *"God forbid,"* he was answering the question, *"is Christ the minister of sin?"* Jesus Christ is rather the giver of righteousness and eternal life.

Consequently, Christ keeps the law through us, and in us, which is done by our faith in Him and what He did at the Cross. Wherefore, when we fly to Him, Moses and his law vanishes away, so that his sepulchre can nowhere be found of sin and death, which can hurt us no more (Deut. 34:5). For Christ our instructor is Lord over the law, sin, and death: so that they which believe in Him, and of course we speak of the Lord Jesus Christ, are delivered from the same.

A PARTICULAR DESIGN

The law of Moses was designed to show man exactly where he was spiritually, which in fact was and is a sad state. Even though God commanded man to keep the law, He gave man no power to do so, and this was done for purpose.

Man's problem all along has been and is pride. Consequently, if God had given man the power to keep the law, it would have only resulted in man being lifted up more in his own pride, with the situation then being worse than ever. So God gave no power for man to keep the law, and for the obvious reason. Man was supposed to realize his inability, his lack of strength, and thereby to throw himself on Christ. Before Calvary, this was done through the sacrifices. To be sure, the sacrifices could not take away sin, and could not afford any type of salvation; nevertheless, the sinner in the offering up of sacrifices was to have faith in what those sacrifices represented, which was the coming Redeemer, which all Jews knew about, or were supposed to know about. Faith in that would save them (Gen. 15:6).

The whole idea is that man cannot make it without Jesus Christ. He must look to Jesus for salvation. He must look to Jesus as the Baptizer with the Holy Spirit. He must look to Jesus for overcoming strength and power. It is Jesus all the way and what He did at Calvary and the resurrection.

The Holy Spirit works only in the legal confines of Jesus Christ and what He did for us with His one atonining sacrifice. The Holy Spirit will not function outside of that capacity, will not help us in other ways as religious as they may be, but only through the sacrifice of Christ (Rom. 8:1-3).

WHICH I DESTROYED

"For if I build again the things which I destroyed, I make myself a transgressor" (Gal. 2:18).

The interpretation of this verse is not difficult if our interpretation of Galatians 2:17 is valid. The legalizers had accused Paul of encouraging sin because Paul's doctrine, they say, throws over the law for God's grace. This Paul denied.

Nevertheless, he replies, sin could be encouraged if having once come to God by faith in Jesus Christ, the one coming should then return to law as a basis for victory or relationship. Actually, it refers to a situation precisely like the one into which Peter had fallen. How is it that returning to law promotes sin?

The simple reason is that the Holy Spirit whose help the believer must have, that is if we are to maintain our position as an overcomer, simply will not help us to keep the law, whether the Law of Moses, or a religious law of our own devising. He will only help us as we depend on the sacrifice of Christ (Rom. 8:1-3).

IF I BUILD AGAIN

The phrase, *"For if I build again the things which I destroyed,"* in the strict sense is referring to Peter's action of declaring the Levitical legislation regarding the eating of certain foods as null and void, which was scripturally correct. He proved that by eating with the Gentiles and then turning around and declaring these things valid by his act of withdrawing from that fellowship, which presented a total turnabout. Consequently, what Peter did was sin, i.e., made himself a transgressor. It is the same with modern Christians.

When the believer, through ignorance or otherwise, turns away from Christ, i.e., the grace of God, to a law of his own devising in order to overcome sin, instead of victory he will actually find the direct opposite—more sin.

Let me explain: Let's say that a believer has a problem with an uncontrollable temper. It could be cigarettes, alcohol, jealousy, lust, envy, greed, or pride. In other words, it could be anything, but we will use the temper problem.

He is now a Christian with the divine nature within his heart and life; consequently, he instantly knows this is wrong; his temper is hurting his testimony and causing all types of problems. In other words, him losing control of his temper is sin.

EFFORTS

Loving Jesus as he does, and woefully ashamed of his actions, he sets about to obtain victory over this problem. Oftentimes he will attempt to do so in many and varied ways: He'll think that he must pray more or perhaps fast one or two days a week; perhaps he must witness to more people about Christ; he must study his Bible more—surely, these things will solve his problem.

If he is a Pentecostal or charismatic, he will get in a prayer line somewhere in order for a preacher to lay hands on him, and if the power of God comes upon him, and he is "slain in the Spirit," he will think this is the answer to his problem.

In fact, all of these things we have mentioned such as prayer, etc., are excellent in their own right; however, these things were never intended by the Lord to give us victory over sin. It is somewhat like using a handsaw as a hammer. While the handsaw does an excellent job at what it is designed to do, it does not serve too well as a hammer.

In effect, the believer has now made a law out of these good and wonderful things, thinking surely he will now be helped.

In fact, he will be helped, because prayer and fasting, as well as the study of the Word, and other such like things, are always a great help. Nevertheless, it will not be the help he's looking for, which is victory over sin. To his dismay, he will find that not only does he still have this problem of an uncontrollable temper, but in fact it is even worse.

WHY IS IT WORSE?

It is worse simply because he has resorted to law whether he realizes it or not, thereby abandoning the grace of God. Consequently, he doesn't have the Holy Spirit to help him, which the Holy Spirit will not do under these circumstances. As a result, he is doomed to failure, irrespective of all of these things he is doing in order to bring about victory.

You see, there is something in man, even in believers, that wants to *do* something. And the doing is always wrong, because it is outside of Christ and His cross. No matter how much willpower he uses, no matter how much effort he makes, the end result is going to be failure, despite all these other things he is doing.

Many believers become frustrated at this stage, simply not knowing what to do. They've tried everything they know, and the problem is not getting better, but rather worse.

None of us think of prayer, fasting, or study of the Bible as law. In fact, they aren't laws; however, the truth is, we make a law out of these things, that is if we depend upon them for victory, which has already been won in Christ.

I pray that the reader can understand what I'm saying.

By no means are we denigrating prayer or the study of the Word of God; we're only stating that these things must be done for the proper reasons. Then they bring good, beautiful, and wonderful results.

AN INSULT TO CHRIST

As wonderful and helpful as these good things are, by us adding them in our efforts to overcome sin, whether we realize it or not, we are saying that Christ did not finish the task at Cavalry and needs our additions.

This is what I mean by our efforts being an insult to Christ. The truth is, Jesus paid it all, and we mean *all*: He defeated every demon and power of darkness at the cross; He satisfied the claims of the broken law, thereby satisfying God; He also broke the grip of sin whenever these claims were satisfied; consequently, Satan has no more hold on the believer.

A VICTORIOUS OVERCOMER

The following in brief is the answer for victory over sin: The believer should not try to be victorious or to be an overcomer. If he tries such, he will fail for the simple reason that he is frustrating the grace of God. The truth is, the believer is already a victorious overcomer in Christ. It is given to us freely upon salvation.

We don't have to do anything to receive it, but simply maintain it. It is ours—a free gift from Christ; it comes with salvation.

The believer should study Romans 6, 7, and 8. In the Romans 6, he will find that we were literally baptized into the death of Christ when He died at Calvary. We will also find in Romans 6 that we were buried with Him and then raised with Him in newness of life. Consequently, we are now a new creation in Christ Jesus, and Satan has no more hold over us. In other words, exactly as Romans 6:14 says, *"Sin shall not have dominion over you: for ye are not under the law, but under grace."*

This means that the cross of Christ was not only the necessary vehicle for our salvation, but as well it pertains to our everyday victory in Christ.

The believer must understand what happened at Calvary, which we have just given in brief, and must have faith in this which Jesus did, literally reckoning himself to be dead indeed unto sin, but alive unto God through Jesus Christ our Lord (Rom. 6:11).

Once again, it's all a matter of faith. The believer is to believe that Jesus paid the sin debt, and that He also broke the grip of sin.

When the believer understands this and then believes it, and keeps believing it, actually confessing it (Rom. 6:11), victory is his.

THE HOLY SPIRIT

When our faith and confidence is in what Christ did at Calvary and the resurrection, the Holy Spirit will then help us overcome a temper problem or any other problem we may have (Rom. 8:1-3). What we found to be impossible for us, is no problem whatsoever for the Holy Spirit, for He is God.

The idea is that our faith and confidence is now in the price paid by Jesus at Calvary, which the Holy Spirit always honors. So the answer is not greater willpower, or dependence upon anything else for that matter, but rather on the finished work of the great sacrifice of Christ, which guarantees not only our salvation, but also perpetual victory. This is the only answer for the sin problem. All sin must be taken to the cross, and we mean *all*.

Then, we will actually pray more, study the Word more, and all these other things, which will now have even a greater purpose and meaning, because all of this now is in the right context.

A TRANSGRESSOR

The phrase, *"I make myself a transgressor,"* is exactly what happens when we revert to law, thereby taking ourselves away from the grace of God.

The very term *grace of God* means that we as human beings need something that we cannot supply for ourselves, and in fact, are not worthy of it at all, but upon faith it is freely given to us by God. As someone has said, "Grace is unmerited favor." I like to state it as being the goodness of God given to undeserving saints.

We do not merit such, we are not worthy of such, but upon faith in Christ, God gives us all the grace we need in order for whatever is needed. There are enough problems in the Christian life for the simple reason that we live, one might say, in an alien society, without us ignorantly or otherwise making ourselves a transgressor. Yet this is exactly what many Christians do, in fact I think most do.

The problem is, most believers simply do not properly understand what they should understand about the great sacrifice of Christ at Calvary. Please don't misunderstand, this subject is so vast, so great, with such height and depth, it would be impossible for it to be exhausted. Nevertheless, all that most believers know about this greatest of all acts is this: "Jesus died for my sins." That is about all they know. And to be sure, Satan takes full advantage of our ignorance.

THE BELIEVER SHOULD CONSIDER THIS

There are hundreds of millions of unbelievers attempting to quit drinking, quit nicotine, or quit a host of other things that they know are killing them. They use willpower, secure the help of a psychologist, or whatever, but with no satisfactory results. However, when the believing sinner comes to Christ, thereby becoming a new creation, his dependence is to be totally in Christ and what Christ did for him at the cross. And if one were to ask believers that question, most all would claim that their dependence is in Christ and the cross, when in fact it isn't, at least for many of them.

We are fooled so easily because these things we select, such as prayer, witnessing to souls, etc., which we think will get us victory over sin are, in actuality, very good things; they are spiritual things, so we think surely they are the answer. In truth, these things are definitely answers for many things, but not for victory over sin. That can come only by our faith in Christ and what He did for us at the cross.

When we start depending on other things, in effect we are not depending on Christ and the cross, whether we think so or not. We are depending totally on willpower, which is the same thing we depended on before coming to Christ. Just as surely as we failed then, we will fail now. Paul said this himself, *"For to will is present with me; but how to perform that which is good I find not"* (Rom. 7:18).

In other words, willpower within itself is not sufficient, even for the believer.

Paul found the answer which he gave to us in Romans 6 and 7.

THE SPOTLESS RIGHTEOUSNESS
GIVEN FREELY BY CHRIST

The argument of verses 17 and 18 is this: Man is guilty and needs a spotless righteousness. This righteousness can be obtained, not through law keeping, but through Christ believing. A professor of the doctrine of salvation by faith who preaches salvation by works, re-erects the legal structure which he himself cast down when he came to Christ, whether he realizes it or not, and so fools himself to be a transgressor in having thrown it down. In other words, if the law could not save us, which it couldn't, why do we return to the law in order to obtain victory over sin, which in fact cannot give any victory. To do so, makes us a transgressor both ways: we are abandoning grace, which is a sin, and reverting to law, which is another sin.

We must understand that faith in anything other than Christ and the cross, and I mean anything, constitutes a transgression and never can be accepted by God.

The law is divinely perfect; man is hopelessly impotent, hence it is useless for him to seek righteousness by the law. Christ who is the righteousness envisioned by the law, becomes such to whosoever believes upon Him; and thus He glorifies the law and at the same time redeems the sinner, which God intends. Please understand, only Christ can glorify the law, because He alone kept the law. Man cannot do such, I don't care how hard he tries.

THE POPULARITY OF CEREMONIES AND ORDINANCES

Man delights to return to those things which gratify the flesh. Consequently, he eagerly accepts whatever appeals to him. Hence, the popularity of *"religious ceremonies and ordinances."* But to rest upon them, even though they may be good within themselves, is to rest upon the flesh. If Christ be everything, then there is neither room nor necessity for other things. Those who occupy themselves with these find in them a fatal sustenance. Their effect is to veil the person and the protections of the great high priest, the Lord Jesus Christ.

Do you understand what we are saying?

This does not mean that ceremonies or ordinances such as the Lord's Supper, or water baptism, or fasting or prayer, etc., are wrong within themselves—they aren't. They definitely have a purpose, but they are not to be used outside of that purpose. Once again, we go back to taking a handsaw and trying to make a hammer of that tool; it won't work!

If we improperly use these things, or improperly look to these things, these things become larger and larger and Christ becomes smaller and smaller.

DISTASTEFUL AND REPELLING

Man likes to have some credit and some position. He likes that which he can see and handle. He refuses to be treated as vile and incapable of good, and is angered that he and his religious efforts should be condemned to annihilation. He will willingly practice efforts to punish himself, for that ministers to his own self-importance; but to accept the absolute judgment of death upon his nature, his religious energies, his moral virtues, and to be commanded to be silent, and as a dead sinner to trust the life-giving Savior, and to find in Him all that is needful for righteousness and worship, is distasteful and repelling. But this is the doctrine of verses 19 and 20, which we will arrive at now.[1]

FOR I...

"For I through the law am dead to the law, that I might live unto God" (Gal. 2:19).

The "we" of Galatians 2:17 which included both Paul and Peter, has changed to the "I" of Galatians 2:18. This personal form of expression now continues as Paul begins to unfold the full nature of the justification that is his because of his being *"in Christ."* In this verse, "I" is emphatic by being in the first position in the sentence. It contrasts with the similar position given to *"in Christ,"* which begins in Galatians 2:20 (the Greek text says, *"in Christ"* instead of *"with Christ"*).

Paul has argued that if he should return to the law after having come to God through faith in Christ, he would make himself a transgressor, which is exactly what Peter had done, and all will do who go that route. But this Paul does not do.

Actually, the opposite is true, because in coming to God in Christ, he died to the law so completely that he could not possibly return to it. *"Through the law"* probably justifies seeing in this brief sentence a capsule version of Paul's explanation of the law's purpose and developed in greater length in Romans 7.

A.C. Gaebelein said, "The law cannot bring life, for no one has ever fulfilled it, except Christ. The law brings death, which it was designed to do, for by it all stand condemned. Nevertheless, even in doing this, law performs a good function. For in the very act of destroying all hope for salvation by human works, law actually opens the way to discovering new life in God, which it was intended to do. It is only when a man will die to his own efforts to achieve salvation that he will receive the gift of salvation that God offers."

DEAD TO THE LAW

The phrase, *"For I through the law am dead to the law,"* does not mean that Paul is a lawless individual. He still holds to the great ethical principles of love and justice, for instance, which are eternal in their significance. These are the great underlying moral principles that inhere in God's character and in His government.

When Paul says that he has died to a thing he means that he has ceased to have any relation to it, so that it has no further claim upon or control over him. It is law as conceived of as a body of legalistic statutes, to which he has died.

Paul's attempt (and all others as well) to fulfill the requirements of the Mosaic legislation as a means of salvation, had taught him his own inability to meet its demands, and its inability to make him righteous. Thus, he finally abandoned it as a means of justification, and accepted Salvation in Christ (Rom. 8:1).

THE LAW IS NOT DEAD, BUT HE IS DEAD TO THE LAW

Paul found that what the law did was to reveal sin, provoke sin, and, in a certain sense, create sin, for where there was no law sin was not reckoned. He found that the law provided no remedy for sin, and neither was it meant by God to be a remedy. It was rather meant by the Lord to condemn man hopelessly, for no one can fulfill its requirements, with him thereby throwing himself on Christ. It exercised a double power over him, for it made him a sinner and punished him for being one.

Even though the law of Moses was set aside, and for the simple reason that it was all fulfilled in Christ, in no way does that mean that the moral requirements of the law are not incumbent upon all men everywhere. God's requirements, and that's what they are, do not change. Even though the ceremonial part of the law is now rendered unnecessary by Christ, the moral part of the law does not change simply because moral absolutes cannot change. However, the law, morally and otherwise, was totally satisfied in Christ, and by faith in Christ, the believer is judged as a law keeper instead of a lawbreaker.

THE FALSE MESSAGE

The false apostle said, "Except you live to the law, you are dead to God," but Paul says the contrary, *"Except you be dead to the law, you cannot live unto God."*

When the word *law* is used, it is confusing to many believers or professing believers. If they think of the law of Moses, they have little knowledge of that, so they brush it aside as not pertaining to them.

However, what they do not realize is that Paul was definitely speaking of the law of Moses, but as we explained in commentary on verse 16, it can refer to any kind of law. By that we mean this: anything—the church, water baptism, our own good works in any capacity—can all be made into a law even though they really aren't "law" to begin with.

The idea is this: if the law of Moses—which was definitely given by God and therefore perfect, at least in what it was designed to do—could not save anyone or afford salvation in any capacity, then how in the world do we think or believe that puny laws of our own making can do any better?

Christians brush this aside because they think it applies to Israel of old, or possibly to Paul, but not to them, but please believe me, it applies to you.

For instance, almost all of Catholic teaching is nothing but law. The same can be said for some Protestant denominations—it is all law. They are saying do this—something other than Christ and Him crucified—and you will be saved. The truth is, if we trust in anything other than the finished work of Christ, we are unsaved. To be sure, that finished work does not include religious ceremonies or ordinances, or anything else of that nature. It is complete within itself—the death of Christ on the cross and His resurrection and our faith in that (Jn. 3:16).

THROUGH THE LAW

What did Paul mean by the statement, *"through the law"*?

This phrase could probably be explained by Paul's explanation given in Romans 7. Even after his conversion to Christ and being baptized with the Holy Spirit, he tried to find victory *"through the law."* That was all he knew to do. He thought that since he was now in Christ and had the Holy Spirit, which he definitely did, that surely he could keep the law, which he had never been successful in doing.

In his own thinking, he now understands why he could not keep the law before conversion, but he now finds that after conversion, after accepting Christ, he still cannot keep the law. He cannot find victory over sin *"through the law,"* no matter how hard he tried, irrespective of the fact that he is now born again and Spirit-filled. So he asks the great question: *"O wretched man that I am! who shall deliver me from the body of this death?"* (Rom. 7:24).

However what he could not find *"through the law,"* he found *"through Jesus Christ our Lord"* (Rom. 7:25).

Therefore, his trust in Christ now makes him dead to the law, even though the law is not dead. He is saying that the law has no more control over him, makes no more demands on him, is not hanging over his head as a sword of Damocles. He is dead to its demands because they were all fulfilled in Christ. He is dead to its threat because Jesus pulled its teeth by meeting its demands. He is no longer subject to its curse, for Jesus took that penalty upon Himself.

Isn't that beautiful?

The idea is this: Everything that Jesus did was as our representative man, in other words, doing it on our behalf. When He went to the cross, He satisfied the demands of the broken law, and simple faith in Him and what He did for us at the cross gives us His perfection. Let me ask it again: isn't that beautiful?

LIVE UNTO GOD

In Galatians 2:19, the phrase, *"that I might live unto God,"* presents such being done through Christ, which could never be done through the law. The Christian lives unto Christ in order that he may live unto God.

The ultimate object of the Christian scheme is that he may be presented righteous before God. By the law he could not obtain this righteousness, however, it is obtained in Christ and Christ alone.

Wuest said:

Faith in Christ was the means whereby Paul's complete and irreparable break with the law was effected. The Lord Jesus lived under the law, fully obeyed that law, assumed the guilt and penalty which the human race incurred by having violated the law, and in dying under the law satisfied its requirements. Thus, He passed out of the realm where law in its legalistic aspect had control over Him. All believers are identified with Christ in His death and also in His resurrection, and thus have passed out of the realm of divine law so far as its legalistic aspect is concerned. Consequently, Paul says that he has thus died to the law that he might live unto God. Subjection to the law as a means of acceptance with God, in reality prevented him (and us) from living a life of unreserved devotion to God. This is one of the most grievous vices of legalism—that it comes between the soul and God.[2]

THE LAW AS AN EXECUTIONER

The Christian is a paradox, an apparent contradiction, for he is said to be both dead and alive; not half dead or half alive, but completely dead and completely alive. The true believer is dead to sin and alive unto righteousness; dead to self and alive unto Christ; and as Paul states it, "dead to the law but alive unto God." This fact Paul declares without apology.

Dead to the law! What a startling, amazing statement: *"dead to the law!"* Paul does not say that the law is dead. Far be it from Paul to claim that the law is dead. Before his conversion, he knew full well its power over him. The law is very much alive today, even at this present time, in cursing and in condemning sin and threatening judgment to the transgressor. The law is still the ministry of wrath upon the sinner. The words of Ephesians 5:6 are conclusive: *"Let no man deceive you with vain words: For because of these things* (the sins mentioned in the previous verse), *cometh the wrath of God upon the children of disobedience."*

No, the law is not dead, but Paul says, "I am dead to the law." The law does not recognize me as even existing anymore. It cannot touch me, for I am dead, and the law cannot touch dead men.

THE OCCASION

To understand what Paul meant by this startling statement, we must see the occasion on which it was said.

In the verses preceding Paul's statement, he tells how Peter had come to Antioch, even as we've already addressed, and had entered fully into the fellowship of Gentile Christians by eating with them and having fellowship with them, which was strictly forbidden by the law for a Jew. But when certain legalistic law teachers from Jerusalem came up, Peter withdrew himself from the Gentile Christians and placed himself back under the law. This so incensed Paul that he severely rebuked Peter for his double standard, and now he concludes with the statement, *"For I through the law am dead to the law."*

As far as I am concerned, my relationship to the law is ended. Now, just what is Paul saying?

He says that in the eyes of the law I am dead, I am nonexistent. An illustration will serve to show what Paul meant.

AN EXAMPLE

Imagine a man who has committed murder. According to the law, if found guilty he must be put to death. He is arrested, charged with murder, and brought to trial. The court is in session, and the judge is on the bench. The accused man hears the accusation and charge read to him. But before the trial is concluded, the accused man suffers a heart attack and drops dead in the courtroom.

A doctor declares him dead and signs his death certificate. Now what does the judge do?

After the commotion is over, does he call the court to order, and say, "Let us proceed with the trial of this dead man"?

Of course not! You cannot try a dead man, or condemn him to death, for he is already dead. So the judge dismisses the case. It is closed forever, and he proceeds to the next case.

In the case of the criminal in our illustration, he cheated the law; he circumvented the law. It was the prerogative of the law to execute the man, but he died before the law could put him to death.

NOT SO WITH PAUL

But, says Paul, it was not thus in my case. I did not cheat or beat the law, but the law itself put me to death.

Notice three important words in our text, *"I through the law am dead to the law"*: Through or by the law I was put to death. The law itself found me guilty and executed me. The law slew me.

Again allow me to illustrate: Imagine again the criminal before the bar of justice. The witnesses are called and all testify to the guilt of the murderer. The judge declares him guilty and sets the day for sentencing. When that day comes, the judge reads from the law the penalty for murder.

It is death for the criminal, and the judge orders the man to be hanged by the neck until he is dead and sets the date for execution. The sentence is carried out, and on the appointed day the man is led to the gallows and hanged.

The physician declares the man dead, and the case is closed. Now this man is not only dead to the law, but dead *through* the law. The law put him to death. It can do no more. The law is satisfied. This, says Paul, happened to me—*"I through the law am dead to the law."*

A SURPRISE!

This is not the end of the story, however. Three days after this guilty man was executed, you meet this same man one early morning, walking down the street. At first you can't believe your eyes. You look more closely, but there is no doubt about it. The criminal is alive.

You rush to the home of the judge, arouse him from his bed, and excitedly exclaim, "Judge, Judge, remember the man who was executed three days ago. Well, he is alive! I saw him with my own eyes! Call the police, call the sheriff, call out the National Guard and pick up this dangerous criminal! Hurry, Judge!"

WHAT THE RECORD SAYS

The judge is not impressed at all, and says, "Now just calm down, and we will look at the record."

He takes down the record of the trial, the verdict of guilty, the account of the execution, the doctor's death certificate, and finally the words, "case closed."

He looks at you and says, "That man is dead."

But you say to him, *"He is alive! I saw him!"*

"I'm sorry," says the judge, "according to the law this man died three days ago. According to the law the man is dead. He has paid the extreme penalty."

The man is legally dead, and the law cannot punish a man twice for the same crime. If the man is alive again, it is of no concern to the law. The law did not anticipate a resurrection. There is no provision in the law as to what to do in such a case.

According to the law the man is dead, and since the law cannot punish twice for the same crime, he is free—dead to the law—through the law and in the eyes of the law. Now, says Paul, that is what happened to me. I was executed by the law, but was raised again.

WHERE? WHEN? HOW?

Paul, will you please tell us when this happened to you, where this took place, and how were you put to death? Paul has the answer ready. It is found in this verse: *"I am* (have been) *crucified with Christ: nevertheless I live; yet not I, but Christ liveth in me ... "* (Gal. 2:20).

You want to know where I died—it was at Calvary. When did I die?—when Christ died. How did I die?—by crucifixion. That is the meaning of Paul's words, *"crucified with Christ."*

Now to understand this strange statement of Paul's, we must turn to the Word of God concerning the members of the body of Christ. When Christ hung on the cross, people saw only a physical, human body nailed to a cross by the hands and by the feet. But when God looked down upon Jesus on the cross, He saw another body—a spiritual body—united to its head. God saw in Christ the mystical body of believers, who are members of Christ and called His body.

God saw the Head, Christ, and He saw the body of Christ, consisting of individual members, which make up the church, which is His body.

What happened to the head of the church that day on Calvary, God reckons as having happened to all of His members, for the church is a spiritual body: *"For by one Spirit are we all baptized into one body"* (I Cor. 12:13).

God foreknew every one of His chosen ones from eternity as members of the body of Christ:

- *"According as he hath chosen us in him* (Christ) *before the foundation of the world"* (Eph. 1:4).
- *"For we are members of his body, of his flesh, and of his bones"* (Eph. 5:30).

CRUCIFIED

As the body of Jesus hung upon the cross, God looked down from heaven and saw the spiritual body of Christ—the church—hanging there *"in Christ."* This is Paul's meaning when he says, *"I was crucified with Christ."* As a member of the body of Christ in the mind of God I was nailed with Jesus to the tree. But this was not all. When they took Jesus down from the tree, they buried Him, the Head with the body, and since we are members of His body, *"we are buried with him by baptism into death"* (Rom. 6:4).

This does not refer to water baptism, but rather the baptism into His death—in the mind of God this is what happened. We obtain its results by faith.

THE RESURRECTION

But that is not all, for that same body arose. After three days and nights, the tomb was found empty, and not one member was left behind. Since we are members of His body, we too arose with Him, and Paul says: *"If* (since) *ye then be risen with Christ, seek those things which are above"* (Col. 3:1).

THE ASCENSION

But there is still more. Forty days later Jesus ascended into heaven and took that body along, at least in a spiritual sense. In Christ, therefore, in the mind of God every believer is already seated in heaven. In our physical bodies we are still here on earth, but positionally and spiritually in Christ, we are already in heaven seated with Christ.

Listen to Paul's statement: *"But God, who is rich in mercy, for his great love wherewith he loved us, Even when we were dead in sins, hath quickened us* (made us alive again) *together with Christ,* (by grace ye are saved;) *And hath raised us up together, and made us sit together in heavenly places in Christ Jesus"* (Eph. 2:4–6).

Remember then that we are members of the spiritual body of Christ, and what happened to Him happened to every member of His body. Yes, with Paul, every believer can say: *"I am crucified with Christ: nevertheless I live"* (Gal. 2:20).

The law has been satisfied by the Lord Jesus Christ and therefore, as members of Him, God reckons it as though we ourselves had paid the penalty. Yes, indeed, dead to the law, through the law!

ARE WE THEN LAWLESS?

We must again answer the charge of some who say this free-dom from the law is a dangerous doctrine and will result in looseness of living and practicing sin without restraint. Anyone who makes this charge does not understand the grace of God. In fact, it is the opposite of that contention. If we go back to law, it will only guarantee sin and failure; whereas, if we depend on the grace of God, it guarantees victory over sin—and that alone can guarantee victory over sin.

"For I through the law am dead to the law, that I might live unto God" (Gal. 2:19).

Free from the law—yes, free from the law of Moses, but now under the *"law of the Spirit of life in Christ Jesus,"* an entirely different law altogether—a law that makes me *"free from the law of sin and death"* (Rom. 8:2).

Deliverance from the law which could only condemn gives liberty—not liberty to sin, but liberty to serve Christ without fear. The law demanded holiness; the grace of God produces it. If a person is looking to the law to improve himself, as so many of us tend to do, it will never accomplish such. In fact, the opposite will result. Only the grace of God can give us that which we must have—righteousness and holiness in Christ.

WHAT THE LAW COULD NOT DO

The law of God is holy, eternal, perfect, and good. It is the divine pattern of righteousness which God demands of those who would be saved by their own works, merits, and efforts. The law of God is powerful, demanding punishment for each transgression. It is absolutely just in treating all alike, and there is no respect of persons under the law of God.

There are no exceptions: *"the soul that sinneth, it shall die"* (Ezek. 18:4). It is inflexible and rigid, so that it makes no allowance for effort, no matter how sincere, if that effort fails to measure up to every single demand of the perfect law of God.

The law condemns and curses every sinner, even as it is designed to do. It knows no distinction between little sins and big sins as far as guilt is concerned. The demands of the law of God are absolute: *"Cursed is every one that continueth not in all things which are written in the book of the law to do them"* (Gal. 3:10).

It recognizes neither wealth nor influence nor position nor station, but says: *"there is no difference: For all have sinned, and come short of the glory of God"* (Rom. 3:22–23).

The law of God is eternal and stands today as the pronouncer of wrath upon all who refuse to accept, by simple faith in the Lord Jesus Christ, God's means of deliverance from its power and condemnation and curse.

We reemphasize these assertions concerning the law, because we who preach grace and freedom from the law for believers in Christ are constantly accused of making void the law, as though it did not exist anymore, or had no application to this age of grace.

This is a false accusation, but it was already answered by the apostle Paul nearly two thousand years ago.

FALSE ACCUSATIONS

He too had been slandered and condemned for preaching liberty and deliverance from the law. We, therefore, would answer our critics in the words of Paul himself in Galatians 2:21: *"I do not frustrate the grace of God: for if righteousness come by the law, then Christ is dead in vain."*

Paul had been accused of making void the law. In Romans 3:31 he answers the critics:

"Do we then make void the law through faith? God forbid: yea, we establish the law" (Rom. 3:31).

Stop and think about these momentous verses for a moment. Paul says, "If man could obtain righteousness by keeping the law, then it was unnecessary for Christ to die, and He, therefore, died for nothing." Consider carefully the implications.

If any human being could possibly be saved by the law of God, then why did Jesus have to die for those who were able to save themselves? It certainly would be a tragic mistake if God should demand the death of His Son to save those who could save themselves without the sacrifice of Christ. And this holds true even for the believer after he is saved.

If the believer, once saved, was able to keep himself saved by the works of the law, which all of us I think have tried to do at one time or the other, then why do we need Him to intercede daily for us at the right hand of God?

What a terrible accusation to bring against God, to say He wasted the work of Christ on the cross for those who were able by their own works to attain righteousness. If that is so, and even as we have already stated, then Christ died in vain. His death was wholly unnecessary and uncalled for, which is the most ridiculous thought or idea that one could ever begin to contemplate.

WE ESTABLISH THE LAW

Now notice the same truth as expressed in that other verse: *"Do we then make void the law through faith? God forbid: yea, we establish the law"* (Rom. 3:31).

By confessing that the law cannot be kept by us, we are not debasing or downgrading the law or weakening it, but instead we establish the law. By our admission that we were unable to meet the demands of the law of God, we prove its perfection, and that it has succeeded in doing what God intended for it to do. We elevate it high above man's fallible efforts and works. To say that man can keep God's holy law, is to drag it down to our own imperfect level, which would mean that the law is really not very much.

However, I confess that God's holy law is so high, so good, so perfect, and so holy, that I—a poor, weak, depraved sinner—cannot in myself meet its high standards, irrespective of how hard I try.

THE HOLINESS OF THE LAW

I extol the holiness of the law and exalt it, and so establish its perfection by not lowering it to the depths of my imperfection.

I establish the law by admitting that its standards cannot be attained by me—a depraved sinner—and that I, therefore, must turn to another for mercy, pardon, and forgiveness. It must ever be:

> *Not the labor of my hands,*
> *Can fulfill Thy law's demands;*
> *Could my zeal no respite know,*
> *Could my tears forever flow,*
> *All for sin could not atone;*
> *Thou must save, and Thou alone.*
> *Nothing in my hands I bring,*
> *Simply to Thy cross I cling.*

This is Bible salvation. How conclusive are the words of Paul: *"But to him that worketh not* (doesn't try to earn his salvation), *but believeth on him* (Jesus) *that justifieth the ungodly, his faith is counted for righteousness"* (Rom. 4:5).

WHAT THE LAW COULD NOT DO

We have seen that the law is powerful in condemning the sinner, but at the same time the law is also powerless to save the sinner. It is also powerless to condemn the believer in Christ.

The child of God is forever free from its condemnation, for the simple reason that we are dead to that condemnation, having died in Christ. After Paul has given us a picture of the struggle between the two natures within him, he cries out for deliverance: *"O wretched man that I am! who shall deliver me from the body of this death?"* (Rom. 7:24).

Paul does not claim sinless perfection even unto grace. He is still conscious of the presence of his old nature, and admits his defeat. Listen to his testimony: *"For I know that in me (that is, in my flesh,) dwelleth no good thing: for to will is present with me; but how to perform that which is good I find not. For the good that I would I do not: but the evil which I would not, that I do"* (Rom. 7:18–19).

Now remember, this is Paul's testimony *after* he was saved, not before as many teach. He still acknowledges the presence of his old nature and confesses his defeat, if depending upon works of the law for victory.

I DELIGHT IN THE LAW OF GOD

Paul continues to tell us of his earnest striving to please God, but how he fails in his own strength, as all will fail in their own strength: *"I find then a law, that, when I would do good, evil is present with me. For I delight in the law of God after the inward man: But I see another law in my members, warring against the law of my mind, and bringing me into captivity to the law of sin which is in my members. O wretched man that I am! who shall deliver me?"* (Rom. 7:21–24).

Notice Paul says, *"I delight in the law of God after the inward man."* This inward man is the new man, the new nature, the life of Christ which the believer received at conversion. This new nature (divine nature) delights in the law of God. It is the perfect desire of Paul to keep God's law perfectly. The new nature seeks to keep God's commandments. But alas! Paul says, I have to contend with another law—the law of sin and of death which is in my members.

As much as Paul's inward man desired to measure up to the law's perfection, he found his old nature opposing him at every turn, or as he puts it: *"But I see another law in my members, warring against the law of my mind* (the inward man), *and bringing me into captivity to the law of sin which is in my members"* (Rom. 7:23).

ONE'S OWN STRENGTH

And then, recognizing the futility, the hopelessness of gaining victory in his own strength and the utter defeat which results from his trying to keep God's perfect law by himself as long as the old nature is within him, he turns from his own efforts, and cries out: *"who shall deliver me from the body of this death* (the old nature)*?"* (Rom. 7:24).

And then he finds the answer. He gives up all confidence in his own efforts, his own willpower, his own machinations, and he turns the whole matter over to another. And so he concludes: *"I thank God through Jesus Christ our Lord"* (Rom. 7:25).

Jesus is our victory, and even when we fail, it is His victory which is credited to our account. Romans 7 closes with this confession: *"So then with the mind* (my desire) *I myself serve the law of God; but with the flesh* (if I depend on the flesh) *the law of sin* (I will fail)*"* (Rom. 7:25).

This is the answer to the verse with which we began: *"For I know that in me (that is, in my flesh,) dwelleth no good thing"* (Rom. 7:18).

But, thank God, that is not the end of the story. Romans 8 should follow the previous chapter without a break. After Paul admits his failure he cries out in Romans 8:1: *"There is therefore now no condemnation to them which are in Christ Jesus, who walk not after the flesh, but after the Spirit."*

IN JESUS AND WHAT HE DID FOR US AT THE CROSS

God has provided a way that we can be holy, righteous, and victorious over the world, the flesh and the devil. It's not difficult; in fact it's very easy, but at the same time it seems to be almost impossible for most believers. We'll look at that in a moment.

If the believer places his faith in Christ and what Christ has done for us at the cross, and he maintains it in Christ and what He has done for us at the cross, instantly a perfect holiness and perfect righteousness will be accredited to such a person. Also, victory over the world, the flesh, and the devil in every capacity will now be his—in totality. This is why Jesus died.

Our faith in Him and what He did for us at the cross guarantees us all these things that the flesh can never attain to. In fact, it's impossible for us to have these things by the means of the flesh. But that's the problem with most Christians. We try to attain holiness, righteousness, victory, and sanctification by our own strength and abilities, which is a hopeless task; it cannot be done.

That's the reason Jesus came down here to die on the cross. It was because we could not do it within ourselves. But it can be done through Him, and it can be done only through Him.

Paul said, *"I am crucified with Christ, nevertheless I live, yet not I, but Christ liveth in me: and the life which I now live in the flesh, I live by the faith of the Son of God, who loved me, and gave himself for me"* (Gal. 2:20).

The great apostle then said, *"I do not frustrate the grace of God: for if righteousness come by the law, then Christ is dead in vain"* (Gal. 2: 21).

If man can do this thing within himself, Jesus did not have to come down here and die on a cruel cross. But the fact that He had to come, and that He did come means that man simply could not do it. Even the best of us under the best of circumstances could not keep the law of God. But Jesus kept it for us, and paid the price that we can have everything that God wants us to have by simple faith. That's it—just having simple faith in Christ and what He did for us at the cross gives us a guaranteed blessing of unprecedented proportions, wherein is altogether our holiness, our righteousness, our victory, and our sanctification.

NO CONDEMNATION

Some have claimed that there is no condemnation for the believer irrespective as to what he does after conversion, how much he fails, or how much he sins. But that's really not what Romans 8:1 is saying.

The condemnation is taken away from all those *"who walk not after the flesh, but after the Spirit"* (Rom. 8:4). If the believer reverts back to walking after the flesh, there definitely will be failure (and we speak of sin), which brings with it automatic condemnation. All sin must be condemned by God; it simply cannot be otherwise.

Some claim that Jesus took all their sins, which in fact He did.

They then claim that sin no longer affects them in a negative way, but there is nothing in the Word of God that remotely states such a thing. Sin is just as negative to the believer as it is to the unbeliever. If committed, it has to be repented of, confessed, and forsaken (I Jn. 1:9).

What does Paul mean by the word *walk*?

He is speaking of our everyday living for the Lord. It is referred to as "a walk." This is where the rubber meets the road, where the pedal meets the metal: If this Christian experience doesn't play out victoriously in our everyday lives and changing us for the better, then it is no different from the philosophies of the world. However, it definitely does change us and for the better, but only if we *"walk after the Spirit."*

WHAT DOES IT MEAN TO WALK AFTER THE SPIRIT?

First of all, every believer has the Holy Spirit. He is given to us to perform a particular task, and that is to make us into the *"image of the heavenly"* (I Cor. 15:49). However, this is not an automatic process; He cannot do this without our cooperation.

To *"walk after the Spirit"* means to have the help of the Spirit, the leading of the Spirit, and the power of the Spirit. To have all of that guarantees total victory.

Just because the believer has the Holy Spirit—and all believers do—doesn't mean at all that the Holy Spirit is able to do all of these grand and wonderful things that we have just mentioned. He can do them, even as He desires to do them, but He will do so only according to one particular direction.

In Romans 8:1, Paul is speaking about an overcoming, victorious Christian life, which all of us surely want to have, and in fact do have. However, it can only be obtained in one manner.

THE LEGAL CONFINES OF CALVARY

The Holy Spirit will not help us overcome the flesh, the world, and the devil outside of the legal confines of Calvary. He functions solely on the sacrifice of that occasion. Paul gave us these legal parameters in Romans 8:2: *"For the law of the Spirit of life in Christ Jesus hath made me free from the law of sin and death."*

Those are the legal confines of which I speak. It is *"in Christ Jesus,"* which means what He did at Calvary and the resurrection.

We are to understand that we were *"in Christ"* when He died on Calvary's cross, at least this was what was in the mind of God. By faith Christ's victory becomes ours.

When we are trusting in what Jesus did there, and solely trusting in that, the Holy Spirit will then do for us what we cannot do for ourselves—totally defeating the efforts of Satan in every capacity. The demands of the law of Moses were met in Christ, and that means His sacrificial, atoning death on the cross. Consequently, this *"law of sin and death"* has no more hold over me.

However, if we look away from the cross to our own abilities, willpower, strength, or a regimen of laws of our own making, or the making of another man, then the Holy Spirit will not help us in this, and we are doomed to failure, and thereby, condemnation.

So, the key is trusting in what was done at the cross, and to keep trusting in that on a daily basis, and then the Holy Spirit will do the work, which we Christians cannot do within ourselves and on our own, which was proven by Paul's experience in Romans 7.

WHAT GOD SEES

When we trust in what Christ did at the cross, God then sees us in Christ as perfect and sinless, and accepts us not on the basis of our own righteousness which is unacceptable anyway, but on the basis of the righteousness of Christ. This righteousness the law could not give us; it was way beyond our reach. The Scripture says: *"For what the law could not do, in that* (because) *it was weak through the flesh, God sending His own Son in the likeness of sinful flesh, and for sin, condemned sin in the flesh:*

"That the righteousness of the law might be fulfilled in us, who walk not after the flesh, but after the Spirit" (Rom. 8:3–4).

The fact then that the law cannot save the sinner, nor keep the saint, is not the fault of the law, but of sinful flesh. That which the law could not do, was because of man's sinful nature, which makes man weak. And because we could not attain unto righteousness by our own efforts, God sent His Son into the world to do for us what we could not do for ourselves, which was to satisfy the law for us by paying its penalty on the cross, and then, by our evidencing faith in that, He offers His spotless righteousness—all of this, that the righteousness of the law might be fulfilled in us.

Notice, it does not say that it might be fulfilled by us, but *in* us. This is all done by the Holy Spirit.

Have you been trying to earn your own victory in your own way?

Have you been trying to seek God's favor by doing your best?

Oh, Friend, your best is not good enough, and in fact, can never be good enough. Why not accept His freely-offered righteousness and be able to say:

I've tried in vain a thousand ways,
My fears to quell, my hopes to raise;
But what I need, the Bible says,
Is ever, only Jesus.

THE HOLY SPIRIT

There are millions of Spirit-filled people all over the world today being used of God, who love the Lord supremely, but they cannot walk in victory themselves. It's one defeat after another, and they don't understand their situation. They are baptized with the Holy Spirit, they love the Lord with all of their hearts, and they are trying their very best to live the life they ought to live, but they seemingly cannot do so. The reason is the following: whenever someone gives his heart to Christ, the Holy Spirit does come into his heart and life then, and does so instantly and to remain forever. That, however, is not the baptism with the Holy Spirit, which is a different thing altogether.

There is a vast difference in being born of the Spirit and being baptized with the Spirit. When one is baptized with the Spirit, always and without exception that person speaks with other tongues as the Spirit of God gives the utterance (Acts 2:4). The baptism with the Spirit is given for service to help us do the works of Christ. Every believer needs to be baptized with the Holy Spirit, and desperately so. In fact, just before the ascension of Christ, the Scripture says that Jesus *"commanded them that they should not depart from Jerusalem, but wait for the promise of the Father, which, saith he, ye have heard of me. For John truly baptized with water; but ye shall be baptized with the Holy Ghost not many days hence"* (Acts 1:4-5).

That's how necessary the baptism with the Spirit is as it regards our work for Christ.

But that is different than the individual who comes to Christ and is born again, which is always accompanied by the Holy Spirit, and one might quickly say, of regeneration—the Holy Spirit regenerates that person. But that's not the baptism with the Spirit, which is for service to the Lord, but is rather supposed to be for our victory.

In other words, if that born-again person who has not yet been baptized with the Spirit will place his faith exclusively in

Christ and the cross, and maintain it exclusively in Christ and the cross, he will be able to live a victorious, overcoming Christian life. Unfortunately, not many place their faith accordingly, but rather place it in something else altogether, which the Holy Spirit cannot honor.

Assuming that the person does put his faith in Christ and the cross—even though he has not been baptized with the Spirit—he can live a victorious life. This is somewhat confusing to the believer who is baptized with the Holy Spirit. But what he doesn't seem to know is that the baptism with the Spirit is for service—to perform the works of Christ, to take the gospel to the world, etc. But the Holy Spirit who comes into the heart and life of the believing sinner at conversion is there to help that person live an overcoming life and will do so if such a person will place his or her faith exclusively in Christ and the cross. Of course, that goes for the believer who is baptized with the Spirit—he, too, must place his faith exclusively in Christ and the cross. Regrettably, most don't and thereby fail to walk in victory despite the fact that they are baptized with the Spirit or are used of God and able to see the gifts of the Spirit function within their hearts and lives. So it can be confusing to those who cannot walk in victory.

Let us say it again: Everyone who names the name of Christ—the person newly born again, as well as the veteran who has been saved and Spirit-filled for many years—must without fail place his faith exclusively in Christ and what Christ did at the cross, and, at the risk of being overly repetitive, maintain it exclusively in Christ and the cross—then victory can be yours.

In the following passages, Paul is speaking of individuals who have given their hearts to Christ; he is not speaking of individuals who have been baptized with the Holy Spirit with the evidence of speaking with other tongues:

- *"There is therefore now no condemnation to them which are in Christ Jesus, who walk not after the flesh, but after the Spirit. For the law of the Spirit of life in Christ Jesus has made me free from the law of sin and death"* (Rom. 8:1-2).
- *"For they that are after the flesh do mind the things of the flesh; but they that are after the Spirit the things of the Spirit"* (Rom. 8:5).
- *"So then they who are in the flesh cannot please God. But ye are not in the flesh, but in the Spirit, if so be that the Spirit of God dwell in you: Now if any man have not the Spirit of Christ, he is none of His"* (Rom. 8:8-9).

However, most Spirit-filled people read these passages and they think he is speaking of the baptism with the Holy Spirit, but he isn't; he is speaking of every born-again believer who has ever lived. Such a person definitely has the Holy Spirit, even though not baptized with the Spirit. Accordingly, God has made it possible that he can live a victorious overcoming Christian life, but only by placing his faith exclusively in Christ and the cross and maintaining it without fail.

Now, some will read this and say, "That being the case, I don't need to be baptized with the Spirit." My answer is, if you want to do service for the Lord, then you must be baptized with the Holy Spirit (Acts. 1:4).

A charge to keep I have,
A God to glorify,
A never-dying soul to save,
And fit it for the sky.

To serve the present age,
My calling to fulfill,
O may it all my powers engage,
To do my Master's will.

Arm me with watchful care,
As in Thy sight to live,
And now Thy servant, Lord, prepare
A strict account to give!

Help me to watch and pray,
And still on Thee rely,
O let me not my trust betray,
But press to realms on high.

THE NEW COVENANT

CHAPTER 10

CRUCIFIED WITH CHRIST

CRUCIFIED WITH CHRIST

THIS SAME POINT—dead to the law but alive unto God—Paul now repeats in greater detail with the name of Christ prominent. He has died to the law so that he might live for God, but this is true only because he has been joined to the Lord Jesus Christ by God the Father. Jesus died; so did Paul. Jesus rose again; so did Paul, and so have we, spiritually speaking.

The resurrection life he is now living he is living through the presence of the Lord Jesus Christ within him. There are different ways in which Paul's references to having died and come to life in Christ can be taken; he himself uses the images in different ways, even as we have previously stated. At times he refers to the participation of Christians in the benefits of Christ's experiences. This means that Christians experience death and new life because Jesus experienced death and new life for them. And of course for us it is a spiritual experience, and not a literal experience. As well, he refers to an actual participation of the believer in Christ's death and resurrection, conceived on the basis of the mystical union of the believer with the Lord (Rom. 6:4-8; Col. 2:12-14, 20; 3:1-4). This last view is the hardest to understand, but it is the one involved.

WHAT DOES IT MEAN TO BE IN CHRIST?

It means to be so united to Christ by faith that all the experiences of Christ become the Christian's experiences, which are intended by the Holy Spirit. Thus, His death for sin was the believer's death. His resurrection was (in one sense) the believer's resurrection; His ascension was the believer's ascension, so that the believer is (again in one sense) seated with Christ "in the heavenly realms" even as we have previously stated (Eph. 2:6).

This thought is particularly evident in Paul's use of the manner in which he speaks of having been crucified with Christ, more so in the Greek text than in the English. He is referring to something which has happened in the past but the influence continues into the present. Paul died with Christ, and so did we; that is, his "old man died with Christ." This was arranged by God so that Christ might live in us rather than the old Paul—and the old us.

Paul is still living, but he adds that the life he lives now is lived *"by faith."* It is a different type of life altogether than that which he was striving to live under the law. In another sense, it is not Paul who is living at all, but rather Christ who lives in him.

CRUCIFIED WITH CHRIST

In Galatians 2:20, the phrase, *"I am crucified with Christ,"* is as stated in the Greek in the perfect tense, which speaks of a past completed action, having present continuous results. Paul uses it to show that his identification with Christ at the cross was a past fact, and that the spiritual benefits that have come to him through his identification are present realities with him.

By this statement he also shows how he died to the law, namely by dying with Christ who died under its penalty. The law's demands were satisfied, as stated, and therefore have no more hold on Paul. Thus, to Paul, being crucified with Christ also meant death to self. When Paul died with Christ, it was the Pharisee Saul who died. What he was and did up to that time passed away, as far as he was concerned. The old Saul was buried, and the old life with him. Consequently, the dominating control of the Adamic nature had its power over him broken.

PRESENT RESULTS

Even as we have already stated, the phrase *"I am crucified with Christ"* as given in the Greek stipulates something which happened in the past, but then continues to have present effect upon our daily walk with God. This is what many in the church do not understand.

They think the cross pertains only to their salvation experience, in other words when they were saved. They do not realize that the effects of what Jesus did at Calvary continues to have visible results in our everyday lives, and we speak of sanctification, that is if we have faith in that which was done, and understand what was done. In essence, that's what Jesus was speaking about when He said, *"take up his cross daily, and follow me"* (Lk. 9:23).

TAKING UP THE CROSS DAILY

First, the taking up of the cross refers to our trusting in what was done there for our salvation and as well our sanctification, which refers to our continued everyday victory in Christ. This, the cross, is the answer and in fact the only answer to the difficulties, problems, and ills of man. It doesn't matter what the problem is, the solution is found in the cross and the cross alone. As stated, it is the only answer.

Humanistic psychology holds no answers, and neither do the heathenistic religions of the world. Only what Jesus did on that cross. Through faith in the cross alone can victory be had over the sins of the flesh, whatever those sins may be.

As well, Jesus used the word *daily* as it referred to taking up the cross, and meant for it to be a daily affair. In other words, we are to trust on a daily basis for our victory, in what Christ did at Calvary, now nearly two thousand years ago. Please allow me to say it again: this is the only avenue of victory provided for us, and the only avenue in which the Holy Spirit will work.

This means that the charismatic churches who teach that the cross only pertains to our salvation, and has no more bearing on our present living, are completely off base. Many of these churches, and regrettably they number into the thousands, will not even sing any songs about the cross in their services, or the blood of Christ, calling such "past miseries," and the "greatest defeat in human history." By such thinking, Satan has succeeded in cutting them off from the only victory possible.

THE CROSS

What Paul speaks of is something more than merely *"dying with Christ"* i.e., imitating the death of Christ after a spiritual manner (it also involves a special reference to the cross.) It is through the power of the cross and through contemplating the cross and all that is associated with it, that the Christian is enabled to mortify the promptings of sin within him, and reduce such to a state of passiveness (powerlessness) like that of death (I Cor. 1:17-18, 25; 2:2; Gal. 6:14; Col. 2:10-15).

This is one of the most significant theological concepts. When a man enters into Christ, he literally enters into His death. In effect, he dies with Christ. This is more than a figure of speech, merely describing the psychological separation or deliverance from sin. It means that by faith the man makes Christ's death his own. The future result is that he does not face eternal death for his sin, those sins being completely eradicated.

Even as we have stated, there is also a present benefit.

The power of sin is broken in a man's life, because he died to sin with Christ. Of particular significance to the present context is the fact that death with Christ is the only way (faith in what was accomplished at the cross) that those enslaved by the law can find freedom.

It is imperative that the sinner's death with Christ not be confused with crucifixion of one's essential selfhood or what is often termed self-crucifixion. It is rather the old, inner self, helplessly and hopelessly depraved by sin that dies. Paul's terminology is strange to modern ways of thinking, yet it depicts a truth that is well-known in human experience. In reality, the new self in Christ is not to be destroyed, but rather remains in Christ. That is the ideal and what the Holy Spirit intends (Lk. 9:23-26).

THE CRUCIFIXION OF JESUS

The death of Jesus on the cross is a historical event. We may debate the exact configuration of the cross and dispute the precise location of Jerusalem's public execution grounds. But we cannot debate the clear teaching of the Bible about the meaning of the cross in God's plan and in our lives today.

Let us say it again: The meaning of the cross is the meaning of the new covenant. Actually, what Jesus did at the Cross is what formulated the new covenant, what made it a viable force. If one doesn't understand the cross of Christ, then one really does not understand the new covenant. The very fact of our understanding necessitates that it be based entirely upon the foundation of the cross of Christ.

THE MEANING OF JESUS' CRUCIFIXION

The story of the crucifixion is told in all of the Gospels (Mat. 27; Mk. 15; Lk. 23; Jn. 19). What at first seemed to the disciples to be a tragedy was recognized after the resurrection as the source of salvation and hope. In his first recorded evangelistic sermon after the ascension, Peter presented Jesus' crucifixion as something determined by God's purpose and foreknowledge (Acts 2:23).

To be sure, Peter did not understand that much about the crucifixion, but he did know it was determined by God. The Jews and the Romans were both instrumental in carrying out the physical act, but still, that was only a part of it. In fact, forgiveness can be found only in the crucified and risen Lord (Acts 2:38-39; 4:10-12).

The first message called on the people of Jerusalem to put their trust in the person of the crucified and risen Saviour. Later, Paul explained that the cross is God's means for reconciling all things, whether things on earth, or things in heaven, by making peace through His blood, shed on the cross (Col. 1:20). Through the crucifixion we have been offered life, and those who put their trust in Christ have been forgiven for all their sins. All that could condemn us was washed away at Calvary (Col. 2:13-17).

In addition, the barriers that divide humanity and that create hostilities were abolished, for people of every culture are brought to God through the cross (Eph. 2:16). Because of the crucifixion we have peace with God and access to the Father, and have become members of God's own household (Eph. 2:17-19).

Jesus' crucifixion and resurrection were God's only way to bring all these benefits to humanity. In view of all that Jesus has accomplished, it is no wonder that Paul confronts Jews who did not grasp it at all, and were tempted to turn back to an Old Testament faith to find in Old Testament law the means for completing their salvation.

Will they crucify Jesus again? Are they shamelessly implying that the cross did not accomplish all that God says it has? (Heb. 6:6).

THE CROSS, THE CHRISTIAN MESSAGE

When the apostle Paul evangelized Corinth, he refused to rely on his training and rhetorical skills. He preached the gospel simply and plainly and relied on the divine power inherent in the message of the cross (I Cor. 1:17; Rom. 1:16).

Actually, I believe that Paul was somewhat discouraged when he left Athens to come to Corinth. He had not seen the response, and I speak of the favorable response that he desired at Athens. A few people came to Christ, but there is no historical record of a church being established in Athens. So Paul, coming to Corinth, knowing that it was the most jaded city in the Roman Empire and understanding that his success in Athens had been very limited, how in the world could he penetrate this shell of bondage and darkness in Corinth? I believe he was concerned about the matter, and I'll give it Scriptural proof in a moment.

I believe as he walked, no doubt, from the port where his boat had docked, to come into Corinth with these things heavily on his mind, the Holy Spirit gently spoke to him and said, If you want success in Corinth, preach the cross. And if the cross will work at Corinth, it will work anywhere in the world.

Well the cross did work at Corinth——a great church was established there. And Paul did exactly what he was told to do. The reason I feel he was thus perplexed is because of what he said in his epistle to the Corinthians: *"I determined not to know anything among you save Jesus Christ, and him crucified"* (I Cor. 2:2).

Thank God the message of the cross has worked anywhere in the world it has been preached, and it is timeless—what worked two thousand years ago will work now.

Those who perish will think the cross is foolishness, but those who are being saved will recognize it as being the message which has the stamp of God's own authority (I Cor. 1:18).

Because the cross is central to the Christian gospel, Paul often uses *"the cross"* as a term for the gospel itself (I Cor. 1:18; Gal. 5:11; 6:12, 14; Phil. 3:18).

THE CHRISTIAN'S CRUCIFIXION WITH JESUS

The New Testament speaks of our crucifixion with Jesus (Rom. 6:6; Gal. 2:20; 5:24; 6:14).

The key to understanding the reference is the concept of identification.

The union that each believer has with Jesus is so close that everything that happened to Jesus is considered to have happened to us. Through our union with Jesus and by the divine power that raised Jesus from the dead, we experience not only crucifixion but also renewal and keeping power (Rom. 6:1-14; 8:1-4).

Marriage provides an illustration of identification. A poverty-stricken woman who marries a millionaire becomes a millionaire when the wedding takes place. Even if the couple later divorces, the law treats his millions as though she had participated in earning them, and that participation will be reflected in the divorce settlement. But God never divorces us. All that

Christ has done—and all that He now is—is ours through our relationship with Him.

THE CHRISTIAN'S DAILY CROSS

Lawrence Richards said:

This enigmatic concept must be important, for all three Gospels report Jesus' encouragement to His disciples to take up their cross and follow Him (Mat. 10:38; 16:24; Mk. 8:34; Lk. 9:23; 14:27). In all of these reports the word *cross* is used symbolically. When Jesus was faced with imminent crucifixion, He prayed in Gethsemane, 'Father... take this cup from Me. Yet not what I will, but what You will' (Mk. 14:36). Here the cross is the ultimate symbol of Jesus' commitment to do the will of God, whatever suffering that might bring for Him. Taking up our cross to follow Jesus simply means that we are to imitate daily Jesus' total willingness to do the will of the Father, whatever that will may hold for us. As well, and to which we have already alluded, it speaks of trusting fully in that which was accomplished at the cross, thereby receiving its afforded victory paid for by Christ. The world little believes this great truth, and sadly much of the church follows suit. Consequently, it is a reproach in their eyes for one to trust solely in the cross for life and victory; nevertheless, this is the only thing in history that affords life and victory. Such comes from no other source.[1]

NEVERTHELESS I LIVE

The phrase, *"nevertheless I live,"* presents Saul the self-righteous Pharisee as having died, at least in Christ, but Paul the great apostle lives. The counterpart of death with Christ is always resurrection and a new life in Him. The man of faith walks in *"newness of life"* (Rom. 6:4), in the *"likeness of his resurrection"* (Rom. 6:5), and *"alive unto God"* (Rom. 6:11). He brings forth *"fruit unto God"* (Rom. 7:4), and serves Him in *"newness of spirit"* (Rom. 7:6).

It is vital to grasp the full impact of this wondrous truth. Death to sin is significant because it makes the new life possible. Deliverance from sin is the opening of the door to a glorious new life in Christ, and is found only in the cross of Christ.

YET NOT I

In Galatians 2:20, the phrase, *"yet not I,"* presents a life that is no longer self-centered (which characterizes all unbelievers), but a Christ-centered one. His new life is a person—the Lord Jesus living in Paul. And through the ministry of the Holy Spirit the Lord Jesus is manifest in his life. The new life is no longer, like the former one, dependent upon the ineffectual efforts of a man attempting to draw near to God in his own righteousness. The new life is a person within a person, living out his life in that person.

Instead of attempting to live his life in obedience to a set of rules in the form of the legal enactments of the Mosaic law, Paul now yields to the indwelling Holy Spirit and cooperates with Him in the production of a life pleasing to God, energized by the divine life resident in him through the regenerating work of the Holy Spirit. Instead of a sinner with a totally depraved nature attempting to find acceptance with God by attempted obedience to a set of outward laws, it is now the saint living his life on a new principle, that of the indwelling Holy Spirit manifesting forth the Lord Jesus.

CHRIST LIVES IN ME

The phrase, *"but Christ liveth in me"* presents Christ as the source of all the life now enjoyed. Of course, Christ does not physically dwell in the believer as should be obvious. However, this of which Paul says is of far greater dimension than a mere philosophical idea.

The truth of what Paul says is this: When Jesus died on the cross, the believing sinner died in Him, which means that Jesus became our substitute. Our identification with Him through faith grants us all of the privileges which the cross affords— salvation and victory. When the believer exhibits faith in the cross, Jesus in turn comes to live in the person. The idea is this: as the believing sinner was in Christ when He died (at least in the mind of God) upon continued faith by the believer, Jesus now lives in the believer. The Holy Spirit, as given to the believer, guarantees the positive effects of Calvary.

A HYPOTHETICAL SITUATION

While it is a guaranteed fact that all believing sinners were in Christ when He died (at least in the mind of God), which is a necessity if one is to be saved, hypothetically, Christ is not allowed to live in the hearts and lives of many believers. While that is not literally correct, for it cannot be literally correct, still the great benefits of Jesus living in the believer are not realized in the hearts and lives of most Christians.

The reason is simple: Many believers—having accepted the cross as it regards their salvation—still try to maintain a life of victory after salvation by reverting to works. Consequently, Christ is made of no effect, with believers living their lives as if Christ did not reside within them. That being the case, the Holy Spirit will not function, and believers are doomed to failure, which probably characterizes most modern Christian lives.

Most all Christians are clear on the salvation process but unclear on the continued victory process, thereby reverting to works. The secret is to keep trusting in the cross on a daily basis and believing that it is not only afforded salvation for our born-again experience, but as well continues to provide power and strength for our daily walk before God guaranteeing continued victory. In the Greek, the word *lives* is *zao,* and means "to live," or literally "to live a life." Jesus is in us in order to live through us the kind of life we must live and desire to live. He is not there as an idle bystander, but at times, sadly, He is reduced to that by our lack of faith in the cross.

THE LIFE WHICH I NOW LIVE

The phrase, *"and the life which I now live in the flesh,"* refers to being in the flesh because that's what we are—not living according to the flesh, but according to Christ. Between the old life under sin and the new life of living, there is the no man's land of life under self. Although the believer has been freed from the grip of sin, he is still lord of his own life.

Thus, Paul uses his personal example to set forth the ideal that God expected of them. Such a life involves a crisis capitulation as the believer surrenders his sovereignty to God.

This is returning to God what man usurped in the garden of Eden. Elsewhere it is described graphically in the imagery of a love slave presenting itself voluntarily to his master (Rom. 6:19), and as a priest presenting his sacrifice on the altar (Rom. 12:11).

The implications of this crisis must be lived out in a lifelong process, which Paul often refers to as walking or marching by the Spirit. This new life under the Spirit of God is lived in the flesh, which here means in the present earthly body—with all of its limitations, weaknesses, and temptations. It is also lived by faith.

FAITH

In Galatians 2:20, the phrase, *"I live by the faith of the Son of God,"* presents to us a part of this great truth which is at times ignored, and as a consequence causes great problems.

Paul witnesses that as he was justified by faith, so he lives this new life of the Spirit by faith in the Son of God as well!

The believer's surrendered sovereignty must not be confused with the sinner's death with Christ. Also, Paul never uses death or crucifixion as a metaphor of destruction of man's God-given selfhood.

In Pauline terms, man's will does not die but is surrendered or presented to God.

All the way, the believer's life must be one of total dependence upon Christ, who loved me and gave Himself for me.

It was by faith in Christ that I first became partaker of this life; it is by faith in Christ that I continue to partake of it. By letting go of my faith in Christ, I instantly lose this life in Christ—His victory.

The believer must do three things as it regards continued victory in one's life:

1. Understand that the cross was not only for his salvation, but also his continued victory.
2. Appropriate the benefits of the cross on a daily basis, trusting in what Jesus did there (Lk. 9:23).
3. Have faith on a continuing basis and understand that the cross of Christ is the means by which all these wonderful things are given to us by the Lord, and that what Jesus did has a present result in his life and will overcome every power of darkness. In other words, this is not automatic, even as Paul says, it requires faith. Now the Holy Spirit can work.

In respect to all of this, Paul refers to Jesus in His role of deity as "the Son of God," the magnificent title by which he recites Christ's personality.

Consequently, Jesus possesses an absolutely commanding claim to His people's adherence, which we dare not decline.

WHO LOVED ME

The phrase, *"who loved me, and gave Himself for me,"* presents the acknowledgement that everything in the Christian's life finds its source in the love of Christ, which caused Him to die for us. There is no other motivation of grace. This emphasis upon love becomes a veritable creedal confession.

Christ died for the whole world, proving that He loved the whole world, but each individual Christian has a right to appropriate His death to himself. The death of Christ was prompted by love, not for the abstraction of humanity, but for men as individuals.

This great love evidenced in such a manner is completely beyond the comprehension of mortal man. In fact, the entirety of the basis of Christianity is built upon the foundation of love, which spawned grace, which of necessity grace must have, that is if it is to be true grace.

This statement, as given by the Holy Spirit through Paul, presents this great gift of God on a very personal basis. He personally gave Himself to each one of us as individuals, even as sinful and wicked as we were, but thank God through Him no longer are.

THE GRACE OF GOD

"I do not frustrate the grace of God: for if righteousness come by the law, then Christ is dead in vain" (Gal. 2:21).

The last sentence of this chapter is introduced abruptly and from a point of view. In the preceding verses, Paul has answered the objections of his critics. Now he objects to their doctrine, showing that if they are right, then Christ has died in vain. The heart of Christianity lies in the grace of God, and in the death of Jesus Christ.

As John R.W. Stott notes, "If anybody insists that justification is by works, and that he can earn his salvation by his own efforts, he is undermining the foundations of the great Christian salvation in Christ. He is nullifying the grace of God (because if salvation is by works, it is not by grace) and he is making Christ's death superfluous (because if salvation is our own work, then Christ's work was unnecessary)."[2]

Gaebelin said, "Paul's logic is incontrovertible. Yet many still pursue the fallacious logic of the legalizers. They suppose that to earn their salvation is somehow praiseworthy and noble, when actually it is vainglorious and ignoble. True nobility (and humility) is to accept what God offers. One must either receive God's offer of salvation, which can only be received in His way, or insult Him."[3]

FRUSTRATION OF THE GRACE OF GOD

The phrase, *"I do not frustrate the Grace of God,"* presents the fact that there is no salvation for the sinner who depends in the least upon good works as a means of acceptance with God.

The word *frustrate* is from the Greek—*apatteo*— and means "to do away with something, laid down, presented, or established, to act toward anything as though it were annulled, to thwart the efficacy of anything, to nullify, to make void."

All of these meanings could be applied here to the act of adding law (works) to faith as the ground of a sinner's justification. One may preach that Christ died for our sins, but if he adds works to faith as the means of the acceptance of the salvation Christ procured for the lost sinners at the cross, he has thwarted the efficacy of grace, for the fundamental meaning of grace is that salvation is given free, without money and without price (Isa. 55:1).

The idea is that if we do not permit the grace of God to operate in us, we will not be overcoming Christians. Religion says, "I can do it." Relationship says, "Christ can do it through me."

A TWOFOLD STATEMENT

If the sinner attempting to be saved tries to bring about such results through his own good works, he automatically frustrates the grace of God, and salvation is forfeited.

If, after coming to Christ, the believer attempts to maintain his life of victory by reverting to works, he automatically frustrates the grace of God, which means to stop its effectiveness, which means that he is doomed to failure in whatever it is that is troubling him. I suspect that most Christians would claim that they readily know and understand this, but at the same time, I greatly suspect that most Christians do not know or understand this. In fact, I don't think that most preachers fully understand it, and, not knowing what to do for those who are troubled by the powers of darkness, they recommend a psychologist.

The truth is, and as negative as it may sound, the church world as a whole is little trying to properly divide the Word of Truth anymore, but is rather looking to other things.

The denominational church world has pretty well denied the Holy Spirit. Consequently, there is very little left but the "letter."

The Pentecostal world has pretty well gone the way of the seeker sensitive.

The charismatic world is pretty well seeking riches, hence the "greed gospel."

Consequently, Satan is having a field day. Admittedly and thankfully, there are exceptions to all of this, which we have stated above, but I think the majority falls into this sphere.

Our answer for all things is in the Word of God. That means rightly dividing the Word, and not corrupting its contents (II Pet. 1:3-4).

RIGHTEOUSNESS AND THE LAW

In Galatians 2:21, the phrase, *"for if righteousness come by the law, then Christ is dead in vain,"* presents the simple meaning that if we can effect salvation on our own by our works and efforts, then what Jesus did at the cross at such an awful price was completely unnecessary.

As well, if humanistic psychology is the answer for the ills of man, even as the modern church proclaims, then again, why did Jesus have to come down and die on a cross?

If justification can be secured by the observance of any law—ceremonial or moral or laws we devise out of our own minds—then there was no need of the death of Christ as an atonement. This is clear and plain.

If man by conformity to any law, effort, or wisdom could be justified before God, then what need was there of an atonement?

It follows from these statements as given by Paul, which are overly obvious, that man cannot be justified by his own morality, his good deeds, his forms of religion, or his honesty and integrity. If he can be, then he needs no Saviour; he can save himself, which is the contention of Satan and most of the world anyway.

It follows, also, when men depend upon their own morality and good works, they feel no need for a Saviour, and this is the true reason why the mass of humanity rejects the Lord Jesus. They suppose that they do not deserve to be sent to hell. They have no deep sense of guilt. They confide in their own integrity and feel that God ought to save them.

Confiding in their own righteousness they reject the grace of God, and despise the plan of justification through the Redeemer.

THE NEED OF A SAVIOUR

To feel the need for a Savior, it is necessary to feel that we are lost and ruined sinners; that we have no merit on which we can rely; and that we are entirely dependent on the mercy of God for salvation. Thus feeling, we shall receive the salvation of the gospel with thankfulness and joy and show that in regard to us, Christ did not *"die in vain."*

DELIVERANCE FROM THE LAW

Almost thirty-five hundred years ago, God gave to Israel on Mount Sinai two tables of a law, which no one since then has ever kept perfectly. This law was the faultless expression of the holy will of God, and sinful man was unable to keep it.

Some fifteen hundred years after God gave this law to Israel, there had not been one single person who could claim complete obedience to this law. This meant that all men were and are lawbreakers, for one transgression was enough to bring a person under its curse.

We repeat without apology the all-inclusive indictment as given by the apostle Paul: *"For as many as are of the works of the law are under the curse: for it is written, Cursed is everyone that continueth not in all things which are written in the book of the law to do them"* (Gal. 3:10). This verse universally and individually condemns every man, for the demands of this law are entirely out of reach of the best human who has ever lived, with the exception of Jesus Christ.

It was impossible for a sinner born with a depraved heart to please God by obedience to His perfect, holy law. Again and again the Bible states that no flesh can be justified by the works of the law. In fact, the law was never intended by God to justify anyone.

Paul says in Galatians: *"If there had been a law given which could have given life, verily righteousness should have been by the law. But the scripture hath concluded all under sin"* (all were found to be unrighteous) (Gal. 3:21-22). It is well to ponder those words.

THE NECESSITY OF THE DEATH OF CHRIST

If it were possible for a sinner to have made himself acceptable in the sight of God by a life of perfect obedience to God's law, then there would have been no need or no occasion for the grace and the mercy of God. It would have made the death of Christ wholly unnecessary. For this reason Paul says: *"I do not frustrate the grace of God: for if righteousness come by the law, then Christ is dead in vain"* (Gal. 2:21).

What a charge to hurl against a righteous God! If it were possible for man to attain righteousness by keeping the law, then God made a colossal mistake in sending His Son to die on the cross. We repeat, if it were possible to be saved by one's own merit, works, and obedience to God's law or any other law or effort for that matter, then there was no need of sacrificing the Son of God to save those who could have been saved by those other means. This is the force of these words: *"if righteousness come by the law, then Christ is dead in vain"* (Gal. 2:21).

Then the death of Christ on the cross was wholly unnecessary and uncalled for. Therefore the question arises over and over again: If the law could neither justify, sanctify, nor satisfy, then why did God give a law which He knew no one would be able to keep? Is it not debasing to the law to say that it could not save the sinner? What is wrong with the perfect law of God, if it can do absolutely nothing for the sinner as it regards the obtaining of salvation?

Listen, there is nothing wrong with the law; the trouble is with the sinner. The standard of the law is perfection and holiness. Paul says in Romans 7: *"Wherefore the law is holy, and the commandment holy, and just, and good"* (Rom. 7:12).

A HOLY LAW?

The law of Moses is holy; therefore, unholy sinners cannot keep it. The law is just; therefore, it condemns the unjust sinner. The law is good; therefore it condemns the evil wicked heart of the natural man.

The law of Moses or the law of God, whichever one we prefer, for both are the same, was given for a particular purpose. That purpose was to reveal the sinfulness of sin, not to enable man to get rid of his sin. The law makes us see sin, but it cannot take away sin.

D.L. Moody used the illustration of the mirror. He compared the law of God to a mirror in which he might behold himself as he really is. Without a mirror, one is unable to have an accurate picture of himself; no one has ever seen his own face. Because our eyes are set back in sockets and can only look forward and sideways, but not backward, no one has ever seen his own face, unless we see it in a mirror of some nature. When we look into a mirror, however, we actually do not see our face; we see only the reflection of it. A photograph is a picture of one's face. But one doesn't actually see one's face. Now a perfect mirror will give a perfect reflection. Without a mirror, one might imagine his face to be perfectly clean, when in reality it is the opposite. However, when he looks into the mirror, he sees that it is dirty, soiled, and possibly even filthy.

MAN

Before God gave His holy law, man was unable to see just how he actually looked in the sight of God. He knew something was wrong, for his conscience told him that. But he had no idea of just how sinful and filthy he really was. He had no conception of the real sinfulness of sin. At Sinai, at the giving of the law, they said, *"all that the Lord has said, we will do."* Poor, blinded, diluted souls!

They had no realization of how depraved they actually were, how utterly helpless to keep the law, which they were about to receive. So in order to show them their real condition, God gave them a perfect law as the standard of God's requirement for holiness. It was a revelation of how short they had to come before God.

The law then, instead of showing them how good they were, or how good they should be, or how good they might be by obedience to the law, only increased the sinfulness of sin, by exposing what was actually in the heart of all men. It was not a very pretty picture!

PAUL

The apostle Paul had to learn by experience this great lesson, that the law, instead of giving life, was a minister of death. It only defined sin, which told man how sinful he actually was, as well as how helpless he is in trying to overcome within his own strength, which in fact was and is impossible.

It seems strange to refer to the perfect, holy law of God as a minister of death, but that's exactly what it was and what it was designed to be.

In fact, before his conversion, Paul was a zealous law keeper, at least he thought to be such. In fact, as touching the outward observance of the law, he was blameless. No one could point the finger of accusation at him, at least as it regarded his zeal and effort. But then Paul came face-to-face with Jesus Christ, thereby seeing in a moment's time what true righteousness really looked like, and in a flash Paul saw that all of his righteousness, which he claimed under the law, was only filthy rags. Therefore, he says in Romans 7:10, *"And the commandment, which was ordained to life* (meaning the perfect life and living demanded by God), *I found to be unto death* (meaning that the commandment could not be kept)" (Rom. 7:10).

KEEPING THE LAW

Paul found that the law, which he so diligently sought to keep in order to earn salvation, was instead his executioner and condemned him to death. It means that the law of Moses, even as all laws, had a penalty, and in this case, that penalty was death, i.e., "spiritual death," which means "separation from God."

In view of that, he says that the law, instead of giving life, slew him: *"For sin, taking occasion by the commandment* (the Ten Commandments), *deceived me* (sin deceived me), *and by it* (the commandment of the law) *slew me* (its penalty of death was upon me because despite my efforts I actually was not keeping the law)" (Rom. 7:11). It was then that Paul realized the high standard of God's law and adds in verse 12:*"Wherefore the law is holy, and the commandment holy, and just, and good"* (Rom. 7:12).

THE PURPOSE OF THE LAW

The purpose of the law was to show the real, awful nature of sin. It did not manufacture sin, but it revealed the true nature of man's heart, which was depravity and therefore a built-in helplessness. Continuing Paul's argument in Romans 7, we read:

Was then that which is good made death unto me? (Is the law the cause of my sin?) *God forbid. But sin, that it might appear sin* (the law defined what sin was), *working death in me* (condemned me because I could not keep its precepts) *by that which is good* (the law was good); *that sin by the commandment might become exceeding sinful* (the law showed me just exactly how bad and awful that sin actually was and that I was a sinner and could by no means by my own efforts change myself)" (Rom. 7:13).

Notice that last phrase, *"that sin by the commandment might become exceeding sinful."*

Before the law, man might claim ignorance, but once the law came, it showed man exactly what God required, and how helpless man was to obey those requirements, which stops self-justification in its tracks. Paul stated the same truth in Romans 5: *"Moreover the law entered* (was given by God), *that the offence* (sins) *might abound* (to show me how sinful I actually was and had been all along)" (Rom. 5:20).

A MIRROR

The law then became like a mirror to reveal the true condition of the sinner as he actually is. As stated, without the mirror man could not see himself as he really is. But that is all a mirror can do—show the filthiness of the face and the need for cleansing. It cannot do the washing. To take the mirror and try to use it for a washcloth will only smear the dirt and spread it all over one's face. To rub the mirror over your soiled complexion will only make matters worse. We must turn from the mirror to soap and water.

So, too with the ministry of the law—it was given to show man his true condition and his need for cleansing; beyond this it cannot go. We must now turn to the grace of God, and in true repentance and confession of our guilt seek for cleansing by the water of the Word, and the regenerating power of the Holy Spirit.

TO SHOW THE NEED OF SALVATION

We repeat, and shall repeat: The ministry of the law is not to save but to *show* the need of salvation. When God gave the law to Israel, they did not know the gravity of their sin. They imagined they were capable and able to earn and merit the favor of God by their own behavior and good works. So God gave them a set of conditions, a set of rules, a pattern for living to be observed if they were to merit God's favor. For sixteen hundred years Israel lived under this law, and yet in all of those sixteen hundred years, not one single Israelite was saved by keeping that law because they all failed as to its requirements.

Without exception all who were saved were saved by grace through faith in God's atoning sacrifice. When God gave the law on Mount Sinai, He also gave the pattern of the tabernacle and the ordinances for the bloody sacrifices. These sacrifices and the tabernacle pointed to the coming Redeemer. Had God given only the law on Sinai—without His provisions for pardon in the pattern of the tabernacle with its bloody, atoning sacrifices—not a single Israelite would have been saved.

FROM SINAI TO CALVARY

To the believer who comes to Christ and abandons all hope of saving himself, Christ becomes the end of the law, meaning that He totally kept the law in every respect, thereby fulfilling it all with His life and death on Calvary. Perfect obedience to the law is not to Christ the condition of salvation, but rather confession of failure and acceptance of grace, resulting in one's salvation.

"For Christ is the end of the law for righteousness to every one that believeth" (Rom. 10:4). He perfectly kept the law, actually doing it for us. Accepting Him by faith, God grants to us the status of law keepers instead of law breakers, which we actually are.

Notice well, *"Christ is the end of the law for righteousness"* to the believer. He does not say that the law ceases to exist, but for the believer, the law is ended as a means of obtaining righteousness through obedience to it. He is now saved by grace. So today we are not under law, but under grace. The believer is not under the law—its threatenings or its penalties. We are *"dead to the law"* (Gal. 2:19), free from the law, and delivered from the law—all by Christ.

Free from the law, O happy condition,
Jesus hath bled, and there is remission;
Cursed by the law, and bruised by the fall,
Grace hath redeemed us once for all.

Once for all, O sinner, receive it;
Once for all, O brother, believe it;
Cling to the cross, the burden will fall,
Christ hath redeemed us once for all.

With the death and resurrection of Christ, the dispensation of law ended, and when Jesus cried, *"It is finished,"* He had met all the demands of the holy law, paid its penalty, and to us who believe, the righteousness of the law is imputed to us and fulfilled in us.

CALVARY

But someone will ask the question, "Do we not need the law today to show us what sin really is?"

My friend, may I ask you, honestly, do we need to go to the law to see what sin is and what sin does? To be sure, the moral part of the law still stands to condemn the sinner, but we now have a much more convincing demonstration of the true nature of sin. It is seen not at Sinai, but at Calvary. After sixteen hundred years of the thunderings of the law, not one single individual to whom the law was given ever kept it. Instead, at the end of those sixteen hundred years, they committed the capital crime of the ages by nailing the only one who ever kept the law perfectly to the cross of Calvary and condemned Him to die as a criminal and a law breaker.

Mark this fact well: after living for centuries under the law, Israel ended up committing the crime of all crimes—crucifying the Son of God. Ah, my friend, if you really want to see what sin is in all of its naked depravity, then come with me to Calvary. See the perfect, sinless Son of God bleeding, dying in agony and shame because of our sin.

There is the picture of sin. There we see what sin really is, and what sin deserves, for He bore our sin on that cross. If you want to know what sin is, go to that scene at Calvary. You will never truly repent of your sin until you see what sin did to the Saviour on the cross.[4]

I saw One hanging on a tree,
In agonies and blood,
Who fixed His languid eyes on me,
As near His cross I stood.

REFERENCES

CHAPTER 2

[1] Arndt; Gottfried Quell and Gottlob Schrenk, commentary on Romans; J. B. Lightfoot, *Commentary on Galatians*; J. Buchanan, *The Doctrine of Justification*; C. Hodge, *Systematic Theology*; V. Taylor, *Forgiveness and Reconciliation*; and L. Morris, *The Apostolic Preaching of the Cross*.

CHAPTER 3

[1] Albert Barnes, *Barnes' Notes on the New Testament* (Grand Rapids, Kregel Publications, 1966).

[2] Kenneth S. Wuest, *Wuest's Word Studies from the Greek New Testament: For the English Reader* (Grand Rapids: Eerdmans, 1997).

CHAPTER 4

[1] Martin Luther, *A Commentary On The Epistle Of Paul To The Galatians* (Columbia University, B. Blake, 1838), 66.

[2] Albert Barnes, *Barnes' Notes on the New Testament* (Grand Rapids, Kregel Publications, 1966).

[3] Martin Luther, *A Commentary On The Epistle Of Paul To The Galatians* (Columbia University, B. Blake, 1838), 72.

[4] Martin Luther, *A Commentary On The Epistle Of Paul To The Galatians* (Columbia University, B. Blake, 1838), 73.

[5] Kenneth S. Wuest, *Wuest's Word Studies from the Greek New Testament: For the English Reader* (Grand Rapids: Eerdmans, 1997), Galatians 2:7.

[6] Kenneth S. Wuest, *Wuest's Word Studies from the Greek New Testament: For the English Reader* (Grand Rapids: Eerdmans, 1997), (Galatians 2:8).

CHAPTER 5

[1] Joseph Barber Lightfoot, St. Paul's Epistle to the Galatians: A Revised Text, With Introduction, Notes, and Dissertations (Macmillan, 1866).

[2] Martin Luther, *A Commentary On The Epistle Of Paul To The Galatians* (Columbia University, B. Blake, 1838).

[3] Kenneth S. Wuest, *Wuest's Word Studies from the Greek New Testament: For the English Reader* (Grand Rapids: Eerdmans, 1997).

[4] Albert Barnes, *Barnes' Notes on the New Testament,* (Grand Rapids, Kregel Publications, 1966).

[5] Martin Luther, *A Commentary On The Epistle Of Paul To The Galatians* (Columbia University, B. Blake, 1838), 77.

[6] G.D. Watson, *Soul Food* (Old Paths Tract Society, 1971).

[7] *The Christian's Friend and Instructor: Christian Magazine, Vol. 17, 1890 Edition* (Irving Risch, 2015).

CHAPTER 6

[1] Kenneth S. Wuest, *Wuest's Word Studies from the Greek New Testament: For the English Reader* (Grand Rapids: Eerdmans, 1997).

[2] H. D. M. Spence, *The Pulpit Commentary: Galatians* (Funk & Wagnalls, 1909).

CHAPTER 7

[1] Martin Luther, *A Commentary On The Epistle Of Paul To The Galatians* (Columbia University, B. Blake, 1838), 60.

[2] Kenneth S. Wuest, *Wuest's Word Studies from the Greek New Testament: For the English Reader* (Grand Rapids: Eerdmans, 1997), Galatians 2:14.

[3] Ibid.

[4] H. D. M. Spence, *The Pulpit Commentary: Galatians* (Funk & Wagnalls, 1909).

[5] Martin Luther, *A Commentary On The Epistle Of Paul To The Galatians* (Columbia University, B. Blake, 1838), 84.

[6] William M. Ramsay, *A Historical Commentary on St. Paul's Epistle to the Galatians* (New York, G.P. Putnams Sons, 1900), 306.

[7] Kenneth S. Wuest, *Wuest's Word Studies from the Greek New Testament: For the English Reader* (Grand Rapids: Eerdmans, 1997), Galatians 2:15.

CHAPTER 8

[1] Frank E. Gaebelein (Ed.), *The Expositor's Bible Commentary: Romans through Galatians, Volume 10,* (Grand Rapids, Zondervan), 448-449.

[2] Kenneth S. Wuest, *Wuest's Word Studies from the Greek New Testament: For the English Reader* (Grand Rapids: Eerdmans, 1997), Galatians 2:16.

[3] Martin Luther, *A Commentary On The Epistle Of Paul To The Galatians* (Columbia University, B. Blake, 1838), 90.

[4] Martin Luther, *A Commentary On The Epistle Of Paul To The Galatians* (Columbia University, B. Blake, 1838), 91.

[5] M.R. DeHaan, *Law or Grace No 954* (Zondervan, 1984).

CHAPTER 9

[1] George Williams, *The Complete Bible Commentary* (Grand Rapids, Kregel Publications, 2008), 913.

[2] Kenneth S. Wuest, *Wuest's Word Studies from the Greek New Testament: For the English Reader* (Grand Rapids: Eerdmans, 1997).

CHAPTER 10

[1] Lawrence Richards, *New International Encyclopedia of Bible Words: Zondervan's Understand the Bible Reference Series* (Zondervan, 2016).

[2] John R.W. Stott, *Only One Way: The Message of Galatians* (Inter-Varsity Press, 1973).

[3] Frank E. Gaebelein (Ed.), *The Expositor's Bible Commentary: Romans through Galatians, Volume 10,* (Grand Rapids, Zondervan),448-449.

[4] M.R. DeHaan, *Law or Grace No 954* (Zondervan, 1984).

ABOUT EVANGELIST JIMMY SWAGGART

The Rev. Jimmy Swaggart is a Pentecostal evangelist whose anointed preaching and teaching has drawn multitudes to the Cross of Christ since 1955.

As an author, he has written more than 50 books, commentaries, study guides, and The Expositor's Study Bible, which has sold more than 4 million copies.

As an award-winning musician and singer, Brother Swaggart has recorded more than 50 gospel albums and sold nearly 17 million recordings worldwide.

For more than six decades, Brother Swaggart has channeled his preaching and music ministry through multiple media venues including print, radio, television and the Internet.

In 2010, Jimmy Swaggart Ministries launched its own cable channel, SonLife Broadcasting Network, which airs 24 hours a day to a potential viewing audience of more than 2 billion people around the globe.

Brother Swaggart also pastors Family Worship Center in Baton Rouge, Louisiana, the church home and headquarters of Jimmy Swaggart Ministries.

Jimmy Swaggart Ministries materials can be found at **www.jsm.org**.